..."I read the news today"

GREAT ROCK & POP

Headlines

COMPILED BY

Tony Jasper

WILLOW BOOKS
COLLINS
8 GRAFTON STREET
LONDON
1986

Willow Books
William Collins Sons & Co. Ltd
London · Glasgow · Sydney · Auckland
Toronto · Johannesburg

First published 1986
Text and compilation © Tony Jasper 1986
British Library Cataloguing in Publication Data
'I read the news today': great rock and pop headlines
1. Music, Popular (Songs, etc.) — History and criticism
I. Jasper, Tony
780'.42'0904 ML 3470

ISBN 0 00 218196 7

Made and printed in Great Britain by William Collins & Sons Ltd., Glasgow

DEDICATION

To Richard, Clare, Tom and Emily, Margaret Robertson and
Sylvia Carter, Myra and Richard

Tony Jasper would like to thank the following for their help and assistance
during the compilation of this book: Louise Haines; Gill Gray and the staff
at the British Newspaper Library; John Kilpatrick; Peter Jones;
Marion Powers; John Bull; J. C. Enos; the editor and features staff of the
Manchester Evening News; Di Mansour; Karen Rydzewski; Hetty Gilmour;
Denise Blake-Crockett; T. M. Forsyth; Andy McDuff; D. Curtis; the *Daily Mirror*
and *Evening Standard* libraries and staff; Donald Wintersgill; Jack Hutton; Malcolm
Richards; Elfie Carper; WEA Press Office (UK); the editor of the *Islington Gazette*;
and the many, many fellow music writers whose names occur during the
following pages.

For permission to use the extracts reproduced in this book the author and publishers
would like to thank: the *Daily Mail*; *Daily Mirror*; Scottish *Daily Record* and
Sunday Mail; *Daily Star*; EMAP Publications; *Evening News* (Associated Newspapers); *Guardian*;
Holborn Publishing Company; IPC magazines; London Express and News Services;
Mail on Sunday; *Manchester Evening News*; *Philadelphia Enquirer* and *Daily News*; *Rolling Stone*;
Syndication International; *Time*; and *Washington Post*.

INTRODUCTION

This book is not intended as a complete history of pop and rock but rather it offers a selection of some of the headline-making events from that spectacular cultural phenomenon that dawned in the 1960s in reaction to the austerity of the post-war years.

Many hundreds of artists have achieved fame and fortune since 1960 but it is not always the most successful who have received the greatest Press attention. Included in this category of those who, in spite of having seen their albums sell by the million, are not covered by this book are: Dire Straits, the Moody Blues, Supertramp, Genesis, Robert Palmer and Emerson, Lake and Palmer.

Indeed, many of those whose names were constantly on the front page possessed more talent for projecting their image than for playing music. The attraction of the myth that all rock-'n'-rollers drink heavily, take drugs and indulge in free love was and still is strong. Stories of cocaine snorting, bouts of vandalism and crashed cars are commonplace. The lawyer quickly became a permanent member of the pop star's entourage.

Others have led more settled lives with their families while some have been unable to cope with the immense pressures of the music world and have had nervous breakdowns. It is an unfortunate fact, however, that with pop as with real life the newspapers are more attracted by bad news. The shock-horror stories have more appeal to the reader than, so they say, do tales of happiness and contentment. Certainly a large number of the headlines in this book are on the sensational side and one has to ask why the world of pop finds it so necessary to outrage and rebel. Does the sensational make for better publicity than quality music? If so those responsible should consider the squandering of life and talent that lies behind some of the dramatic headlines.

Although the years between 1955 and 1960 saw the birth of the original rock-'n'-roll and are for many the Golden Age of music with such stars as Elvis, Bill Haley, Jerry Lee Lewis, the Everly Brothers, Little Richard and Eddie Cochran, space has not permitted us to include headlines from this era. Another reason for their omission is that newspapers did not devote as much space to contemporary music then and many of the most significant events are not adequately recorded.

This book is meant for a wide public and not just for record buyers, and better-known artists have more headlines than others. Similarly, some events deserve more coverage because of their impact. The deaths of John Lennon, Elvis Presley and Bob Marley, for example, as well as the headline-grabbing nature of punk. One must add the awe-inspiring ventures of Band Aid, the USA for Africa recordings and, of course, Live Aid.

Above all, we hope that this collection of headlines, photographs and some text will bring back memories and provide a nostalgic journey through the last 25 years of pop and rock.

Tony Jasper, May 1986

THE SUPREMES

BEATLES NEW TRIUMPH: WIN FIRST GOLD DISC

RECORD AND SHOW MIRROR. Week-ending January 9, 1960.

☆☆☆☆☆
☆☆☆☆☆☆
☆☆☆☆☆☆☆
☆☆☆☆☆☆

S TOO OLD 5?

ROCK 'N' ROLL NO LONGER THE GOLDEN BOY

d the varying degrees of
ght on the disc jockey
ticeable change to the
t. That is to say, rock
s no longer the golden

de with regard to the
at some changes are
s old by comparison
g into disc service
velvet shirts, tight
en he becomes a

! Maybe just a
llege style outfit
Good

more Motown
e Marvellettes,
he Velvelettes,
onder.

t, the girls put
o map. We've
them

Is he too old at 25?

AWN SOUND

EARL VAN DYKE

attraction in t

Rolling Stones fined for a 'public insult'

WESTON

LANGHAM

Gaye, one of the
nrst people to sign with
Tamla—he played drums for
Earl Van Dyke for a while—
heard three young girls singing
and they became his backing
group, the Vandellas.

Martha Reeves was a girl who
was pop music crazy and used to

them
ere, but the whole Tamla
building thought the wait
was worth just every minute
of it.

Detroit is a swinging city. The
coloured people are great ones at
church singing, choirs, glee clubs,
school concerts, local talent contests.

There's always plenty of music
in Motor Town. Berry Gordy has

As the decade dawned few could have foreseen the revolutionary changes that were going to take place in the music industry even before it had run through half of its ten years. While the media acknowledged the rise of the pop star and the growing importance of the recorded disc as opposed to 'live' music, the emphasis was still on the showbusiness or light entertainment side of the music industry. This is well illustrated by the title of a popular weekly called *Record and Show Mirror*. The paper contained record reviews, a limited chart service and some popular concert notices but, overall, it devoted more space to film and theatre and to covering 'respectable' pop stars who mainly appealed to the over-thirties. British radio reflected a similar state of affairs. One has the impression that record artists were second-rate figures unless they had established a reputation on the club, cabaret and stage circuit.

Indeed, those pop stars whose unorthodox conduct it was felt could lead to anti-social behaviour from their fans were soon taken up by those who promoted family entertainment rather than teen appeal. Tommy Steele might appear to have been Britain's first rock-'n'-roll star but he was essentially manufactured. He had no intention of leading a teenage revolt against the establishment or of spearheading a new music movement. Cliff Richard was the same when it came to his relationship with the younger generation. He soon stopped singing rock-'n'-roll. Both Steele and Richard were hugely talented but they were not destined to cause havoc.

Adam Faith, Billy Fury and Cliff Richard appeared on countless television pop shows and became known as a musical 'holy trinity'. Faith daringly admitted on television that he had had pre-marital sex and survived the ensuing storm. Most viewers were impressed by his intelligence as he talked animatedly on the normally rather sober interview programme *Face to Face* with John Freeman. Pop stars were not usually considered bright by the biased oldies who had much to lose if the pop bandwagon took off.

Stars such as the 'holy trinity', Marty Wilde, Joe Brown, Eden Kane, Emile Ford, Vince Eager, Helen Shapiro, the Shadows, plus a number of one-hit wonders like Tommy Bruce, Lance Fortune and Michael Cox, helped keep television ratings high and 'package' shows, which featured a variety of artists, on the road. American rock-'n'-rollers were still popular but did not visit Britain often enough to keep the ever-growing pop audience happy. Fats Domino, Elvis, Jerry Lee Lewis, the Everly Brothers, Del Shannon, Johnny Preston, Brian Hyland, Johnny Burnette and Johnny Tillotson all had hits during this period and some occasionally crossed the Atlantic.

The industry was to change drastically once the Beatles got under way. They had a minor hit with *Love Me Do* in 1962 and were among a large number of groups from Liverpool who were trying to make it nationally. The next year, 1963, the Beatles went to number two with *Please Please Me* and Beatlemania began. Kids suddenly had money to spend as the austerity of the post-war years lifted. New groups and artists proliferated and the Merseybeat sound, with acts like Gerry and the Pacemakers and Billy J. Kramer, took off. The British Press realised that they had to cover pop and its stars for it sold papers even if it was the image that people found interesting rather than the music.

Sometimes provincial newspapers found they discovered the news first. Such was the case of the *Richmond and Twickenham Times* when, on Saturday 13 April 1963, they ran the story of a group, the Rolling Stones, who were packing out the Craw Daddy Rhythm and Blues Club at the Station Hotel, Kew Road, Richmond. Within days Patrick Doncaster of the *Daily Mirror* was giving the group national coverage while Peter Jones of the *Record Mirror* ensured that record fans knew as well.

The music scene had come of age.

1960-1964

ELVIS TOO OLD AT 25?

ROCK 'N' ROLL NO LONGER THE GOLDEN BOY

And, if some changes are being made with regard to the rock, why, it's practically inevitable that some changes are planned for old Elvis Presley. (At 25 he is old by comparison with the schoolboys they've been pressing into disc service these days!) Anyway, the talk is—no more velvet shirts, tight pants and pastel suede shoes for Elvis when he becomes a civilian once more.

The wiggling and gyrating is gonna be 'out! Maybe just a hint of a quiver, they say, but in his trim college style outfit ol' Elvis is gonna make like (Lawd help us!) **Pat Boone!** To keep him from becoming, possibly, neurotic or something they're going to let him grow his sideburns again—talk is, that's what he misses most in the army—but, to counteract this, they're going to stick an empty pipe in his hand or breast pocket. Give him that "older fella's poise."

Don't say you haven't been warned. If all this comes to pass, those first post-service photos of Presley are going to be earth-shaking . .

Is he too old at 25?

Friday, March 4, 1960.

AND TALKS ABOUT MARTY WILL...

CLIFF RICHARD

to **DEREK JOHNSON** who flew to Germany to interview Presley before he returned to the U.S.

ELVIS PRESLEY treated me to one of his smouldering, heavy-lidded glances, and the corner of his mouth curled into a faint smile. "I don't know if I shall manage to get to the top again," he said. "I only wish I did know. I hear that trends have changed, so it might be pretty difficult for me. But I'll tell you this—I'm sure gonna try hard."

I was talking to Elvis in the Ray Barracks, Friedburg, some thirty miles north of Frankfurt, just before the singing phenomenon flew back to America this week for his discharge from the Army. This was the first time Elvis had been able to speak freely since his arrival in Europe—and I was there on behalf of the NME.

Three exclusive NME pictures of Sergeant ELVIS PRESLEY, taken during the farewell press conference he gave before leaving Europe—and the Army—this week. Derek Johnson was there to represent NME readers and reports that Elvis was very interested in the paper and its readers—in fact, Elvis shares with you the information in the NME each week, and was consequently only too happy to add to that information this week!

Elvis entered the US Army in March 1958 and was discharged two years later, in March 1960. While he was in the army RCA continued to release a backlog of Presley material. Before he left for home the Army organised a huge Press conference at which Presley described how much he had enjoyed his time in service. There was much speculation in the Press whether Elvis would regain his previous popularity.

The 'Old Groaner' wasted his breath forecasting the end of singles. Some 51 million were sold in 1959 and by 1964 the figure had risen to 73 million. Even so, White Christmas remained one of the biggest-selling singles of all time.

THE TOP RECORD & MUSICAL WEEKLY

No. 109   Week ending April 23, 1960
Every Thursday, price 6d.

Eddie Cochran tragedy—body flown to States

Gene Vincent's injuries are not serious

THE body of American rock singer Eddie Cochran, who was killed in a car crash on Easter Sunday at Chippenham in Wiltshire, was to the States on Wednesday. Vince Eager, who was to have go... America with Cochran, has decided not to go.

Eddie Cochran was travelling in a hired car to London Airport where he was due to catch a plane for America. With him in the car were Gene Vincent, songwriter Sharon Sheeley and theatrical agent Patrick Thomkins. All four were taken to hospital in Bath.

Gene Vincent, who was asleep at the time of the crash, suffered a broken collar bone, and was well enough to phone his wife on Monday. He was discharged from hospital on Tuesday and flew back to the States with the body. He will return in time to start his new tour at Hanley on April 30.

Miss Sheeley—she and Eddie Cochran were unofficially engaged and were to have married shortly—has a fractured pelvis and other injuries. It is not known at present how long she and Gene Vincent will be in hospital.

...ACK GOOD

Singles are dead says Bing

BING CROSBY, in London last week with his wife Kathryn on his way to the Olympics in Rome, may not be figuring in the Top Ten, but the "Old Groaner" has no intention of retiring from the music scene.

"I guess my records don't sell as well as they used to," he said. "But people still seem to want me to make them. I've just finished an album back home with Louis Armstrong and Billy May. The numbers are standards and some others by Johnny Mercer.

"I still find it very stimulating to work with people like Billy and Louis. Billy's music has such a great sense of humour.

"I'll tell you one thing, though. The singles market is dead, there's no doubt about that. Albums are the only thing left to do.

New ideas are getting hard to find, says BING CROSBY (DISC Pic).

WORLD'S LARGEST EVENING SALE

The Evening News

PICTURE EDITION

FOR SMALL-ADS

© Associated Newspapers Ltd., 1960   NO. 24,402   LONDON, FRIDAY, JUNE 17, 1960   PRICE 2½d.

TOMMY STEELE STORY IN PICTURES

Wedding in Soho Church to his Dancer Bride

THE boy from Bermondsey marries his girl from Leeds at St. Patrick's Church, Soho-square.

It is the heart of show business, Soho, and the right place for the wedding of Britain's top young star and a girl who made her name as a dancer at the Windmill.

For Tommy Steele leapt to the top of the entertainment world in a single year—and has stayed there.

He met his bride in a dressing-room at the Chiswick Empire and their courtship took place in a series of variety tours.

Tommy Hicks was born on December 17, 1936, in Bermondsey.

"Tommy Steele" was born less than four years ago in a Soho coffee-bar just down the road from the church where he marries.

INTRODUCED
To The Queen

Tommy Steele hit British show business like a tornado. Within a year he was at the top.

He had been introduced to the Queen, and had led the finale at the Royal Command Performance.

He had made his first film and become almost a legend.

Some of this was achieved by the ingeniously clever publicity of his agent, John Kennedy. Tommy Hicks was on leave from the Merchant Navy strum-

An early picture of the Cockney boy catching up on fame.

ming his guitar round the Soho coffee-bars when Kennedy devised a series of stories to get him into the public eye.

But Tommy had been an entertainer much earlier. As a Bermondsey schoolboy he liked writing and made up plays for his class to act.

But he was no scholar, and leaving school at 15 went to sea as a bell-boy on the big liners sailing to and from Quebec.

was to become his dresser—he composed revues.

So the idea of breaking into show business came to the young merchant seaman with the shock of yellow hair and the effervescent personality.

He played occasionally with a small group that included Lionel Bart, who gave him tips on the niceties of song-making.

John Kennedy, Hugh Mendl, who signed him up for Decca, and Larry Parnes, who joined in his business management, had a good proposition on their hands.

That was in the autumn of 1956. In January, 1957, he was singing at the Cafe de Paris.

In that amazing year he toured Britain, France, Italy, Belgium and Denmark with his group—the Steelmen.

Among his records were "Butterfingers," "A Handful of Songs," "Shiralee," and "Singing the Blues," and Lionel Bart, who has now had his own personal success with the show "Fings Ain't Wot They Used T'Be."

Since then he has toured Scandinavia and South Africa.

At times his appearances have almost caused riots—as at Dundee, where he was badly mauled by screaming girls.

His first film was "The Tommy Steele Story," his second "The Duke Wore Jeans."

EARNINGS
In Show Business

His third—"Tommy the Toreador"—had its premiere in aid of the boys' club to which Tommy once belonged.

He takes a serious interest in the problems of young people.

Tommy's earnings were estimated at £20,000 in his first year. He is thought to have made something like a quarter of a million pounds in the four years he has been in show business.

Much of that goes in the running of his personal organisation.

Some has been spent on moving his mother and father from Frean-street, Bermondsey, into a pleasant but simple house at Ravenscourt-park, Catford.

His brother Colin has now left to make his own show business career, mainly in Italy.

His brother Roy hopes to be a jockey, and his sister Sandra is now 11.

Tommy has been living at Cat-

ADAM FAITH COLLECTING FOR OXFAM YESTERDAY

By Daily Mail Reporter   DE 63

POP SINGER Adam (Faith) has joined the Daily Mail £500,000 Oxfam drive. He is telling his thousands of fans: "Please don't send me a Christmas card this year. Give the money you would have spent to the Oxford Committee for Famine Relief."

[Adam], 23, yesterday launched his personal campaign towards raising money for the world's hungry people.

He arrived home in Esher, Surrey, at 8.30 a.m. after working at Oxford.

About four hours later, still without sleeping, he was out with an Oxfam collecting tin and an Oxfam poster.

★★★ 'Just friends'—but she admits... ★★★

I LIKE ADAM

IS there a romance between America's pop song princess, Connie Francis, and Britain's current rock 'n' roll rage, Adam Faith?

Connie's answer—before she flew home last week—was that well-worn routine reply: "We are just good friends." But when she saw me react to this piece of corn with a slight yawn, she hurried on to qualify it.

"But I think Adam's wonderful," she said. "We've been seeing each other secretly since I first met him at the Variety Club Golden Disc lunch.

"He has been showing me around London, and it has been so marvellous that I shall be sorry to go home."

Mature

WHEN I asked what made nineteen-year-old Adam so wonderful, twenty-one-year-old Connie curled her legs up on the settee in a luxury suite at The May Fair Hotel.

Dreamily she answered: "I think the main attraction is that he's so mature for his age.

"I don't have to pretend I'm interested in conversations about football, cricket, movies and subjects...

for she looked more like a ballerina than a singer.

Connie beamed. "I'm so glad to hear you say that," she said. "I think that what a singer does with the hands and body is all important.

"I spend three hours a day in New York rehearsing with dancing teacher Bob Audy.

"Clothes are also vital. For my act, every piece of clothing is chosen without my even seeing it until I get dressed for a show. But I do go shopping sometimes.

● Connie and Adam, they both insist "We're just good friends"—go out sightseeing together in London. Said Connie: "It's been marvellous."

POP PROFILE

Connie

by JACK BENTLEY

VERDICT ON THE NEW PRESLEY

Sure, he's the greatest—but the new style, I don't like says Marty

THE phenomenal, unpredictable Elvis Presley has made it! Gone is the wild rocker, the sideburns, the body gyrations. In their place is a mature, subdued, clean-cut Presley with the main accent on his voice.

And the result? Over 350,000 copies of "Are You Lonesome Tonight?" were ordered before its release, an all-time record for his disc, "It's Now Or Never."

For the second consecutive time a new style Presley disc has leaped straight into the top position of our charts—an incredible feat.

But who would have believed it of Presley?

Little praise greeted the first disc he made after his two-year Army stretch, "Stuck On You." His follow-up, "Mess Of Blues," although a good seller was disappointing because Elvis, it seemed, had nothing new to offer.

Something new had to be found for him.

He gambled on recording the Italian favourite "O Sole Mio," under the title "It's Now Or Never," and wham, Presley was back.

It was a gamble! A big gamble. But all those around him, including himself, realised that the gamble must be taken.

What is the reaction to this new styled Presley in the business itself? I have been talking to a number of artists and important recording executives to get their personal views and opinions.

Here is what they had to say— and some of the comments are not what you might have expected!

Tess Conrad

"IT'S very appropriate that the KING himself should start something completely different as far as teenage music is concerned. I'm all for it. Not that I particularly prefer this new Presley to the old but just the same I think it is a great Presley.

Adam Faith

"I THINK he is great. It is an adventurous return. As for as starting a new trend is concerned, well, anything Elvis does starts a new trend, doesn't it?

Pete Murray

"I THINK the man who has guided Presley into this new style is the most brilliant man in the business today. For I feel sure had Elvis continued to record the kind of stuff he was doing before his army days he would most certainly have had it.

Marty Wilde

"I DON'T like the new Presley. First of all I want to make it quite clear that I am his number one fan. I worship the ground he walks on. He is the greatest. BUT I don't like what he is doing now.

But I must say Elvis is singing far better today than ever before and the records themselves were sufficiently made.

Cliff Richard

"AS soon as Elvis came out of the Army his voice improved. It's now much stronger and much more powerful. He has a fantastic way of controlling his voice which he proved in 'It's Now Or Never'.

Norrie Paramor

"I CERTAINLY don't think this will start a trend back to simple waltzes again! I understand that

Colonel Parker is responsible for persuading Elvis to do that dramatic recitation in the middle of the disc and I think it was a great idea and a very courageous one, too.

Pain that has made Billy Fury mellow

The Evening News, Wednesday, July 13, 1960

I am learning to sing, not shout
says Marty Wilde

The golden boys

QUOTE: WHEN YOU CAN GET APPLAUSE YOU DON'T WANT 'SCREAMS' ANY MORE

QUOTE: I THINK ELVIS WILL BE 'THE GREATEST'

QUOTE: ROCK 'N' ROLL CAN'T DIE

MARTY AND HIS WIFE JOYCE—NOT FORGETTING THE POODLE — RELAX IN THE GARDEN OF THEIR SUMMER BUNGALOW AT BOURNEMOUTH.

Born a rather plain, and very British, Reg Smith, Wilde was one of the biggest artists of the late 1950s and early 1960s. The occasional visits of American stars could not satisfy the growing interest in pop and Wilde, with his cover versions of US hits, responded to the demand. He was a resident performer on *Oh Boy!* and hosted *Boy Meets Girl*. His marriage to a member of the Vernon Girls lost him support among female fans and he never achieved success in the United States.

His son Ricky was later hailed as the British answer to Donny Osmond but found greater triumph in the 1980s as producer to sister Kim.

10s, a night singing in coffee bars—if he was lucky.

"I want to go on learning," he said. "That's being young. I'm now learning to sing instead of shout. And I'm getting applause instead of screams, that's the really big thing. Oh, I can still get screams —you've only got to move your body about—but when you can get applause you don't want screams any more.

"Sometimes the boys and I go through some of the old songs and we always end up laughing.

"Yet you know if I had to

am now and going back to the time I used to enter talent contests, I'd go back to the talent contests, I was really happy then.

It was an Elvis Presley disc that started Marty Wilde on the road that has brought him more money than any other British rock 'n' roll singer.

A friend who was broke sold Marty a Presley LP that he neither liked nor wanted. But he gave the friend 15s. for it, played it, and suddenly wanted to sing like Presley.

Last year he was earning £1,000 a week. It's anyone's guess what he will gross this year.

Last December he married petite Joyce Baker, one of the Vernon Girls. They have a flat in Chiswick. She is now expecting a baby.

His marriage seems to have made little difference to his fans—except, of course, that they now applaud instead of scream.

"They've grown up with me, I suppose," he said.

He got his name from Larry Parnes—Marty after the film title and "Wilde" because of his occasional wildness.

BIG PLANS FOR BILLY FURY

BREAKING INTO THE BIG TIME in tearaway style proving more than ever a real solid Show Business attraction is yet another bright member of the Larry Parnes stable—BILLY FURY.

Fury was an early pop hero of British fans. His manager, Larry Parnes, claimed he was the 'champion teenage idol' long after Tommy Steele and Cliff Richard had become family favourites *The Sound of Fury* has been regarded by critics as one of the few genuine British rock-'n'-roll albums. However, Fury, in common with other artists of the time, mainly made cover versions of US hits.

Throughout his life he suffered from ill health. At 14 he had rheumatic fever and later underwent several major heart operations. He toured the club circuit in the 1960s, made fresh record contracts and several career returns during the next two decades but sadly he died from heart disease in 1983.

Clark   **Shapiro**   **Scott**   **Francis**   **Shelton**

THE GIRLS ARE COMING BACK
As 'quality' returns to the charts, so do the girls
...and the music business couldn't be more pleased

Some adults called the new pop age 'dirty' and were horrified by pop stars' dress and hair. They were also worried about their possible influence over the young. Song titles like *Let's Spend the Night Together* and *I Can't Control Myself* were highly criticised even though no one minded Sinatra singing *Strangers in the Night* or the Dubliners *Seven Drunken Nights*. However, pop's overall image was more respectable than these headlines might suggest.

Towards the end of 1985 there was a considerable hue and cry in the United States over the state of rock lyrics with the Moral Majority pressure group demanding that records are given a rating similar to that in films. Below is *Rolling Stone*'s filthy fifteen.

LAST week, to everyone's pleasure and some people's surprise, a girl crashed into our charts at number 11. Her name: Helen Shapiro. Pet Clark also slid gracefully in with "Romeo." And Shirley Bassey who was lingering at 17 looks set to get yet another disc, "Reach For The Stars," into the parade.

What's happening in the business? The trend that is bringing quality discs back is also opening up the charts to the girls. Look at the list who have had hits since the beginning of the year, when Matt Monro had his break with *the* ballad "Portrait Of My Love."

Apart from those I've already mentioned there was Connie Francis with a rock-a-ballad ("Many Tears Ago"), Brenda Lee, Anne Shelton and Linda Scott.

Last year? Apart from Francis and Lee nothing to write home about. But that's not the end to it. The cabaret and TV scene has also had a touch of girl craziness. Instead of visiting rock stars we've had Patti Page, Eydie Gorme, Rosemary Clooney is currently here. Jo Stafford is filming a TV series, the great Ella has called.

End at last?

The long domination of males seems to be coming to an end. And you know, I can't say I'm sorry. And even more important, the business generally is pleased.

But to look into it a little closer I spoke first of all to Pye A and R man _____, who _____ depends on the interests of John and Bob Allison. 21-year-old John and his 19-year-old brother Bob live in Parsons Green with their parents, two sisters and younger brother Peter. Until recent...

Nigel Hunter

associate themselves and their own feelings.

"Helen does all these things admirably. She's very individual in vocal style, and has a tremendous personality. I'm especially pleased at the swift success of her second disc, because this is always so vital after a hit debut."

John agrees with the theory that girls predominate amongst the buyers of pop singles.

"That's why artists like Cliff and Adam do so well. But there's room for girls, too, providing they get through sympathetically to the record fans. Cliff creates the impression that he's singing to each girl individually.

"Helen singing a plea not to be treated like a child or to a boy she loves but who doesn't seem to know of her feelings for him also appeals to girls because these are real-life situations in which they can picture themselves."

As well as the meaning of the songs, it's also the sound of the record itself which can influence pop fans into buying. John Schroeder cited the case of Anita Scott's "I Told Every Little Star."

"That was a good oldie brought right up to date and given a really distinctive sound which put it across."

Terrific impact

...the publishing side... Music...

DISC
THE TOP RECORD & MUSICAL WEEKLY

No. 123   Week ending July 30, 1960
Every Thursday, price 6d.

POP LYRICS ARE BAD
TV report causes outburst in the music world

LAST week a report was published by a Joint Committee set up by the BBC and the ITA into the effect of TV on children. In that report pop music, and in particular the lyrics of pop songs, were criticised in no uncertain terms as "drivel," "degraded" and "injurious." And now DISC has discovered that a number of very influential people in the music business think THAT THE COMMITTEE WAS RIGHT!

First, Russell Turner, BBC TV producer associated with "Six-Five Special," "Juke Box Jury" and the forthcoming "Sugar Beat":

"I agree with the committee. Modern songs are musically and lyrically appalling. Three-quarters of the current pop releases come from America, and they're muck. I realise that our record companies are obliged under contract, to issue them here, but they are muck nonetheless, and damaging to teenagers."

Hit songwriter Johnny Worth, who penned "What Do You Want?" among others, also thought the condemnation songs warranted the condemnation expressed by the committee:

"I often hear a number and think to myself, 'What a terrible lyric!' I believe I can honestly say I'm not guilty in this respect.

"I don't see that all pop songs should get such a slating, though. After all, a lot of folk songs are a bit bawdy, to say the least. It's largely a case of what's in people's minds. 'One Night Of Love' is a lovely song with lovely lyrics, but its title might be considered questionable."

Disc jockey David Jacobs was another who thought the Committee were largely in the right.

(Continued on back page)

This is what the Committee said

"TOO many of the lyrics broadcast are merely drivel and have a generally debasing tone which is to be deprecated. Much of the emphasis in these lyrics is not on sentimentality, which has its generally innocuous place, but on a degraded attitude to sex. Some of them cannot be defended as simply harmless. Tolerance of what is just silly should not extend to what is clearly injurious.

"The Committee also feels that the lighter music performed, distinct from either serious or pop music, might have greater variety. There is a tendency to reflect too slavishly the fashion of the moment, whether it is beat music or any other kind."

MUSIC NEWS

Furor over rock lyrics intensifies

The Filthy Fifteen

ARTIST	SONG	RATING
JUDAS PRIEST	"Eat Me Alive"	X
MÖTLEY CRÜE	"Bastard"	V
PRINCE	"Darling Nikki"	X
SHEENA EASTON	"Sugar Walls"	X
W.A.S.P.	"(Animal) Fuck Like a Beast"	X
MERCIFUL FATE	"Into the Coven"	O
VANITY	"Strap On Robby Baby"	X
DEF LEPPARD	"High 'n' Dry"	D/A
TWISTED SISTER	"We're Not Gonna Take It"	V
MADONNA	"Dress You Up"	X
CYNDI LAUPER	"She Bop"	X
AC/DC	"Let Me Put My Love Into You"	X
BLACK SABBATH	"Trashed"	D/A
MARY JANE GIRLS	"My House"	X
VENOM	"Possessed"	O

X = Profane or sexually explicit   O = Occult   D/A = Drugs or alcohol   V = Violent

13

OUR NAME IS JUST PART OF THE PUBLICITY, ADMIT TOP HIT PARADE SINGERS

THE FAMILY THAT NEVER WAS

The 'Allison Brothers' with their mothers at the airport: Mrs. Alford, Brian Alford, Colin Day and Mrs. Day

By Daily Mail Reporter

THE dapper Allison Brothers, winners of second place in the Eurovision Song Contest, confessed last night: "We're not brothers at all."

The two singers, dressed identically and with similar hairstyles, had just arrived at London Airport from Cannes.

Amid a welter of welcome-home publicity—with free records, photographs, potted biographies, and autographs—21-year-old John Allison (real name Brian Alford) said:

"The name was given to us by a publicity agent we had some time ago. We've known each other since children, but we're not related.

"We knew it would come out some time and now we're glad." Bob Allison, 19 (real name Colin Day), told me: "Now we just be called 'The Allisons.' We were told to call ourselves brothers and did so."

In the fantasy world of the teenage girl the pop idol must, in principle at least, be available. Any facts to suggest otherwise, such as marriage, girlfriends or even boyfriends, are not to be mentioned.

One way of ensuring this is to promote the family image. Britain's Eurovision entrants of 1961, the Allisons, were thus portrayed as brothers. All was fine until the truth came out and the hype machine was exposed.

BOB DYLAN: A DISTINCTIVE FOLK-SONG STYLIST

26 September, 1962 Dylan began a two-week engagement at Gerde's, New York. The New York Times writer Robert Shelton attended. He was impressed not so much by Dylan's voice, which he described as 'anything but pretty', but by his originality and inspiration. A few days later the New York Times ran this four-column headline:

Shelton wrote:
'A bright new face in folk music is appearing at Gerde's Folk City. Although only 20 years old, Bob Dylan is one of the most distinctive stylists to play in a Manhattan cabaret in months … When he works his guitar, harmonica or piano, and composes new songs faster than he can remember them, there is no doubt he is bursting at the seams with talent … Dylan's highly personalised approach toward folk song is still evolving. He has been sopping up influences like a sponge …. Mr Dylan is vague about his antecedent and birthplace, but it matters less where he is going, and that would seem to be straight up.'

TWITCHING THE NIGHT AWAY

DAILY MIRROR, Thursday, June 13, 1963   PAGE 25

PATRICK DONCASTER
The Mirror's DJ

IN the half-darkness, the guitars and the drums started to twang and bang. A pulsating rhythm and blues. Shoulder to shoulder on the floor stood 500 youngsters, some in black leather, some in sweaters. You could have boiled an egg in the atmosphere.

They began to dance. And it was no place for Victor Silvester.

They just stood as they were. Their heads shook violently in what I can only describe as a paroxysm. "A sudden attack," says the dictionary of this word.

THRASHING

That's what it looked like in a sweating jazz club that meets in the Station Hotel at Richmond, Surrey.

Their feet stamped in tribal style. If they could, the dedicated occasionally put their hands above their heads and clapped in rhythm.

Suddenly there would be shaking figures above the rest of the on-the-spot dancers, held aloft by their colleagues, thrashing and yelling "Yeh, yehs."

No one needed a partner. It was simply shake, rattle and roll on your square foot of the floor.

In its fervour it was...

a revivalist meeting in America's Deep South.

Responsible for this extraordinary scene in suburban Surrey are five long-haired lads known as the Rolling Stones — who roll out the rhythm and blues on guitars and drums.

Their names: **Mick Jagger**, 19, studying at the London School of Economics; **Brian Jones**, 19, who used to be a lorry driver and lights up sixty smokes a day; **Keith Richard**, 19, who used to be a Post Office worker; **Bill Wyman**, 21, who likes poetry as well as rhythm and drummer **Charlie Watts**, 21, an advertising agency man, who collects pocket handkerchiefs. He has 100.

TWITCH?

What do the fans call this dance? (I am told it happens nowhere else in Britain.) Nobody seems to know or care. They just do it.

It could well be the Parox... or the Twitch ... or the Sudden Attack. If you wish to try it out, all you need is a lot of people in a crowded room and the Rolling...

Or you might just like to listen. Which is quite exciting, anyway.

THE fanatics of the light fantastic—Is it light any more? — are in considerable confusion.

There are so many dances that they are tripping over each other.

DECIDE!

So it is no surprise to have land on my desk a disc with the title: "Us Kids Have Gotta Make Up Our Minds."

Make up their minds, that is, on what dance to do. The disc might help you sort things out. Artist: American **Sonny Parks**, who warbles in on the Warner Bros' label.

PS: He hadn't caught up with the Twitch when he made this one.

LET'S take it a little easier and lend an ear to Mr. Bobby Darin and Mr. Acker Bilk.

Mr. Darin is most fetching with a cute num... wrote...

ROLLING STONES
... from left to right: Keith Richard, Bill Wyman, Mick Jagger, Brian Jones, Charlie Watts. Five long-haired lads responsible for an extraordinary scene in suburban Surrey.

In the 1950s Cliff Richard used to wiggle his leg like Elvis and affected an agonised Presley mood. The 1960s' Cliff adopted a more sophisticated dress and style. The smouldering look gave way to smiles.

However, new, sullen and supposedly anti-social stars were soon to appear. The *Daily Mirror* was the first national newspaper to announce the arrival of the Stones who were the chief exponents of this trend and were regarded by some as insolent and foul-mouthed. Even the music press had sharp words for them despite its admiration for their music. *Melody Maker*'s Ray Coleman asked: 'Would you let your sister go with a Rolling Stone?'

NEW MUSICAL EXPRESS   Friday, August 9, 1963

Third Gold Disc, and now—

CLIFF TOPS SIX OVERSEAS CHARTS IN A WEEK!

CLIFF RICHARD, who will be seen receiving his third Gold Disc on tomorrow's edition of "Lucky Stars Summer Spin" is currently topping the charts in six foreign territories—an unprecedented achievement for a British artist. He is now expected to film his edition of the Ed Sullivan U.S.-TV show here on September 22.

Cliff received the Gold Disc for a million sales of his "Bachelor Boy"/ "The Next Time" single from recording manager Norrie Paramor during the telerecording of ABC-TV's 100th "Lucky Stars" show on Sunday and it is included in tomorrow's programme screening.

Cliff's six round - the - world chart-topping positions are all with "Lucky Lips" — an outstanding achievement for the disc that failed to make the number one spot in Britain!

In "Billboard's" world-wide chart reports, it is the best seller in Norway, Israel, South Africa, Hong Kong, Sweden and Holland, where

The Shadows are recording background music for a new British film, "French Dressing," which has just been completed by Kenneth Harper—producer of "The Young Ones" and "Summer Holiday."

Drummer Brian Bennett has written the title number, which the group will play over the credits. They will also record it commercially—possibly for inclusion in an EP of music from the film.

Harper and director Sidney Furie have just returned from Mexico and Puerto Rico where they have been seeking locations for Cliff's next film.

his "Summer Holiday" gives him a second Top Ten placing at number eight.

In America, "Lucky Lips" has climbed six places this week to the...

Big Three join Joe Brown tour

THE Big Three and Jess Conrad have been added to the six-night tour which Joe Brown headlines with Dee Dee Sharp in October. As previously reported the package opens at Grantham Granada (19th).

The Big Three will be on all the dates except Greenford Granada on the final night (25th).

In addition to the theatre bookings, Dee Dee Sharp will also play ballroom dates during her british visit at Scunthorpe Baths Hall (October 31), Malvern Winter Gardens (November 2), Oldhill Plaza and Handsworth Plaza (8th), Lincoln Drill Hall (9th) and Dunstable California (16th).

Dee Dee will appear for three days at Belfast's Boom Boom Room from November, 11-13.

Craig Douglas Sunday shows

TWO more Sunday concerts this month have been set for Craig Douglas—Isle Of Man Marina (18th) and Llandudno (25th).

He appears at Chester Royalty for a week of cabaret from Monday, and at Malvern Winter Gardens on August 17;

You'll see this galaxy of talent on the 100th edition of the "Lucky Stars" show tomorrow (Saturday). Eating pieces of celebration cake, while CLIFF RICHARD admires the Gold Disc for "The Next Time"/ "Bachelor Boy" presented to him by a-and-r manager NORRIE PARAMOR (left), are the SHADOWS — Bruce Welch, Licorice Locking, Hank Marvin and Brian Bennett. Below: The original "Spin-A-Disc" team is on the left—BILL BUTLER (extreme left, back row), JANICE NICHOLLS and JANET CARN, with original compere BRIAN MATTHEWS between them. And behind ALMA COGAN and PETE MURRAY are (from left) the SEARCHERS, the TREMELOES, and BRIAN POOLE.

Report that Sinatra sells

NEW MUSICAL EXPRESS

THE BEATLES ON 'JUKE BOX JURY'

MORE fantastic television plans for the Beatles! December 7—the day of their Fan Club Conve—will probably become National Beatle Day with all four on BBC-TV's "Juke Box Jury" par a live transmission from the stage of Liverpool Odeon. Final plans for David Jacobs and a outside broadcast unit to travel to Merseyside for the date are still being set.

Earlier that afternoon, the BBC may also film the Beatles on stage at the theatre, performing specially for fan club members. Further negotiations await the return of their manager, Brian Epstein, from America.

. . . latest disc sensation

Despite the continued success of "She Loves You," a new Beatles' single will be issued end of this month and on advance orders alone the group may qualify for its second disc. The group also makes history with an advance order of well over a quarter-on its second LP "With The Beatles"—two discs prior to release ! The Merseysiders will receive awards from EMI chairman Sir Joseph Lockwood isc achievements.

NEW SINGLE : The Beatles' fifth single will be issued on November 29. It features two more songs by John and Paul, "I Wanna Hold Your Hand" coupled with "This Boy." Advance orders for the disc reached 700,000 on Wednesday—only three days after dealers were told of it.

This unexpected release is almost certain to enable the group to maintain their lead over Cliff Richard in the NME's 1963 chart championship.

NEW ALBUM : By Wednesday night advance orders for the Beatles' second album, "With The Beatles," had reached the staggering figure of 265,000—another unprecedented achievement in the history of the British recording industry ! The LP will not be in the shops for another two weeks.

PRESENTATION : At a private ceremony in London on November 18, Sir Joseph Lockwood will hand the Beatles a silver LP to mark sales well in excess of a quarter-million of their first album, "Please Please Me."

Special arrangements are being made by Arthur Muxlow told the NME : "They will also receive—probably from recording manager, George Martin—a miniature silver which, although only two inches in diameter, will actually Twist And Shout."

award marks two more Beatles' achievements— million sales of their EP "Twist And Shout" (the selling EP in Britain) and their distinction in rst recording stars to top the LP, EP and singles same time.

U.S. wants ou Caravelles

THE Caravelles, whose debut disc "You Don't Have To Be Baby To Cry" clinched its to number 6 in this week's U 100, published by "Billboard are being sought for appearance America either next month or

Two major U.S. agencies are nego tiating to handle the Caravelles there and the duo have already been invited to appear on Ed Sullivan's spec tacular TV show.

They are almost certain to visit America within six weeks of com pleting their tour with Billy J. Kramer on December 8.

● "You Don't Have To Be A Baby To Cry" has reached No. 2 in the Australian hit parade.

MAX BYGRAVES' 'LUCKY STARS'

MAX BYGRAVES will make a guest appearance in ABC-TV's "Thank Your Lucky Stars" on Saturday, December 7.

The sequence which Buddy Greco will be screened on the same date. Also in the line-up are the Spotnicks, who Gene Vincent is set for December her November 23 bill.

Susan for Ball ?

Susan Maughan is likely to join Gerry and the Pacemakers at the Dockland Settlements Ball in honour of Princess Margaret at which Dietrich is now unable to attend the Temperance Seven are joining the cabaret for the event at the Savoy Hotel in London.

Hollie

The Hollie Following December Empire booked Hall (3rd), Kings Lynn bridge Rex (10th).

Further details ConnP Hall (12th), A (14th), Bolton Pa Astoria Memorial Music Hall (27th).

SHAD

ANOTHER made with the Sh Locking after all with the group Richard g recorded for To di interrupt rehearsals week for "Wonderful Life.

breakthrough in guitar design . . .

Disc banned—and hows

rrow's "Thank Your e telerecording on o'clock Club " be allowed to sing he show.

new Val Guest pro ircus " which stars

rôle he joins a beauty compe ncludes Linda s, the Duchess an Hartnell, for Joe and Comedy

DAILY MIRROR, Tuesday, November 5, 1963.   Page 17

PRINCESS MARGARET CHEERS THE BEATLES

FOUR young men, with shaggy-dog hairstyles and velvet-collared suits, are being presented to Princess Margaret. But they really need no in...troduction. For they are . . . the Beatles. From the left—Ringo Starr, John Lennon and Paul George Harrison and Paul McCartney.

It happened last night at the Prince of Wales Theatre, after the curtain was rung down on the Royal Variety Show.

The Beatles were a hit with everyone.

Princess Margaret clapped and cheered them as the audience went wild with delight. And outside the theatre, the Beatles' faithful, screaming fans called—joined to 200 police specially drafted in cope with the spreading beatle mania.

See Centre Pages.

The Beatles Triumph

"om the HMV la om Karl Baron on ..ched the Springfields, has ut group, the Companions, has who previously recorded as a solo will make its disc bow on Fontan ..nnett and the Rebel Rousers under the supervision of Ad anager John Burgess. The di "You're Really Got A Ad Parlophone on No recorded by I same lab

---

BEATLEMANIA

Night of triumph for four young men at the Royal Variety Show

NEW th

They loved them—Yeah, Yeah, Yeah!

By Don Short

LEADING Beatle John Lennon bawled into the microphone at the Royal Variety Show last night:

"Those in the cheaper seats please clap—and the rest of you rattle your jewellery."

The 1,200 people in the audience at the Prince of Wales Theatre paid from one to twenty guineas.

And the four lucky lads from Liverpool were then they had broken down their traditional "stuffed-shirt" barrier.

From then on the usually sedate audience made it quite clear that they had been bitten by the Beatle bug. And that they were ENJOYING it.

Snapping

In the royal box Prin cess Margaret, in a red and gold brocade gown, was snapping her fingers in time with the music.

The Queen Mother smiled happily—and clapped with the rest of

The Beatlemania fever increased with the group thumping out their hearts out with "She Loves You," "Yeah, Yeah," "Twist and Shout," and "Till There Was You."

Last night EVERYBODY loved the Beatles—Yeah, Yeah, Yeah.

It was their greatest triumph yet. Most of their teenage fans were locked outside the theatre. The Beatles were on their own. And they made it.

Backstage, after their performance, the Beatles were dazed at their triumph. Said Ringo Starr: "I went in a little over the shock."

Then came the royal party.

The Queen Mother asked: "Where are you playing next? "

Paul McCartney said: "It was fantastic. We never dreamed this would happen."

John Lennon: "The audience were really with it."

And George Harrison added: "We're still getting over the shock."

Then came the introduc tions to the royal party.

The Queen Mother asked : "And next ? " Harrison replied : At Slough, on Sunday night, Ma'am." The Queen Mother replied: "Oh, that is quite near us."

And Princess Margaret chimed in with: "Oh, Slough, Slough, quick quick Slough, I have read quick your visit today."

Then came the two strong-Jones, Tony Arm must be the only photo grapher who hasn't photo graphed you.

The Beatles told how it was quite welcome to do so.

Other big hits in the first half of the programme were American singer Buddy Greco and Susan Maughan with a new hair style and new dress.

Compere Dickie Hender son kept the royal box in smiles linking up the Varying acts.

Ballet star Nadia Nerina closed the first half of the programme.

Smile

Television addicts, glee fully welcomed Wilfred Brambell and Harry H. Cor 1. Little Charlie Drake, who was also on the bill, got a smile from the Queen Mother when he wise cracked: "Sorry your horse didn't do very well over the week-end, Ma'am."

The Queen Mother's horse, Silver Fame, finished second at 6-1 in Saturday's Grand Sefton at Liverpool.

Among the other star performers were Marlene Dietrich, Harry Secombe, Tommy Steele, Max By graves and Joe Loss.

THE QUEEN MOTHER with four of the stars at last night's Royal Variety Show in London. From the left are comedian Charlie Drake, ballet star Nadia Nerina, TV's Dickie Henderson and bandleader Joe Loss.

REAL GONE! A fainting girl is carried away.

MARLENE'S PALS

Marlene Dietrich, filmland's queen of hearts for thirty years, makes friends with the Beatles, pop princes of 1963, at rehearsals for the show.

75 PER CENT PUBLICITY, 20 PER CENT HAIRCUT AND 5 PER CENT LILTING LAMENT

SUNDAY MIRROR, February 23, 1964

EATLE CRUSH

FAB. FANtastic.
OUT. It was
incredible re-
London Airport
r seen. It was
BEATLES.

this exclusive pic-
cials taken for the
Mirror by Deso
nn, shows the
that faced them
they flew in from
a yesterday
look at those fans.
inistry of Aviation
te put the number
00 to 12,000.
raming, Banner-way-
jam-packed on the
op of the Queen's
ling.
stly girls. But there

were others. Mums with
babies in arms. Dads with
children on their shoulders.
It was pandemonium.

The screams worked up to
fever pitch when the
"Beatle Clipper" jet
touched down and those
haircuts appeared.

In a mad rush to get

another glimpse of their
idols, teenagers smashed
the glass panel of the door
way leading to the stairs.
It was chaos. Splinters
showered frightened girls.
Some were cut, some
bruised, and many fainted.
Forty casualties were
given first aid. One girl
was taken to hospital. The

survivors of the rooftop
stampede clambered on to
cars outside the VIP
lounge and crushed roofs,
bonnets and boots.

The Beatles knew no-
thing about the chaos.
They were with reporters.
Said Paul: "A better re-
ception than in America."

Asked whether they had
a special message for the
Prime Minister—who had
described them as his
"secret weapon"—and their
parents, they said: "Hello
Alec and hello Mum."

Then they were smuggled
out a side entrance.
● Last night Paul went to
see actress Jane Asher,
18, at a Canterbury theatre.
He said later: "It seems
corny to say it, but we're
just good friends."

Sunday Mirror Reporter

The Americans went mad about the Beatles in 1964. The hype machine did its work well and American kids were well primed about this exciting new British group. Thousands of screaming fans met the Beatles at Kennedy Airport when they arrived on 7 February and New York's traffic was nearly brought to a standstill as the fab four made their way to the city's centre. The British Prime Minister had been due to arrive on the same day as the Beatles but it had been Sir Alec Douglas-Home who put back his visit a day.

When the Beatles returned to Britain on 22 February it seemed as if all London's classrooms had emptied out to meet them at Heathrow. British fans' fears were confirmed when the four spent more and more time in the United States and sadly toured less in Britain.

BEATLES NEW TRIUMPH WIN FIRST GOLD DISC

THE staggering success of the Beatles continues! Only days before they face their biggest-ever audience—on this weekend's "Sunday Night At The London Palladium"—it was learned that the Beatles are now assured of their first Gold Disc for their current single, "She Loves You." And this week sales of the group's "Please Please Me" album passed the enormous figure of 250,000.

More than three-quarters of a million copies of "She Loves You" had been sold in Britain alone by this week—and as the disc continues a big seller at home, foreign sales are now sure to bring the total to a million.

Virtual world-wide release is being set for the disc. It is already proving a hit in Scandinavia and has been issued in America, where the nation's disc-jockeys are giving it considerable air-play.

Other countries in which the John Lennon-Paul McCartney composition will be released are Australia, Israel, France, Benelux, Italy, Germany, South Africa, Sweden, Denmark, Finland and Iceland.

"She Loves You" is the Beatles' fourth single, and their third British chart topper this year.

They're back!

A POLICEMAN finds his ear uncomfortably close to a scream. It happened at London Airport yesterday. It was the wildest reception ever seen there. Who was flying in? That's right—the Beatles. Now turn to Pages Two and Three.

DAILY MIRROR, Monday, February 24, 1964 PAGE 13

STOWAWAY GIRL CRASHES THE SECURITY BARRIER FOR A RIDE WITH HER IDOLS IN A 1912 ROLLS

Daring Sue drops in on the Beatles

HOLD MY HAND! Susan grabs the car's side—a heartbeat away from George.

A booted leg rests on the side of the Rolls-Royce as 16-year-old Susan Sims lands among her idols.

By DON SHORT

CAMERAS whirred as the Beatles came down the Thames in a high-powered motor cruiser yesterday—to disembark for a ride in a 1912 vintage Rolls-Royce.

John, Paul, George and Ringo — who were being filmed for a TV programme called "Big Night Out"— climbed into the car.

Then suddenly, 18-year-old Beatle fan, Susan Sims, dashed into camera focus. She grabbed the side of the car, then tumbled in.

Susan had slipped through the tight security ring at ABC TV's riverside studios at Teddington.

There she was in the picture – disappearing with the Beatles in the Rolls, too late for anyone to stop her.

And she will appear like that when the TV programme is screened.

Producer Philip Jones clapped a hand to his head and shouted: "How did she get in?"

Nearly 500 other Beatle fans screamed and shouted behind wire fences as police drove after the car.

Tears

But Susan was close to her idol, George Harrison, at last.

At the studio, George got out, with Susan hanging on to his coat.

Then a police sergeant caught up with her. And her big moment was over. She burst into tears. George consoled her. And as she was led away Paul told her: "Don't worry, luv."

A stern-faced policeman asked her: "How did you get in?"

All she could answer was: "He held my hand. George held my hand."

She wore red cowboy boots and placards over her raincoat declared: "I Love the Beatles," "Our Beatles Are Home," and "George, I Love You." A silver key ring, inscribed "For George's 21st on the 25th," was round her neck.

Outside the barrier, where police had escorted her, Susan, a children's nurse from Miles-lane, Cobham, Surrey, sobbed:

"Paul and Ringo stopped me from hitting the floor when I jumped in.

"I met them once before in Bournemouth. It took me two days to hitchhike there and Paul told me off."

Then Susan told how she had got in. "There was a tree on the bank and I climbed in over that."

Frantic

More Beatle fans found the same way over later in the afternoon. And there were frantic chases round the studio before the security gap was closed.

An ABC television spokesman said: "We can't cut out the Rolls-Royce scene as it would spoil the continuity. So I am afraid the young lady will be seen in the programme."

"I hope she won't be calling back for a fee."

TWIST and SHOUT
A police sergeant prises Susan's grip loose from George's coat while she presses her head to his chest.

ALL MY LOVING
... but all there can be for unhappy Susan is a consoling hand before the Beatles go on their way.

SHE LOVES YOU The end of the trip, but Susan still keeps hold of George Harrison's coat as he gets out of the car . . . . . George is the Beatle Susan adores.

Friday, September 3, 19

NEW MUSICAL EXPRESS

NME HAS ONLY REPORTER PRESENT WHEN —
Elvis meets Beatles

ELVIS PRESLEY was playing bass guitar, with the benefit of a little instruction from Paul McCartney; John Lennon was on rhythm guitar. The record they were backing was Cilla Black's "You're My World." Suddenly John exclaimed: "This beats talking, doesn't it?" And that's how it was—the world's No. 1 solo star and world's No. 1 group were meeting for the first time and communicating through music.

The get-together took three days of planning and was shrouded in secrecy to avoid two armies of Beatles and Presley fans gathering in one spot. The Beatles had accepted Elvis' invitation to spend last Friday evening (August 27) at his home.

It was my great privilege to be the only journalist invited. There is not a picture in existence to record the great event. No one with a camera was allowed inside.

Colonel Parker escorted the Beatles to Presley's Bel Air home shortly after 10 pm. Police stopped traffic to prevent fans tailing them. The Colonel's associate, Tom Diskin, and I collected Brian Epstein from Los Angeles Airport, to which he had flown specially from New York to be present, and we arrived at the house a few minutes after the Beatles.

> CHRIS HUTCHINS brought the two greatest pop attractions on earth together and tells NME readers in a vivid word-picture what happened at Elvis' Bel Air home.

...thought my number was really up

THE THOUSANDS WHO ASKED YESTERDAY:

How's Ringo?

PHOTONEWS

Picture by HARRY BENSON

RINGO STARR'S tonsils are out, he's feeling fine, and supping up ice-cream, tea, and lightly cooked eggs. The Post Office, however, is feeling slightly battered. So many girls rang the Beatle fan club to ask about him that London's Covent Garden telephone exchange was jammed. Five operators were intercepting and answering inquiries, with the aid of chalked-up bulletins in the exchange.

While Ringo was resting, a medal was on the way to him from two girls in Dayton, Ohio, inscribed: "Medal for Bravery; my tonsils are out." Their doctor-employer keeps a stock of the medals—for his child patients.

AT THE END OF THE HOT LINE— COV 2332

by ANN LESLIE

IT is two o'clock when I arrive at Hot-Line Headquarters, the tiny office of the Beatle fan club who own Cov. 2332, the telephone number via which anxious and devoted Beatle-people can inquire about Ringo's progress.

I push past a small crowd in the bookshop below; then up the stairs past where some wit had plastered "Betting Office" over the "Ladies" sign, and on to where countless Beatle fans have scrawled "I love you,

Ringo" and "I'm the one you winked at on the 2nd July" over the margarine paintwork.

The office is almost submerged in adoring debris—sacks of letters, telegrams, embroidered cushions, cuddly toys. Struggling through this debris are two girls, two men.

WHITE PHONE

There is an unnerving and unexpected quiet. I am introduced reverently to a white telephone which every moment gives strangled couple of quickly cries. No one

answers it: "We've got a phone-answering gadget on it how—yesterday it was murder" they say.

"Tried to get three extra lines put in—too late.

"It's a whole system breaks down every 20 minutes or so. And the poor exchange is jammed —half the time you can't get through on any Covent Garden number.

"Ringing from the States they are. All through the night there [2.10 p.m. I eavesdrop on the phone-answering machine

With supervisor hovering in background, five girls at Covent Garden exchange intercept and

---

CHRIS HUTCHINS is in America

LIVING with the BEATLES

NME is the only music paper to have a staffman with the Beatles on their tour. Here he tells of their greatest concert triumph and of being

PRISONERS ON FLOOR 33

Part of the 56,000 crowd (the whole lot are on the centre pages?), which cheered and went hysterical over the BEATLES at Shea Stadium, New York, on Sunday night. (*NME* Exclusive picture).

The BEATLES in action, surrounded by protectors and sound system men on the field at Shea Stadium. (*NME* Exclusive picture).

THE most spectacular concert in American history! An invitation to a party from Frank Sinatra! Royalty treatment from civil authorities! And a police force that cordoned-off a square mile of New York City!

These are just a few of the thrills the Beatles have encountered during their first four days of this historic American tour.

During those four days John, Paul, George and Ringo have been the sole occupants of the 33rd floor of New York's War-wick Hotel.

To get within half a mile of the hotel you have to prove to police at specially erected barriers that you are either staying there or are visiting another building nearby. Even the hotel's employees have to show a Beatle pass to get to work!

At the Warwick itself there are guards in the lobby, riding in the lifts and on Floor 33.

BUT THE SAME SECURITY WHICH HAS KEPT THE FANS OUT IS ALSO KEEPING THE BEATLES IN!

On the night we arrived (last

Los Angeles teenagers invaded canyon home

NEW MUSICAL EXPRESS *

Fans waved from helicopters!

FOR five days the Beatles basked in the glorious Californian sunshine by the swimming pool of their rented house in Benedict Canyon. Although the house was several miles out of town beyond Beverly Hills it seemed as though every fan in Los Angeles made a pilgrimage at one time or another to stand and wave at the gates for a few seconds before being moved on by the police (writes CHRIS HUTCHINS).

Some came by helicopter they had saved for months to charter and waved from the sky. Others walked up the long steep hill in the intense heat.

One little girl took 4½ hours to climb the hill on crutches and hand to the guard at the gate a ring she had made for Ringo and a letter. Then she turned round and started the journey back.

The Beatles rarely slipped out and only did so by night. Early in their stay George and Paul went to a Byrds' recording session and heard the American group wax its new U.S. single "The Times They Are A-Changin'."

There were frequent visitors to the house including Joan Baez who spent most of Monday chatting to John by the pool.

Car broke down

The Beatles travelled

LIVING with the BEATLES

burning, so don't be surprised that only two Beatles arrived home tanned.

Each evening a chef prepared steaks on a charcoal grill in the garden for their dinner. They rarely went to bed before

The BEATLES received a fan deputation at Atlanta, Georgia, where they were inundated with gifts, including life-sized figures of themselves, two of which Ringo and John are holding. In the background, arrowed, is NME's Chris Hutchins, who has written this series and who organised the historic Elvis-Beatles meeting, described by him on the next page.

COLONEL TE... BOYS ABOU... ELVIS ...

WHEN he visited their Colonel Tom answered questions from Beatles about why Elvis P... no longer tours or records film songs.

"Elvis is unavailable personal appearances because his filming commitments. I've sent his gold Cadillac on a... of America. Matter of fact i... successful I'm thinking of put... his gold suit on tour!" he...

On the question of recor... Parker said: "What differ... does it make to the fans wha... Elvis makes them in Nashville Hollywood? They still buy... even after ten years."

SMALL FACES

NEW to

Friday, Septembe...

YEAH! YEAH!—RINGO MARRIES
MAUREEN at 8.15am

By MAUREEN CLEAVE

Beatles drummer Ringo Starr married 18-year-old hairdresser Maureen Cox at Caxton Hall, Westminster, today. It was a quiet, breakfast-time wedding. And then they drove off to Hove for their honeymoon.

Eight-fifteen. It must be the earliest hour any Beatle has ever risen.

John Lennon had this to say: " It was very early and we all felt a bit ill, except Ringo. He looked extremely well. He kept going because he was getting married.

'There was an Austin Princess for them and my Rolls and George (Harrison) came on his bicycle. He fancies this cycling now and at the end we put his bike in the back of my Rolls."

Off-white suit

" Ringo wore a lightish grey tweedy kind of suit with the pants sort of raised up in the front and the jacket sort of dropped down at the back.

" He had a white carnation and so did Brian Epstein. Nobody got us any. We were going to wear radishes, actually.

" Maureen had on an off-white suit of sort of lacy wool and her hair was up and done in a sort of string bag at the back. It looked good, actually.

" She had orchids.

" Some fellow said, ' Are you Richard Starkey and are you Maureen Cox?' and they said yes and I clapped at the end. Nobody cried.

" We'd threatened Mrs. Starkey that if she did she wouldn't be one of the gang.

" Then we all signed the register and went off to breakfast."

And so ends John Lennon's description of the wedding.

Apart from John and George Harrison and John's wife, Cynthia, the couple's four parents were there and Beatles's manager Brian Epstein was best man

On holiday

Paul McCartney is on holiday at present, said Mr. Epstein.

The notice of marriage was given late on Tuesday afternoon in Ringo's real name—Richard Starkey.

The wedding was planned in secrecy and at 8 a.m. today the Superintendent Registrar, Mr. Barry Digwood, and his assistant, Mr. Donald Boreham, were waiting.

The couple were a few minutes late and it was nearly 8.15 before the ceremony was under way.

As the party left they were ushered down the steps by a surprised doorman.

He said: " I could hardly believe my eyes when I saw Ringo. I helped them into their cars and off they went."

The couple were married by licence and the notice of marriage was given without either of them appearing at Caxton Hall beforehand.

Pop girl Dusty to be sued

£6800 ACTION AFTER ROW OVER S. AFRICAN TOUR

Evening Standard Reporter

British pop singer Dusty Springfield learned today that she is being sued for damages by the promoters of her recent South African tour. The 23-year-old singer was ordered to leave South Africa three weeks ago after performing before multi-racial audiences.

News of the action came in a report carried by the Johannesburg daily newspaper Die Transvaler.

The promoters seek the return of £1800 paid to Miss Springfield and Die Transvaler says the promoters also claim £5000 damages.

The South African Government refused to extend Miss Springfield's visa after she performed before white and coloured audiences.

Said Miss Springfield's manager, Mr. Vic Billings: " This is complete news to me. I can't understand it. We left on good terms with the South African promoters.

" It was agreed that neither Dusty nor they had broken the contract. They had booked her into halls catering for multi-racial audiences which the Government wouldn't allow —so it wasn't Dusty's fault.

" The £1800 was deposited in a London bank in Dusty's name before she left for South Africa. It's there, but we can't touch it until the authorisation to clear comes from the promoters themselves in Johannesburg. That seems unlikely at the moment."

TV BAN ON TWINKLE'S SONG

By JACK BELL

TWINKLE, the 17-year-old singer with the long blonde hair and sparkling rings on her fingers, has had her first record banned by " Ready, Steady, Go!" Rediffusion's top TV pop show.

The song, called "Terry," has been banned because it tells the story of a boy who gets killed on a motor-bike after a quarrel with his girl friend.

It has reached thirty-fourth position in the show's popularity chart.

The "Ready, Steady, Go!" programme editor, Mr. Robert Bickford, said: " I think it is sick, unsuitable and morbid. We don't want to encourage American-style 'sick' numbers on this programme." The song was written by Twinkle—real name Lynne Ripley—of Kingston Hill, Surrey.

Listen

Mr. Philip Solomons, publisher of the song, said last night: "They must clear their ears out at ' Ready, Steady, Go.' They must listen to what the lyrics say. The girl in the song pleads with the boy to be careful. It's really a plea for road safety.

"Twinkle is not a nasty little girl. She is intelligent and educated.

"She is recording the song in French, Spanish, German and Italian. It goes on release in America next week."

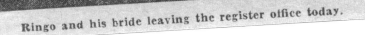

Ringo and his bride leaving the register office today.

THREE STONES TO FACE 'INSULT' CHARGE

ROLLING Stone Mick Jagger and two of his pop group are to face summonses alleging insulting behaviour.

They are due to appear in court at West Ham, London, on July 22.

The summonses against Jagger, 20, bass-guitarist Bill Wyman, 23, and guitarist and harmonica-player Brian Jones, 21, were issued following a complaint by garage attendant Mr. Charles Keeley and one of his customers, Mr. Eric Lavender.

The action follows an alleged incident at an all-night garage in Romford-road, Stratford, last March.

After the Stones called at the garage, Mr. Keeley and Mr. Lavender lodged a complaint at Forest Gate police station.

Mr. Lavender was formerly warden of the Durning Hall Youth Centre, Forest Gate.

THE ROLLING STONES RUN INTO NEW TELEVISION ROW

By RAY HILL

THE Rolling Stones pop group, temporarily banned by the BBC after a row over a recording session, were involved in another rumpus last night.

The Stones turned up at the Alpha Studios, in Birmingham, to record their "Little Red Rooster" for next Saturday's "Thank Your Lucky Stars" on ABC-TV.

A Press party had been laid on to "Meet the Stones." But they shook their flowing locks and said: "Not for us."

They also refused to attend a photographic session to have their pictures taken with Petula Clark.

After angry words had been exchanged, they agreed to see reporters in their dressing-room.

Mick Jagger, the group's lead singer, told me: "We don't want any trouble with anyone—the BBC, ABC or anyone else.

"The police wanted to get us out of this building because of our fans, so we decided not to meet the Press or anyone else for drinks.'

The group's row with the BBC is over their failure to turn up for a recording session. The BBC has decided not to offer them any more contracts until that has been sorted out.

Mick Jagger said: "If the BBC are upset we're sorry—we don't want anyone to be upset with us.

"If necessary we will apologise."

Holiday

He went on: "The contract must have been signed for us while we were in the States. I didn't know anything about it.

The Stones's supposedly 'put-on' vulgar act of the 1960s hid their talent from many though it proved a gift to newspaper headline composers. They became musical superstars but their personal lives were the subject of frequent media interest. Jagger was associated with many girls and sometimes drugs. Keith Richard led a similar life style and, like his group vocalist, made several court appearances. For all that they couldn't help giving electrifying stage performances and recording some of rock's finest songs.

CROP OF THE POPS

DAILY MIRROR, Wednesday, April 22, 1964   PAGE 21

Free trim for next Hit Parade champs

A FREE haircut awaits the next artist or group to be top of the pops.

The man who offers to snip a little bit off the top is Mr. Wallace Scowcroft, leader of Britain's hairdressers.

For, he says, the professional pride of hairdressers is being outraged by teenaged customers who slavishly follow the long-hair styles of their pop idols.

"If pop groups had their hair well cut the teenagers would copy them—instead of just asking for a bit off the neck," Mr. Scowcroft said yesterday.

Then 50-year-old Mr. Scowcroft, who is president of the National Federation of Hairdressers, put his head in the lion's mouth, so to speak.

The Rolling Stones are the worst," he said. "One of them looks as if he has got a feather duster on his head."

Long locks at the top . . . Mick Jagger of The Ro'ling Stones.

---

300 FLOCK TO COURT AS 3 POP STARS ARE ACCUSED

The Rolling Stones . . . Charlie Watts, Brian Jones, Keith Richards, Mick Jagger, Bill Wyman.

Rolling Stones fined for a 'public insult'

By MARY MALONE

NEARLY three hundred women and teenaged girls waited outside a court yesterday for the arrival of the Rolling Stones pop group.

Three members of the group — singer Mick Jagger, 21, and guitar-players Bill Wyman, 23, and Brian Jones, 21—appeared in court at West Ham accused of using insulting behaviour at a London garage.

Sixty teenagers packed the public gallery, on each side of which stood three policemen. Outside, fifty policemen were on duty controlling the crowd.

Charlie Watts, the group's drummer, listened to the case from the back of the court.

The fifth member of the group, lead guitarist Keith Richards, gave evidence for the three accused.

Jagger, Wyman and Jones denied using insulting behaviour by urinating against a wall at the Francis service station in Romford-road, Forest Gate.

They were found guilty and fined £5 each. All three gave notice of appeal

---

The big crowd—most of them women and teenaged girls—waiting for the Rolling Stones to arrive at court.

STONES ARE MORONS— MAGISTRATE

By GORDON GREGOR

A MAGISTRATE yesterday described the Rolling Stones as "complete morons with hair down to their shoulders, and wearing filthy clothes."

White-haired Mr. James Langmuir, Stipendiary Magistrate at Glasgow-Central Juvenile Court, made his comments during a case involving a 16-year-old youth.

Mr. Langmuir asked the youth, who had admitted breaking a shop window near a theatre where the Rolling Stones had been appearing:

"What is the attraction for you with complete morons like that?"

And he went on: "I am surprised that you go along and mix with these long-haired gentlemen. They have their hair down to their shoulders, wear filthy clothes and act like clowns.

"You buy a ticket to see animals like that?"

Animals singe[r]

HIS 'TOO-YOUNG' FANS BANNED FROM COURT

Express Staff Reporter

FORTY young girls were banned from a courtroom yesterday when a pop singer was accused of smuggling.

Eric Burdon, 24-year-old lead singer with The Animals, was escorted by his fans when he appeared before Uxbridge, Middlesex, magistrates.

But the police stopped the girls, aged between 11 and 15, from entering the court.

"A youngster must be over 14 years before being allowed into an adult court," said a police officer.

Burdon was fined £200 with £21 costs after admitting fraudulently attempting to avoid Customs duty payable on a camera at London Airport.

SHEATH KNIVES

Miss Elizabeth Thomas, prosecuting for Customs and Excise, said when asked if he had anything to declare Burdon produced [th]ree sheath knives, an antique gun, 200 [ciga]rettes, and three records.

[The ca]meras were taken out of his [case ... Miss] Thomas, and the [... sa]id he was satisfied with [... no]t satisfied with [... the other ... had bought.]

Animals singer Eric Burdon yesterday . . . has to pay £221

Jordan given [sentence]

QUOT[E]

HOW WE LEARNED TO STOP WORRYING AND SURVIVE THE BOOM!

MELODY MAKER, Jul[y]

(Hollies) explain success secrets

THE pop scene is at a crossroads. With no clear trend in sight and a general lull, several things become clear.

One is that it is no longer automatic for a group or singer to have permanent success after one hit record. Quality of individual records matters more than reputation or personality.

Long hair

Another is that music is as important as visual attraction. Long hair seems to have exhausted its power over record sales.

A third certainty is that the Hollies have lasted the pace. This group's success story is one of the most remarkable to come out of the British beat era.

They are image-free — some say colourless. The "soul" groups that make the "in crowd" sounds and rave about obscure artists, look on the Hollies with a cynical smirk.

They think they are musically a bit of a joke. Unfortunately for the wise guys, the jokes on them.

The Hollies are currently enjoying rich chart success which is the result of a steady, if unspectacular climb, to a happy peak.

Theirs is popularity rather than fame.

by RAY COLEMAN

Since they mushroomed into professionalism from Manchester in the foggy days of 1963, Graham Nash (rhythm guitar), Allan Clark (singer), Tony Hicks (lead guitar), Eric Haydock (bass guitar)

and drummer Bobby Elliott have maintained an extraordinarily solid grip on the hit parade. How have they done it?

In days of images and the pop personality cult, how have five ordinary men made such an impact?

Leader Nash believes it is a triumph of music over personality.

Image

"Yes, we're all completely aware of our lack of an image," said Graham. "I've been tryin[g]

"We survived, I believe, because we refused to get caught up in the band-wagon."

Nash condemned some groups for the attitudes and behaviour.

Knocks

"One big trouble with the whole scene right now is that too many people are having too many knocks at a lot of people for nothing.

"The Kinks knocked [the] Steady [...]

'I don't think Dyla[n] will make it big in Britain now. He was too rude to people who were genuinely interested in him'

GRAHAM NASH

Dylan, I don't think Dylan will make it big, pop-wise, in Britain now. He was too rude towards people who were genu-inely interested in him.

"I think there's too much of this attitude from a lot of people in the business, you know.

"There's no need for bitter-ness. If a lot of groups stopped knocking each other and concentrated on sorting out their problems [...]

else, if we can arrange it — and have it out with each other.

"It's no use brooding. You've got to stop a bad atmosphere dead.

Music

"Sometimes [...]

MANFREDS BOUNCE CZECHS

— IT'S THE BOYS WHO JUMP ON STAGE

"THEY'RE a bit un- used to it really. They appreciate in an entirely different way — a better way," said singer Paul Jones, re- flecting upon the Man- freds triumphant visit to Czechoslovakia.

"They" were, of course, the audience. "It" was the music of Manfred Mann.

"Like so many continen- tal countries, especially Sweden and Finland, it's the boys who are most ap- preciative. The girl's don't scream."

How prepared were the Czech pop fans for Mann- made music?

Familiar

"Well they can't get records over there," said Paul, "but they listen to the radio. There are pro- grammes like 'For Your Tape Recorder.' Some men- tioned listening to Radio Luxembourg.

"They were familiar with 'Do Wah Diddy,' 'Sha La La,' '5-4-3-2-1,' and some knew 'If You Gotta Go'. They'd heard it on Lux's Top Twenty Show.

"We went as sort of jazz group. The Czechoslo- vakian Ministry of Culture said 'We'll have you, you play jazz'."

"In fact the kids weren't too interested in jazz so we pruned out the jazzier num- bers. They're mad on rock and roll.

"The number that went down biggest was 'I'm Tired Of Trying, Bored With Lying, Scared Of Dying'. It's a Chuck Berry type rock number, which they loved. Also 'I Got My Mojo Working,' which we do with a lot of dyna- mics."

"The fans there didn't make a noise during the perform- ance," laughed Paul, "but as we built up a number, or got to the climax of a 'twelve- bar rave-up, then the kids let out great roars — BUT not the mass hysteria of the female kind we get here."

Shuffling

"In Bratislava, there was a forty foot space in between us and the 4,000 strong Halfway through [...] started their

seated mass slowly closing the gap. When they got to the stage they stopped and went on listening.

"I thought they'd start leaping up and pulling out our hair!

"As we were leaving the stadium the coach was sur- rounded. With faces pressed against the windows, they started chanting, 'We want the Manfred.'

"Naturally we were a bit nervous, confronted by this sea of faces. Anyway, we eventually stood up and waved really," said Paul.

"The funny thing is the crowd was 80 per cent males, but I think this is explained when you remember that the Czechs are seven years be- hind us musically

"Their music scene now has just started and is the equiva- lent of ours in 1956. The males are digging Chuck Berry, Bill Haley, and Buddy Holly.

"In the early days all the violence was in the music— and I think this is why there wasn't so much violence on the Czech crowd's part. [...] long came Buddy Holly [...] who started

singing ballads as well as rock, and the music got more and more subdued.

"The less violence in the music, the more from the audience was the result.

"Music for Czech teenagers is still an outlet; when it stops being that, the fans turn to violence for an outlet."

Paul thought back: "The most rioting we got, was about 30 kids, all boys, leap- ing on the stage in Prague. They were really enthusiastic boys.

Rough

"All they did was slap my back and take bits of my sweater — whereas the girls in England take my hair if they have half a chance."

Group leader Manfred chipped in: "The police were rough with the kids. And they were armed, although they didn't use guns of course."

"They stood several deep, in rows and with dogs," said Manfred, "but the kids seem to take no notice, and having all those police didn't seem to ruin the atmosphere."

Said Paul: "I was very impressed by the place. Prague and Bratislava are beautiful towns."

Said Manfred: "I thought their standard of living was below ours. I came back thinking "Good old England," which was frightening be- cause whenever I hear patriotism I think 'Here we go again!'—NICK JONES.

PAUL: "They're mad on rock"

Turning the Rock-around-the-clock back

HALEY'S BACK— WITH KISS CURL

Selby

IF asked to name the most terrify- ing experience of my life I would unhesitatingly nomi- nate the first London concert by Bill Haley and his Comets in 1957.

I really thought the theatre was going to collapse around me. And anyway, if I escaped the falling masonry I would be trampled to death by what seemed like a million screaming, writhing, yell- ing fans.

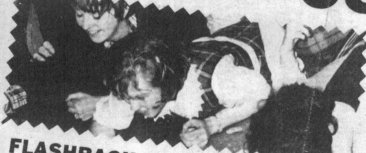

FLASHBACK TO 1957—AND HALEY FANS GO WILD DURING THE COMETS' TOUR

BY BOB DAWBARN

[...] w Haley — still with the famous [k]iss curl and certainly not look- [in]g one day older—is back with [hi]s Comets for a new British [to]ur.

[On]e of the reasons I am so glad [... is] back is that now we have [a] chance to entertain," said [Hal]ey when I reminded him of [a] previous tour. "Everything [wa]s so hectic last time. There [wer]e so many people at the [sho]ws that we didn't have the [chan]ce to do all we wanted to

[...] had the same thing the [Be]atles are experiencing now. [I] understand what they are [goin]g through.

[It's al]most impossible to entertain [so] many people — especially [when] they expect so much. Then [the] promoter says 'Do 20 [minute]s and get off.' And you've

got to try."

Does Bill think there will a return to the rock style of ten years ago?

"It's a fact that groups like mine and people like Chuck Berry, Carl Perkins and Little Richard hadn't toured here in a long time. That meant there was no- body to play our style," says Bill.

"Now with the appearance of those artists it's going to help rock-'n'- roll quite a lot. Of course, it's up to the people, but I would say rock-'n'-roll has a good chance— and I will do everything I can to help it.

"You know, I was one of the first people to try to get the States interested in the Liverpool groups.

"In October, 1962, I played at the Star Club in Hamburg. At that time we had on the bill

Disley

The Sound of Success

THE THUMPING BEAT OF TAMLA—MOTOWN

by Philip Wainwright

The Motown sound was the brainchild of Berry Gordy Jnr. It was a slightly unorthodox but very successful mix of black gospel, soul and white pop. The numerous artists stayed true to their black roots but became enormously popular with the mainly white record-buying public in the United States. Their song lyrics were straightforward and were mainly about the problems of being a teenager. In 1964 there were so many identical titles listed in the R&B and Pop charts that the US magazine *Billboard* was temporarily forced to discontinue separate listings.

Gordy began his famous Tamla label in 1960 but, until the release of *Heatwave* by Martha and the Vandellas in 1963, material in Britain was released under the London American, Fontana, Oriole and Stateside labels. Among the many famous Tamla artists were: Stevie Wonder, Smokey Robinson, Mary Wells, the Temptations, Junior Walker and the All Stars, the Supremes, Diana Ross, the Jackson 5 and Marvin Gaye.

THREE bi-syllabic names, if spoken suddenly to an American, will elicit the response "hit records—top stars—big money." The magic words? You ought to have guessed it, for these names are rapidly gaining similar associations over here, but for all Record Mail's "without-it" readers, they are: Tamla, Motown and Gordy.

Narrowing the field still further, try these names for size: Mary Wells, the Supremes, Martha and the Vandellas, the Miracles, the Marvelettes, the Temptations, Stevie Wonder, Barrett Strong, the Contours, Eddie Holland, Brenda Holloway, and so on, almost ad infinitum. The three magic names are, in fact, the record companies which record these powerpacked chartbusters.

Berry Gordy Jr. is the name of the Mr Big who is responsible for the whole set-up. He is president of the organisation controlling the three labels, and is proud to say, "This is my baby—I started it from nothing. Now we're so big that a letter sent from anywhere in the world will reach us, and the only address you need put is Hitsville, USA. That'll get here."

And that's no idle boast; I tried it with a letter only a couple of weeks ago, and already I've had a reply!

OUTLET

Berry started four years ago, and since then 80 per cent of his releases have made the American charts. It was only recently that his British outlet became the Stateside label, since which time he has begun to emulate his U.S. success with such discs as "My Guy" by Mary Wells, and "Where did our love go?" by the Supremes.

Berry is smart enough to know that the disc-biz is not something that can be departmental.

vue) and there is a publishing company, Jobette, which handles everything that Berry's artistes record. Needless to say he owns that, too.

BIG THREE

And the Gordy group is still expanding; he now has labels other than the Big Three, the most promising of which is the recently formed Mel-o-dy. This, like the others, is based in [the same address]. Berry finds most of

GORDY

THIS WAS THE YEAR OF TAMLA - MOTOWN ..

by Alan Stinton

SOMEBODY once said that in pop music the only thing which can confidently be expected is the unexpected. The point has been proved on countless occasions since, of course, but never quite so convincingly as when, last month, the Supremes took their "Baby Love"—and the Tamla-Motown Sound—right to the top of our charts.

Just how unexpected this particular chart success had been only a month or so earlier can be judged when we realise that "Baby Love" is, in fact, the FIFTY-SIXTH Tamla-Motown single to have been issued in Britain; and yet it is only the Company's third major hit here. The other 53 discs (and they include a score or more of the greatest R and B songs ever put on wax) completed the Atlantic crossing only to be shot down in flames by British apathy.

WELCOME

★★★★★★★★★★★★

USA, beginning with a very brief run-down on some salient facts.

Barrett Strong's "Money" introduced Tamla-Motown to British record-buyers on (of all dates) April 1, 1960. (For the next four years it certainly seemed as though the joke was on any label which handled the Detroit Sound).

London - American's three attempts ("Money," "Shop Around" and "Ain't It Baby") all came to nothing, as did all four brave tries on Fontana ("Please Mr. Postman" etc.)

MARY WELLS had the breakthrough with "My Guy." (R.M. pic.)

THE MOTOWN SOUND

THE SUPREMES

IN a world map of the pop music and jazz scene, you can stick flags in certain towns.

These are the ones that have come to fame: Liverpool, Hamburg, New Orleans, San Francisco, Chicago, Nashville. They have all produced a sound of their own.

Now put a flag into the big bustling city of Detroit, USA. Detroit is already world famous anyway—for motor cars. It is probably the biggest car making place in the world. It's where Ford began and mass production started.

But today, Detroit is making a new name. Away from the automobile assembly lines they are making a new kind of pop music that is hitting the world charts. They call it the Motown Sound.

The Supremes have it and they took it to the top of both the US and the British charts with *Baby Love*. Mary Wells, the Beatles fav gal, showed it with *My Guy* which went to Number 5 here. Martha and the Vandellas flew the flag with *Dancing in the Street*. The Miracles gave us their version of it with *That's What Love Is Made Of*. Kim Weston and Earl Van Dyke came up with *A Little More Love* and *Soul Stomp*. Marvin Gaye chimed in with *How Sweet It Is* and duetted with Kim Weston on *What Good Am I Without You?*

If you want any more Motown names, there are the Marvellettes, the Temptations, the Velvelettes and Little Stevie Wonder.

No doubt about it, the girls put Motown on our pop map. We've seen them and heard them on our TV screens and transistors : Mary Wells, who went a-touring with the Beatles, the Supremes, Kim Weston, Martha and the Vandellas.

I met them when they were here and got from them the story of Motown.

There's a man behind Motown named Berry Gordy, who runs a record label called Tamla, now known as Tamla-Motown. He also runs a big package show of his stars, which at various times includes the groups and gals already mentioned. This is the famous Motown Revue, a top

MARTHA AND THE VANDELLAS

attraction in the US, and it will probably visit Britain this year. The Supremes told me :

"All the Tamla-Motown people were either born in Detroit or grew up in it. We record there and live there still. We all know each other, but now we tour so much we don't see much of each other. We were at school together. So were the Marvellettes. Of course, we are all in strong competition with each other, but when anybody gets a hit we're all glad."

Typical of the Motown crowd is the story of how Martha and the Vandellas came into being.

Marvin Gaye, one of the first people to sign with Tamla—he played drums for Earl Van Dyke for a while—heard three young girls singing and they became his backing group, the Vandellas.

Martha Reeves was a girl who was pop music crazy and used to go along to the Tamla Record building and sort of hang around.

After a while they got to regard her as on the staff and she worked away as a secretary—for no pay ! How pop crazy can a girl get ?

Finally, they took her on the staff and her job—with pay—was

BY HAL LANGHAM

to look after the tapes of songs for artists to learn. Martha used to sing the words whenever she could.

One day the Vandellas were in the studio to cut a new disc when one of them was taken ill. Berry Gordy at once put Martha Reeves into the team and she was so good that he signed her up and made the group Martha and the Vandellas.

Berry Gordy's big day was when he was able to break the news to the Supremes that they were Number One. It had taken five years to get them there, but the whole Tamla building thought the wait was worth just every minute of it.

Detroit is a swinging city. The coloured people are great ones at church singing, choirs, glee clubs, school concerts, local talent contests.

There's always plenty of music in Motor Town. Berry Gordy has made his Tamla label by going out to look for all the new and young talent around.

He's succeeded. And how he's succeeded !

Who knows? The Motown Sound may do a reverse Beatles or Mersey Sound and take over the charts!

EARL VAN DYKE

KIM WESTON

MARVIN GAYE

VALENTINE—16-1-65

The record industry and television companies made so much money during 1963 and 1964 that they were eager to find another teen sensation like the Beatles. The Americans came up the the answer. This was not a case of discovering a group but rather of manufacturing one by carefully creating the right image for the teenage girl market. The four members of the Monkees were chosen for their looks and personalities, rather than for their musical ability, and Monkeemania won the day. When the group came to Britain in 1968, British Rail ran special Monkee trains. The group had hastily learnt how to play instruments for their world tour and massive amplifiers were fitted at group concerts so that no one would miss a note, which may seem an odd idea since most had come to scream instead of listen to the songs. For that, they could buy an album.

The Monkees were the industry's last major teen success of the decade though for a while it seemed as if such groups as the Walker Brothers, Bee Gees, Troggs, Dave Dee and Co, Herman's Hermits and, perhaps the Hollies, might arouse the same fervour that the Beatles and other Liverpool artists had inspired in 1963 and 1964. All of these groups made news in the pop magazines and in some instances reached the pages of the national Press. However, pop was appealing to an older age group that had grown up with the Beatles. Musically competent new acts like the Who, Spencer Davis (especially lead singer Stevie Winwood), though liked by kids, were particularly popular with this age group.

College and university halls and campuses became increasingly important in funding acts and creating new ones. It was a period rich in diversity. The Animals, Fleetwood Mac, the Paul Butterfield Blues Band, Canned Heat, Elmore James, Ten Years After and John Mayall were part of a blues explosion. At the same time American releases on the Stax and Atlantic record labels, by artists such as Otis Redding, Carla Thomas and Wilson Pickett, gave the dance floors something new and exciting. Rock groups began to proliferate and the guitarist came to have as much cult status as the lead singer. Emerson, Lake and Palmer, Black Sabbath, Yardbirds, Cream, Humble Pie, Traffic, Blind Faith and Deep Purple were to become big names alongside many others before the decade ended.

Folk-rock, of which Fairport Convention were the most successful group in Britain, flourished while John's Children, T-Rex, and the Incredible String Band were among the most popular British flower-power groups. Flower-power's ethos was 'making music the way we feel' which with luck coincided with the record companies'. The spread of stereophonic recording added to the drug taker's appreciation of psychedelic or flower-power music. Naturally, the Americans were not totally squeezed out by the British boom. The Mothers of Invention, Captain Beefheart, the Byrds, Love and the Grateful Dead were some of the biggest groups of this period. Solo artists like Joan Baez and Judy Collins consolidated their position while Joni Mitchell, Laura Nyro and Roberta Flack arrived on the scene.

Naming names also means remembering greats like the Velvet Underground, of which Lou Reed and Nico were members, Sly and the Family Stone, who married rhythm and blues with psychedelia, the Band, Doors, the Mamas and the Papas and Creedence Clearwater Revival. There are many more but it was the established groups, such as the Stones and the Beatles, who attracted the headlines, for many of those mentioned above were of interest only to the music lovers.

The enormous upsurge in record buying and in pop generally gave rise to the pirate radio stations moored off the British shore that played hours of exclusively pop music and introduced disc jockeys who became entertainers in their own right rather than just as announcers of the records. Because the pirate radio stations paid the musicians no royalties and were frowned on by some members of the establishment for filling young people's heads with frivolous rubbish, many were forced to close. However, the BBC reorganised itself and Radio One was born.

Festivals became more and more popular as the decade drew to a close. The Monterey Festival in California in 1967 had shown that festivals could be beautiful but the problems of huge crowds, bad organisation and sometimes weather often caused disaster. However, in spite of these problems, the popularity of festivals and all-night concerts demonstrated the tremendous appeal of pop to young people.

DISC WEEKLY, February 6, 1965

Orbison | Stones
Kinks | Gerry | Wayn

DISC

FEBRUARY 6, 1965

PROBY TEARS THEM UP!

SEE PAGE 8 ▶

---

8   DISC WEEKLY, February 6, 1965

PJ SENSATION

Theatres ban him but he may still appear on tour

P. J. PROBY, " problem boy " of the pop scene, sparked off the show business shock of the New Year when his act caused him to be banned from ABC and Rank Theatres during his current tour with Cilla Black.

The fireworks started the first night at the ABC Croydon, when P.J.'s trousers split during his performance. You can see the result on the front page! The same thing happened at Walthamstow on Saturday and at Luton on Sunday.

Upshot was an ABC ruling that P.J.'s act would be banned. And at the ABC, Northampton, on Monday, the show went on without P. J.

But, at presstime, it seemed possible that P. J. would play with the all-star package at the four independent theatres included in the tour.

Says Arthur Howes, impresario who handled the P. J.-Cilla Black tour in conjunction with Brian Epstein:

" So far as I am concerned, P.J. will be on the bill at the Colston Hall, Bristol, this Friday, at Newcastle City Hall on Feb. 11, at Sheffield City Hall on Feb. 19, and at Liverpool Empire on Feb. 21—the final night of the tour. I have not had any intimation to the contrary."

A second tour for P. J. Proby, scheduled in March for Joe Collind and Mervyn Conn Productions, is also in doubt because of the Rank Theatres attitude.

But Mervyn Conn told DISC WEEKLY: " We are definitely going ahead with the tour probably at re-arranged theatres."

PJ, drink in hand, chats to CILLA backstage at the Croydon AB on the opening night of the tour on Friday.

SIXPENCE

WANTED!

UPROAR at Bob Dylan concert

9/4/66

"THIS is my last visit here," said an angry BOB DYLAN at his final British concert at London's Albert Hall on Friday. Sadly, some of the audience didn't seem to care. They hooted, barracked and stalked out in protest when, after the interval, Bob appeared with his electrified backing group. Dylan's excursion into rock-n-roll angered them. They wanted only the pure guitar-accompanied folk singing of the first half.

Dylan handled the aggressors extremely well. "Oh, you beautiful people," he said, sending them up. And, referring to the songs: "Aw, it's all the same stuff . . ."

"Go Home!" "Get the group off!" "Drop dead, Dylan." But he battled on. And though the dreadful reception he got was unforgiveable, the rowdies had some justification.

Shambles of noise

We don't mind a wailing backing group, but MUST it be so LOUD? A lot of Dylan's talent lies in his words, and few could be heard above a caterwauling din, appallingly tasteless, thudding drumming, and electrification gone mad.

The electrified performance was a shambles of noise—a vivid contrast from the first half, which was the great Dylan-with-guitar at his best, singing with more clarity than ever, putting across beautiful songs like "Desolation Row" with a sensitivity sadly lacking from his band-backed mess.

True, some of the second-half had a bit of ferocious appeal. And when he wound up with "Like A Rolling Stone," he sang the words: "You're gonna have to get used to it" as if they had some hidden meaning.

Let's hope he either changes his mind or rethinks his group's function. Dylan is great, but with that sort of row going on behind him, he insults his own talent.

RAY COLEMAN

DYLAN MAKES POP 50, CONCERTS SOLD OUT!

BOB DYLAN was the most wanted and talked-about star in the pop music world this week. The American folk singer jumped into the hit parade at 32 with his first British single, "The Times They Are A-Changin'."

And Donovan, the British singer who has been attacked for allegedly being on a Dylan kick, streaked up the chart 21 places to 15 with his first record, "Catch The Wind".

Big draw

London agent Tito Burns, who is presenting Dylan's one-man-shows, announced that his concert at London's Albert Hall, on May 10, was a sell-out already. The hall seats 6,500.

"I am putting on an extra show on May 9 because of the fantastic demand for the May 10 show," Burns said. "I knew Dylan would be a big draw but I never dreamed it would be this big.

"Manchester Free Trade Hall's Dylan show on May 7 is also a sell-out already. My office phone has been besieged by inquiries for tickets. But people cannot buy tickets from me—the box office opens at the Albert Hall on Monday, March 29 and no telephone bookings will be entertained."

Dylan will star in his own TV spectacular during his British visit. After opening at Sheffield City Hall on April 30, Bob moves to Liverpool Odeon (May 1), Leicester De Montfort Hall (2), Birmingham Town Hall (5), Newcastle City Hall (6), Manchester (7) and London Albert Hall (9 and 10).

The Beatles are expected to attend Dylan's first London show.

Dylan also has a heavy seller in America, "Subterranean Homesick Blues" (see page 7).

DONOVAN SENDS DYLAN A CONGRATS CABLE

● DONOVAN

DONOVAN, whose first single, "Catch The Wind," this week jumped to number 15 in the Pop 50, this week sent a telegram to Bob Dylan.

It congratulated the American star on reaching the chart.

Donovan's own 45-minute ITV spectacular will be screened in six or eight Anglo-American cities.

On BBC-TV "Top Of The Pops" today (Thursday).

His first LP, "Things Thats Been Did And Things Thats Been Hid," is out in the first week in May. It contains a mixture of original material by Donovan and standard folk songs.

Donovan's agent, Aussie Newman is currently negotiating a three-day trip to America from April 16, which will include the Ed Sullivan show as well as other TV and radio dates.

His first single is being rush-released in America on April 16.

EVERYONE'S MOONSTRUCK BY JONATHAN KING!

DISC 7/8/65.

ONE of the reasons "Everyone's Gone To The Moon" is so popular is because you can make up your own words to it. You can walk around singing about "hearts full of cabbage" and nobody will notice you're singing rubbish.

Because the words are so unusual not only do people forget them—but they don't even know what they mean!

So for all moonstruck people everywhere, from the mouth of the genius composer himself—Mr. Jonathan King, comes the true meaning!

"Well, things like the church bit where everyone's singing out of tune means that people rush off to church in the middle of 'Family Favourites' and lunch—so they're in a hurry to get back home.

"And the 'arms that can only lift a spoon' is that all people are interested in is eating and stuffing themselves with food, and they're too lazy to do anything else.

"The part about people going to the sun is really looking back on happier days when they were more intent on enjoying themselves. Really it's a rather bitter little song. The thing that lifts it is that pretty backing.

"I felt I'd like to write something about how horrible the world's getting these days.

"How people don't exercise their minds and just sit about like turnips. I feel that all these things are most important."

＊ WHERE ELSE?

How did Mr. King arrive at that unusual title? "Well, these days where else can you go except for the moon? There's nowhere else left."

After a few short weeks, and with more success to be obviously heaped upon his educated head, Jonathan already feels that he has started a new trend in pop songs.

"People are longing to get lovely smooth sounds instead of just noises from their records.

"The strange thing about my record is that people say it has a childlike quality," he said, sounding extremely puzzled. "And yet no child has appeared for miles in my personal interpretation of this song. Strange."

To date the astonishing Mr. King has been approached by no less than 38 agents—all clamouring to book his talents for tours and "one nighters." And things are happening so quickly that he has already had to pay a long and detailed visit to his accountant.

What sort of a person is Jonathan King, under all that moontalk? His own description of himself is this:

"AN EXTREMELY FUNNY, AMUSING PERSON WITH A RAKISH SENSE OF HUMOUR, WHO LIKES TO TALK ABOUT THIS AND THAT."

JONATHAN — amus...

Dylan was the United States' main musical innovator and influence of the 1960s. A singer-songwriter who inspired many others, he came out of a rather loose folk scene. His lyrics were both introspective and full of social and political observations. His adoption of the electric guitar and the birth of folk-rock met with a storm of protest and illustrates how some fans prefer staying with what they initially find in an artist rather than travelling with him through change. He survived them.

Sonny and Cher are a husband and wife team, but you will see from the picture that this is hardly an adequate description. As my friend in Hollywood wrote in advance of their coming: 'This is no Nina and Frederik deal, I assure you.'

SONNY is 24. He has gentle brown eyes, a ready smile and a militant passion for teenagers. The teenagers' cause is Sonny's cause. His wife is an arresting beauty of unnerving self-possession and enviable style. She has long jet-black hair, dark eyes and is part Turkish, part Armenian, part Cherokee Indian and slightly American. She wears rings on her index fingers and her father is vice-president of a bank in Los Angeles.

She is a tough, elegant, talkative girl of 19, a child-bride. She eloped to Mexico in order to marry Sonny and wore white crepe bell-bottoms for the ceremony. She was then 17.

They have been making records together for 10 months and this week top the American hit parade with one called I Got You Babe, Sonny's composition. It is typical of their work in that it has a message—as many American songs these days. While our songs tend to be bald statements of fact, e.g. I Want To Hold Your Hand, You're Going to Lose That Girl, Everyone's Gone To The Moon, American songs are more persuasive.

disc date

BY MAUREEN CLEAVE

7-8-65 CHER AND SONNY : SONGS WITH A MESSAGE.

Johnathan King, B.A. (Cantab) did not try to hide his academic achievements unlike some pop groups and artists who to this day cultivate a couldn't-care-less image. King came to conquer pop and he remains active in the cause.

DEGREE FOR POP STAR JONATHAN

POP star Jonathan King was awarded an English degree at Cambridge University yesterday.

Then he made a 110-mile dash to Southampton . . . to compere the pop television show – "As You Like It."

But before he left, 22-year-old Jonathan said: "I've no set ideas for the future but I will still be dabbling in pop music."

Jonathan's mother attended the degree-conferring ceremony. But his "good friend" Sandie Shaw was not there. She sent a "congratulations" telegram instead.

Jonathan, was at Trinity College, which Prince Charles joins in October.

He said of his studying: "For the past four weeks before the exams, I shut myself in my room and did nothing but study."

Book

He went on: "I started a book on the drug problem three days ago. Drug-taking is a frightening phenomenon — especially L.S.D.

"I wouldn't dream of taking it.

"I'm sad about Paul McCartney having taken it because he is a creative person, and I think he has a lot of influence over people."

Silver medals from the Queen

ly cord

SAT.
JUNE 12
1965

'S NATIONAL NEWSPAPER
No. 21,721

YEA, YEA—ALL HE BEATLES GET MBES

Ena Sharples

goes one bette

THE Beatles are honoured by Queen in an amazing Birthe Honours list out today.

Also in the list recommended to the Quee Harold Wilson ... Ena Sharples and Dixon of Green.

THE BEATLES, John, George, Ringo and each get the M.B.E. become members of the Most Excellent Ord the British Empire and entitled to wear a medal.

... *even on stage if they want.*

The boys, the first pop group ever to receive such an honour.

the Most Excellent Order of the British Empire.

Paul, John, Ringo and George ... now Members of the Most Excellent Order of the British Empire.

JOHN LENNON SENDS HIS MBE BACK TO THE QUEEN

By JAMES WILSON

BEATLE John Lennon sent his MBE medal back to the Queen yesterday—wrapped in an envelope and delivered to Buckingham Palace in his white Mercedes.

With it was a letter to the Queen explaining why he was returning the award, which he received with the other Beatles in 1965.

The letter said: "I am returning this MBE in protest against Britain's involvement in the Nigeria-Biafra thing, against our support of America in Vietnam and against 'Cold Turkey' slipping down the charts."

"Cold Turkey" is the latest record by John and his wife Yoko Ono. It is now in the charts at number 16.

Copies of the letter—signed "with love, John Lennon"—have been sent to Prime Minister Harold Wilson and the Central Chancery, which is responsible for listing honours awards.

Last night John—his wife by his side—said: "I feel very strongly about peace. This gesture is really a publicity gimmick for peace."

Squirmed

"I did not really want to take the award in the first place, but something in my ego told me I might be able to use it one day —and now I have.

"I always squirmed when I saw 'MBE' on my letters. I did not really belong to that sort of world. It always embarrassed me.

"I think the Establishment bought the Beatles with it. Now I am giving it back, thank you very much."

John, 28, said the decision to return the award came in bed early yesterday.

"I was turning over thoughts of the wars and the report of the atrocities in Vietnam. I have just returned from holiday and was feeling guilty about doing that instead of working for peace.

"I have been thinking about returning it for some time. Suddenly I thought 'now's the time.'"

He continued: "I am sure my fans will realise that this decision is my business."

Why did he return the MBE in an envelope?

John said: "I have been wearing it on my belt along with other hippie things. I lost the box and had to return it in the envelope."

Thirty - four - year - old Yoko said: "I am very proud. This is what I like about John. He is just being very natural. Both of us have the same vibration about this."

A spokesman for Apple, the Beatles' company, said the reference to 'Cold Turkey' in the letter was included as an "after-thought."

Items

"John saw that the disc had slipped a place down the charts and decided to add this to his protest. There is no intention that the other two items and this should have the same significance."

A Buckingham Palace spokesman said last night: "People are entitled to return awards. In fact several people did so when it was announced that the Beatles had been awarded MBEs."

4d.   Tuesday, June 15, 1965   No. 19,144

TWO MBEs SENT BACK BECAUSE OF BEATLES

By MIRROR REPORTERS

TWO men announced yesterday that they do not want their MBE medals any more—because the four pop-singing Beatles have been given the same award.

One of the men is former Royal Air Force Squadron-Leader Paul Pearson, 64—now managing director of a computer firm.

Mr. Pearson, who got his MBE after commanding the Air-Sea Rescue service at Dover during the last war, said at home in Tennyson Court, Warrais Park, Haywards Heath, Sussex:

"I have returned my medal because the latest Honours List has debased and cheapened it as an honour."

He added: "The MBE was created—in my mind, and in the opinion of many others—for service above and beyond the call of duty and money. It has now been awarded to people who have been amply rewarded by the applause of teenagers and their bank managers."

Protest

Mr. Pearson has also written a protest to Premier Harold Wilson.

And in Montreal yesterday, French Canadian politician Hector Dupuis announced that his MBE is also on its way back to the Palace. . . .

Mr. Dupuis, 69-year-old former Liberal Member of Canada's Parliament, got his award in 1945, for his work for deciding who was to be called up for the Forces.

"When I received my award," he said. "I considered I was really unworthy of the honour."

But that, he explained, was before last week's Birthday Honours List gave MBE's to the Beatles.

"I have no desire to be associated with those long-hair, vulgar nincompoops," Mr. Dupuis said. "Neither do I want to be a member of an Order which recognises stupidity and hysteria."

COMMENT from each of the Beatles: "No comment."

Just like a mum, say the Beatles

By DON SHORT

THE Queen was lovely. This was the verdict of Paul McCartney yesterday after the Beatles received their MBEs at Buckingham Palace.

She was "very friendly," he added—"just like a mum to us really."

The Beatles agreed that they were quickly put at ease at the ceremony by the Queen's welcoming smile.

"We had been drilled by some big Guardsman as to what to do," said John Lennon.

All four shook hands with the Queen, who told them it was a pleasure to present them with their MBEs.

'Swinging'

The Queen asked the group how long they had been together.

She laughed as Ringo

The Beatles, Members of the Most Excellent Order of the British Empire, show off their medals after the investiture at Buckingham Palace.

The Who were a Mod band, whose dress typified Mod fashion. Rod Stewart, the Small Faces, Marc Bolan and David Bowie were other products of the Mod world that dressed smartly, rode exquisitely-adorned scooters and collected obscure soul singles from the United States.

I Can't Explain reached number eight in Britain after the group had appeared on *Ready, Steady, Go* and Townshend had smashed his guitar and Moon kicked over his drums. The Who provided the anthem for the us and them syndrome of kids and parents with *My Generation* and its time-honoured dismissal of oldies 'Why don't you f-f-f-fade away'.

The Who had little sympathy with studio-produced music such as *Good Vibrations* and Townshend (right) bitterly attacked the Beach Boys.

'Wilson lives in a world of flowers and chewing gum'

WHO boss attacks Beach Boys

PETE TOWNSHEND this week attacked Brian Wilson, musical brain behind the Beach Boys, for "making pop music too complex."

"Brian Wilson lives in a world of flowers, butterflies and strawberry flavoured chewing gum," the Who star declared.

"His world has nothing to do with pop. Pop is going out on the road, getting drunk, meeting the kids.

"'Good Vibrations' was probably a good record but who's to know? You had to play it about ninety bloody times to even hear what they were singing about."

As the musical brain behind the Who, the group that last year Paul McCartney predicted would probably be the biggest influence on pop music in 1966, Pete Townshend finds himself concerned about the state of pop music in general, and especially about the British pop scene.

His attitude to pop is that it is getting so complicated nobody knows what's happening—least of all the fans. And it is the fans that Pete is most concerned about.

In his manager's office last week he yanked off the scarf that had been half covering his face against the cold like a Bedouin let loose in London, and slumped in a handy chair.

"Look, the kids just don't know what's going on, everything's so involved. Next year is going to be worse. We're going to have a batch of over-produced Beach Boys records and over-produced records in general.

"Andy Warhol leader of America's plastic pop brigade will come over and start on his psychedelic bit and everyone will walk around saying 'oh yeah that's what I thought all the time'. And the first one to explain it like that will cop the money...."

We're just amateurs, say the Us behind The Who

"WE'RE not an Epstein and Bernstein team, we hate the whole mohair suit, fat cigars and gold watch image. We're just a couple of amateurs." So said Chris Stamp and Kit Lambert who manage The Who and the Merseybeats.

It would be difficult to find a more incongruous pair.

Kit is 28, son of Constant Lambert and born in Knightsbridge.

Chris is 23, brother of Terence Stamp, son of a tug driver, and born in Stepney.

Kit went to Lancing College: Chris to grammar school.

They met when they were working in films, and they share what they call "the only slum in Belgravia."

They discovered The Who playing at the Railway Hotel at Harrow and Wealdstone when they were looking for material for a pop feature film.

Asking

"From there we just blundered into management," said Kit. "We hadn't a clue ... about it."

THE WHO . . . discovered by Stamp and Lambert.

BY VIRGINIA IRONSIDE

Tuesday nights thereafter were dead no longer.

Elated with The Who's success (two hit records so far and another record released this week) they decided to take on another group.

In the face of derisive laughs from the industry they coolly signed up the Merseybeats, a last year's group if ever there was one, with nothing but a couple of recent flop records to recommend them.

Now their latest record,

I Love You Yes I Do, has crept into the charts, and they are making TV appearances.

"The field is wide open for new managers," say Kit and Chris. "Now that Epstein has become a remote millionaire and Andrew Oldham has gone respectable.

"To be a good manager you must be a gambler, you must love pop and you must have an over-riding conviction in the people you're managing."

Indeed, Kit was so overcome when he heard that The Who had sold 750 copies of *I Can't Explain* in a week that he threw open the window and shouted the news to the inhabitants of Belgrav...

"There are times, when the Merseybeats ... mobbed in the North, I'm very near to ... admitted Kit. "I ju... meet anyone's eyes ... doesn't ...."

Chris smiled. "I'r ... nut," he said.

TOP TEN

● Doddy's still on top, but it's all change below him, with Chris Andrews in the No 2 spot.
1. Tears .... —Ken Dodd (1)
2. Yesterday Man .... Chris Andrews (6)

FILMS

● Vivien Leigh goes to the top of the West End successes this week, and Zorba the Greek makes a come-back.

WEST END
1. Ship of Fools—Vivien Leigh, Simone Signoret, Jose Ferrer (—).
2. August is the ... Frederica, by ...
3. The Nanny—Bette Davis (2).

BOOKS

● Edna O'Brien's ... amorous capers on holiday in Fr... place, this week.
1. August is the ... Edna O'Brien (4 ...
...ley Head (3a) (1) ...
Theodore Sorensen (Hodder & Stou...
...59.) (4. Airs Above the Groun...
by Mary Stewart (Hodder & Stoughton ...
The House of Elrig, by ...

WHO BOMB THREAT: IRA WARN 'DON'T WEAR UNION JACKETS IN DUBLIN'

Music Echo 14/5/66

● Who in Ireland—with Pete Townshend wearing tricolour jacket

FANATICAL IRISH Republicans threatened to blow up the Who with bombs planted under the stage if they appeared in Dublin's National Stadium last weekend wearing their famed Union Jackets.

Police sped to the show to search under the stage as some seven anonymous callers phoned bomb threats.

The police needn't have bothered. No bomb was found.

The fanatics needn't have bothered either.

The Who discarded their Union Jack coats for the Dublin date and appeared before 2,500 fans in jackets made up of the flag of Eire, the tricolour, which is green, gold and white—specially tailored for them by Dublin's only boutique.

Previously, the Who on their first trip to Ireland, had played to equally enthusiastic audiences in Belfast—where they wore the Union Jack coats.

From June 1-6 the boys are in Sweden for TV and shows.

WHO ARE THE WHO? WELL, THEY'RE MODS WHO PLAY FOR MODS, AND, MOST IMPORTANT, HAVEN'T GONE NICE AT THE EDGES

EVENING STANDARD, SATURDAY, MAY 29, 1965

WHO'S WHO [left to right]: Moon, Peter Townsend, John Entwistle and Roger Daltrey.

Ike

Tina

9/7/66

Mr & Mrs DYNAMITE!

ASK any of the top pop stars what they consider the most outstanding record to enter the chart in recent weeks and chances are they'll scream "River Deep, Mountain High."

This sensational number by the hitherto unknown husband-and-wife duo of Ike and Tina Turner has knocked DJs and artists alike head over heels in ecstasy.

It has swept up the hit parade with a rapidity matched only by some of the best stuff from our really big names. DJs weren't slow to realise its potential even though the record hardly got off the ground back in the States. Radio London, for instance, latched on to it very early and made it one of their famous "Climbers." They weren't disappointed. It blazed a fantastic and fiery trail to the top.

London discotheques soon found it the most requested record among the "in crowd" and stars like George Harrison, Mick Jagger and Georgie Fame were soon spreading the gospel according to Ike and Tina.

Perhaps the most far-seeing fan of "River Deep, Mountain High" was "Top Of The Pops" producer Johnnie Stewart who went to enormous trouble to track the couple down on a massive one-nighter trek.

At his request a film unit approached them in Arkansas and shot that dynamic insert we saw recently on the show.

Tina, known as the "Bronze Bombshell," does all the sensuous singing, while Ike looks after the backing as arranger, conductor, and pianist.

Neither are newcomers to the taking their own 15-piece 1960 and only this week Their hit was produced by of the "sounds" geniuses At the moment Ike and T album specially for the E to bring the couple to B They met in St. Louis and have four children.

Music Echo 21/5/66

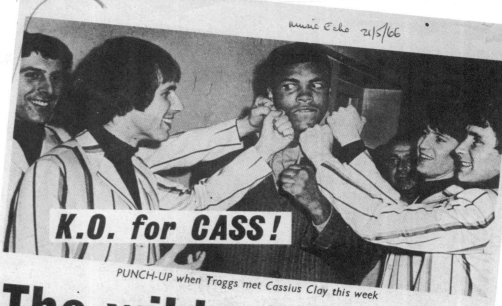

K.O. for CASS!

PUNCH-UP when Troggs met Cassius Clay this week

The wild wild world of the TROGGS!

This week 'Wild Thing' shot up to 3. Here the Andover lads turn themselves inside out!

PETE STAPLES

I AM Pete Trogg—bass guitarist and a fellow who has a great deal of trouble with his hair.

The hair thing is a very sore point with me. It goes the wrong way. Highly curly and unmanageable.

I'm pretty quiet really—until Reg calls me Gladys.

At one time I used to love being on my own. That was because I got claustrophobia when I was with crowds of people. And THAT was because I used to sleep in the airing cupboard at home when I was little.

I used to be an electrician blowing things up with happy abandon. Now I like to spend my free time messing about with boats.

I'm not really a great worrier. I think whatever will be will be. So I don't think about the future—just let things take their course.

I do fairly good imitations of Ken Dodd when roused, and I have a secret ambition to interview Ronnie because I can't work him out.

RONNIE BOND

I AM Ronnie Trogg, drummer and man with the mad grin and Richard Third haircut.

I have to put up with the rest of them taking the mickey out of me 24 hours a day because I always say the wrong thing—like telling people I had double eggs, chips, egg and bacon.

To hide my utter embarrassment with this situation I revert to taking off James Cagney or Spike Milligan.

I love cars. I can't drive but the others say I can always collect the numbers.

I have a bad habit of never having any matches. This is made worse by the fact that nobody else has any either and we all smoke like fiends.

The only thing I miss is the country air. I wake up every morning with a headache and a sore throat feeling tired. It's very rotten air in London. I'm surprised we're all still alive!

I enjoy the group thing tremendously, I couldn't do it if I didn't enjoy it. It's not just the money y'know.

CHRIS BRITTON

I AM Chris Trogg—lead guitarist and the one who wears striped corduroy jackets that look like cotton. Amen.

I am also a fiend for the girls. In fact I consider them to be the most important thing in life—and so I think highly of our fans.

I don't get nervous going on stage. In fact I prefer that than just playing to a few people in private.

I only go to the cartoon films to please Ronnie, but I did fall for Walt Disney's "Fantasia" because of all the hip hippos in ballet skirts.

I worry about whether everything's going to work out on a date. Whether we'll get there on time, whether the gear will work. But not about the real future.

I collect very weird records. I don't really like most pop records. The only one of the Beatles I've got is their old "My Bonnie." But I bought Phil Upchurch's six years ago. I like them when they're not musically quite right.

REG PRESLEY

I AM Reg Trogg, lead singer and songwriter and the man with the most maniacal giggle in the world.

I write most of my stuff on buses and in taxis — anywhere where I'm alone and yet surrounded by people, if you know what I mean.

When I get song ideas I don't write them down but try to remember them and work on them very late at night.

I like being surrounded by people, although sometimes I do get moods when I feel like climbing to the top of Mount Everest (I haven't yet).

After singing, I like swimming. In fact in my early days I broke the school record for the "plunge." Well it was more like drowning than plunging actually. And I always think I won because I'd put my trunks on back to front!

Sometimes I think if I wasn't a singer I'd like to be an eating...

I have a bad...

SHOWPLACE

Tigress Tina roars out

THIS is how 'The Tigress' tore into British audiences at the weekend. As London and Bristol recover today Italy prepares for the sexy roar of Tina Turner. Her blues-rock-soul act with husband Ike and the black-is-beautiful Ikettes is strictly hit-and-run. Business is so good the American pop group has cut its touring time down to three months a year.

Picture : BILL ORCHARD

OPERA

AIRPORT FANS CHASE WALKER GROUP INTO 'GENTS'

DAILY MIRROR, Monday, January 16, 1967   PAGE 3

By MIRROR REPORTER

THE Walker Brothers pop group had to hide in a lavatory when crowds of screaming teenagers chased them yesterday.

Police rushed to London's Heathrow Airport as fans forced their way into the departure lounge of the Oceanic terminal.

The "siege" started after the group—Gary Leeds, 21, and Scott Engel and John Maus, both 22 — were smuggled into the lounge through a back corridor.

More than 1,000 fans had piled into the terminal to try to get a last glimpse of the Walkers, who were leaving for a 15-day tour of Australia.

The fans were barred from the lounge.

Suddenly about forty of them rushed the doors, scattering policemen, passengers and officials. The Walkers hid in the lavatory.

A hundred more teenagers stormed through the lounge doors. Police sent for extra men.

Sobbing

While the Walkers stayed locked in the lavatory, hysterical girls were dragged away, sobbing.

Gary said: "Although we are American, we live in England and regard ourselves as British stars.

"But we never expected a farewell scene like this."

Later the group's plane had to return because of mechanical trouble.

While the Walkers waited for repairs to be done, Scott said: "I am simply terrified about flying. This delay hasn't helped."

Eventually the flight took off—four hours late.

Refuge Locked in the Gents: the Walker Brothers. Outside: the fans.

IS FINED £250

Donovan drugs and a naked girl

28/7/66

"Evening News" Reporter

A DETECTIVE told Marylebone court to-day how £25,000-a-year pop singer Donovan ran stark naked round his Maida Vale flat, swearing and jumping on a policeman's back after smoking Indian hemp.

Twenty-year-old Donovan, who appeared under his real name, Donovan Phillip Leitch, of Alexander Court, Maida Vale, pleaded guilty to being in possession of cannabis resin (Indian hemp) at his home on June 10. He was fined £250—the maximum.

With Donovan in the dock were David John Mills, aged 20 —also known as Gipsy Dave— and 20-year-old Doreen Fabienne Samuel, of Roe Green, Hatfield, close, who was said to have been found naked in Donovan's room.

They were charged with being in possession of Indian hemp at the flat at the same time.

Mills, Donovan's musical director, was fined £250 and the girl, who was described as an interpreter, was placed on probation for 12 months.

'Glad it's all over'

After the hearing Donovan, who wore a green and fawn

Folk singer Donovan to-day

A Scottish folk-rock musician, influenced by mysticism to the extent of travelling to India to study in 1967, Donovan was one of the most successful artists cast in the Dylan mould. His 1967 album *Sunshine Superman* offers classic Donovan while the album's title track and *Mellow Yellow* are probably his most memorable singles.

Scott Engel of the Walker Brothers had great talent but suffered from frequent identity crises and his undoubted potential was never fully realised.

The Bee Gees originally came from the Manchester area but had also lived in Australia. They produced a new sound with their close, high vocal harmonies and, like the Walkers, had thousands of screaming teenage girl followers.

SINGER FOUND GAS-FILLED FLAT

MICHAEL HOUSEGO

Scott Engel, lead singer with the Walker Brothers pop group, was rushed to hospital early today after being found unconscious in his gas-filled flat in Mayfair.

He was taken to St. Mary's Hospital, Paddington, where a doctor stayed by his bed all night.

SCOTT ENGEL
Found unconscious.

NEW MUSICAL EXPRESS *

DEREK JOHNSON looks ahead and suggests —
HOW TO KEEP THE POP FANS HAPPY WHEN THE PIRATES SINK!

ENJOY the pirates while you can, pop fans! Government ban takes effect—and who knows what will happen after that? Despite all their faults and illegalities, the off-shore stations have proved that there is a crying need for a day-long pop music service, and the question that's concerning most pop enthusiasts at the moment is—what alternative provision can be made to fill the gap?

First, let's ask ourselves whether the Government is right to impose such a ban? Obviously, one's first impression is to cry "No!" at the top of one's voice. But look at it rationally—after all, the pirates are outlaws and law-breakers, and really the Government has no alternative but to act.

Goodness knows, they've been putting it off long enough, for fear of displeasing thousands of potential voters. But now, due to international pressures (for make no mistake, this is not solely an internal matter), they have been forced into action.

Why must the pirates go? Well, for one thing, they are cluttering up an already crowded wave-band, and interfering with reception of many legalised stations abroad—as well as with shipping and S.O.S. messages.

The pirates themselves claim that they have carefully chosen their wavelengths to avoid interference, but the fact remains that complaints are pouring in from all over Europe.

Secondly, there is the situation whereby the pirates play records unendingly, without any regard for agreements between the BBC, Musicians' Union and the various gramophone societies—such as the Corporation has to comply with in its needle-time quota.

And this is the main reason why the record companies themselves are violently anti-pirates. Indeed, some (but not all) of the pirates do not even pay their obligated copyright dues.

This, then, is the case against the pirates—it's a very strong case. And it's one with which any sensible person must have a great deal of sympathy.

Nevertheless, the fact remains that the pirates have demonstrated the need for their existence—and if the Government is to clamp down on them, it must, in all fairness, provide a satisfactory replacement.

Driven out

Will the Government's ban be successful? Well, certainly I cannot envisage any Naval boarding parties commandeering the ships although they could effectively take over the forts inside territorial waters). But by making it illegal to advertise with the pirates—or to supply them with food, equipment or any services—they could soon be driven out of business.

The pirates say that they can still obtain revenue, and supplies from "other sources." Well, if they can, jolly good luck to them! Personally, I'm too optimistic—and I find myself compelled to think about what can be done to supplant them when the time comes.

One immediately turns to the BBC in the hope that Auntie might have the answer to the problem. And I feel that the solution could be found within the Corporation, if only the powers-that-be were prepared to adopt a realistic and enterprising approach.

The suggestion which I believe the BBC is kicking around at the moment involves splitting the Light Programme into two—medium and long wave.

Normally, they would operate together—but whenever a speech, drama or a variety show cropped up on medium wave, then the long wave would go its separate way and continue to provide pop music.

The main fault with this project is that the Corporation is committed to providing entertainment for all the family. Thus, a service of this kind would not be restricted to, say, the Top Forty—but would also encompass dance bands, cinema organs and perhaps even piano music. You can't blame the BBC for this—it's their obligation—but it won't suit the avid pop fan.

There is a ready-made solution—but unfortunately I can't see the Corporation swallowing it.

At the moment, the BBC devotes something like 16 hours a day (plus a considerable chunk of its needle-time) to the Music Programme and Third Network—a service which caters

There's only six months to go before that? Despite

for appreciably less than one per cent of the population.

Surely the thing to do would be to take over this wavelength as a pop service. All the "heavy stuff" could then be pushed over to the Home Service, which would still retain many of its specialised programmes, such as schools broadcasts.

The Light would then concentrate on plays, light music, variety, comedy-with-music shows, features and sport—leaving the Third free for pop.

The snag here is that, under its Charter, the BBC is also compelled to cater for minority audiences—and that's precisely what it's doing on the Third right now, even if somewhat disproportionately.

The BBC is rightly very proud of its Third Programme as being unique in the world, so frankly I can't hold out much hope of this pop suggestion being adopted.

Alternative

What has to be done, therefore, is the setting up of a chain of local broadcasting stations dotted throughout the country—expressly for providing a pop service to displace the pirates. Wavelengths would be allocated on VHF, so as to minimise any risk of interference, and the stations would operate under Government licence — existing either by Government subsidy (which I consider highly unlikely) or by local advertising (which seems the more probable—and I see nothing wrong with this, certainly local commercial TV has proved very satisfactory).

The stations would, of course, be subject to a strict code of conduct, both advertising and programme content. This is only to be expected, it is essential—whenever a legalised radio station.

I don't mean that everything would be scripted and censored, to be various show-business agree various royalties, and negot time allotments.

This means that they wo would have to rely on continuous reco would have to inject a m entertainment. In this one record after another a sort of "Saturday Cl

Three floating pirate radio stations may be sunk in six months. L to r: Radio Caroline, Radio London and Radio 270.

Naturally, the contractors would need to show that they had the necessary financial wherewithal to cope with this increased outlay, plus the know-how to operate such a service.

Who, then, should be granted the licences to launch such a project? Quite clearly, the Government should turn to those who have already accumulated vast experience in running pop services—the pirates themselves, plus Radio Luxembourg (London). Provided they are willing, and had the resources, they should be given first crack of the

Whatever happens, it looks as though the days of the pirates are numbered. And public opinion insists that something must be done to replace them—and whether that service is provided by a commercial radio or the BBC, it's got to be POP. So, it's all yours Harold.

ED (Stewpot) STEWART
Radio London

JERRY LEIGHTON
Caroline North

Radio 270 disc jockeys capering ... ip.

Much to kids' disgust, snobbery in British radio circles and Musicians' Union fears that recorded music would replace live bands meant that the playing time of records on air was restricted during the first half of the 1960s. Radio Luxembourg introduced many to American R&B while radio broadcasting ships, which set up home just off the British shore, used American-style DJs and played hit records 24 hours non-stop. Kids adored it but the authorities were not enamoured. New legislation saw the pirate ships removed from British waters but at least it prompted the reorganisation of BBC radio and the birth of Radio One. Many of the disc jockeys from the banned radio stations found jobs on it.

---

he five aces of ur newest national asset

20/10/67

THE BEE GEES ... dollars for Britain.

by JAMES GREENWOOD

THE times they are a-changin'!

First it was the Beatles getting the MBE. Then it was Lew Grade getting the Queen's Award for Exporting.

Now the Bee Gees (the pop group currently at No. 1 in the charts with Massachusetts) have been dubbed by the Home Office "a social and national asset."

What that means, in fact, is that the dollar earnings of ... group of five boys (three ... Australians) have ...

stay for a further period but given them permission to stay and work in Britain indefinitely.

Not long ago a New Zealand girl came over here in similar circumstances and took a job with the Northern Symphony Orchestra.

She became a valued instrumentalist but after two years she went back to insisted she make proper application to settle here.

I wonder what she will think when she reads this story. But of course she wasn't earning dollars for us.

America's love affair with Beatles sours

Evening Standard Reporter

NEW YORK, Thursday.—America's love affair with the Beatles turned sour today as radio stations in several states banned their records in protest against alleged anti-religious remarks by John Lennon.

The announcers of a growing number of radio stations in cities and towns said they would follow the example of an Alabama station manager, Tommy Charles, who called for bonfires of their music and records across the nation.

However, announcers in some areas said they would continue to play Beatles' records, despite the furore which has arisen from a statement by John Lennon that the Beatles are more popular than Jesus, and that Christianity is on the way out.

[The statement was made by John Lennon in an interview with Maureen Cleave which appeared in the Evening Standard and was reprinted in an American magazine.]

Permanent ban

In Ogdensburg, New York State, Donald Ballou, general manager of the local station said he had ordered the Beatles' songs banned permanently.

Ballou said: "I have personally read the article and do not appreciate my child listening to any group that would condemn Christianity. Neither would I allow my audience to listen to such a group."

A mobile Alabama station joined the Ban the Beatles movement, and the announcer said: "Lennon's statement is

not only deplorable, but an outright sacrilegious affront to Almighty God."

'No bigotry'

In Conroe, Texas, the announcer said the Beatles had been banned but added: "We will re-consider if a public apology is made by a spokesman for the group."

However, the manager of one San Angelo, Texas, radio said: "We have taken them off and we don't care if they come out with 10,000 apologies, we will not play them again."

In Salt Lake City, programme director Bill Terry said: "I don't believe in religious bigots any more than I believe in Beatles bigots. I'm playing their records, not their religious ideals."

The campaign was joined last night by the Ku Klux Klan.

At Tupelo, Mississippi, Dale Walton, a Klan Grand Wizard, urged teenagers to "cut their wigs off," and send them to a "Beatle burning" being organised by the Klan on August 15.

● John Lennon is to desert the Beatles temporarily to star in a film on his own. The picture is called How I Won (the) War. Dick Lester, who directed the Beatles in their two films will produce and direct this one

AND THIS IS WHAT MAUREEN CLEAVE WROTE

mind is closed but it's closed round whatever he believes at the time. "Christianity will go," he said. "It will vanish and shrink. I needn't argue about that; I'm right and I will be proved right. We're more popular than Jesus now; I don't know which will go first—rock 'n' roll or Christianity. Jesus was all right but his disciples

GREAT DAVY, WHAT A RAVE!

YES, it was Davy Jones' week all right.

If 5,000 people "got up out of their seats" for Billy Graham at Earls Court, then 50,000 other people got up out of their seats and out of their minds for Davy Jones at Wembley's Empire Pool.

They shouted for Mike, yelled for Micky, screamed for Peter, but went completely berserk for Davy.

The legs on the right are an example of the Monkeemania. Banners, posters, hats, tee-shirts—nothing else mattered.

Hoarse, crying, fainting, sobbing, screaming, running, leaping barriers, and bashing each other on the head with outsize programmes.

Wembley had never seen anything like it—and probably never will again. Today, Disc presents a four-page souvenir of the Monkees in Britain.

MONKEES **Peter**

"You Can't Judge A Book By Looking At The Cover" sings Mike Nesmith, and how true! No one seeing the impassive Monkee breaking out into such a raving song would have judged Mike capable. Memories of Mick Jagger were revived as Mike, complete with sympathy black armband, roared through the R'n'B standard.

VERSATILE Davy takes to the drum kit—and look at that haircut! Davy proved he's quite an expert with the sticks.

Show highlight 2 — Micky "James Brown" Dolenz is helped offstage by Mike at the end of an all-systems-go "I Got A Woman."

DISC 4-PAGE SPECIAL MONKEEMANIA

20 GIRLS FIGHT AS MICKY'S COMB GOES FLYING...

"I SUPPOSE you're wondering why I've asked you all here tonight," smiled an immaculately dressed, beautifully sun-tanned Peter Murray.

The reply from 9,700 assorted bodies packing Wembley's Empire Pool on Sunday left him in no doubt.

Whatever they cried—"Davy," "Micky," "Peter" or "Mike"—it was the fifth and last of the Monkee Marathons, and brother did we know it!

Fifteen minutes before Mr. Murray had appeared on the large rostrum, spasmodic screaming was greeting every last-minute technician or official who dared to trespass on to the sacred Monkee territory.

Disc's photographer Peter Stuart had been to the afternoon concert and volunteered the information that press officer Tony Barrow had found Davy Jones' double and was using him to decoy the fans from the foursome — who made their getaway in a catering van!

In the V.I.P. gallery sat Keith Moon, Spencer Davis, Screaming Lord Sutch, manager Bob Raefelson and, of course, Disc writer Samantha Juste.

GREAT LULU

The scene was set, the lights dimmed, purple spotlights flooded the stage, and on the Enif...

Wembley Recaptured ... by David Hughes

"Tell The World About You," "Respect," "Treat Her Right," "Shout," and "Call Me," and got tumultuous reception for "Let's Pretend" and "The Boat That I Row."

THESE CONCERTS MUST RATE AS LULU'S GREATEST TRIUMPH.

Interval time, and after a short fashion parade of Monkee tee-shirts, a few minutes for peanuts and Pepsi. But, perhaps not surprisingly, few left their seats, loath to miss anything.

It was not long before the "We Want The..." chants...

Peter Murray returned for his important announcement, and retired next to Spencer Davis. The lights were still up, and from beneath the canvas roof at the back of the stage came much scuffling and movement.

Screaming blotted out all hope of conversation, the lights finally dimmed again, and to the familiar "Here We Come" theme, here they were.

Smartly and soberly dressed in red corduroy...

Mr. and Mrs. Elvis Presley . . . pictured together after their wedding in a private hotel suite.

ELVIS MARRIES HIS ARMY SWEETHEART

From BRIAN HITCHEN
New York, Monday

MILLIONAIRE pop singer Elvis "The Pelvis" Presley married his Army sweetheart in Las Vegas today.

Elvis, 33, and his bride, 21-year-old Priscilla Beaulieu, had flown into the Nevada gambling city aboard a private jet from his home in Palm Springs, California, at three o'clock this morning.

With them were six friends, one carrying a white bridal gown.

The couple went immediately to a nearby courthouse, where Elvis bought a marriage licence. They were married later in the private suite of a hotel.

Elvis, who was one of the most eligible bachelors in show business,

slipped a simple gold wedding ring on Priscilla's hand.

Dark-haired, grey-eyed Priscilla is the daughter of an American Air Force lieutenant-colonel. Elvis met her while serving with the Army in Germany.

She was a high-school

girl in Wiesbaden, where her father was stationed.

They dated each other regularly, and when Elvis returned to the United States in 1960 after seventeen months in Germany, Priscilla tearfully waved him goodbye at Frankfurt Airport.

Priscilla's father is now stationed in California and for the past year the couple have been seen several times together.

Elvis said after the wedding: "I still feel nervous."

Even if they've been only occasionally impressed by Cliff Richard in the United States, Cliff Richard is one of Britain's top stars and the Shadows one of its top groups. Chart successes support this view, but while they had countless hits and made films both together and separately, it was obvious their partnership would not survive the 1960s. Cliff became a Christian and was uncertain whether he would remain in the music industry. He stayed with pop and somehow made time for his religious pursuits. Although they would have brief reunions with Cliff at later dates, the Shads instinctively drew apart.

DAILY MIRROR, Thursday, April 13, 1967   PAGE 17

DON SHORT'S DISCS

IT'S ALL OVER

[WHICH IS THE TITLE OF A RICHARD RECORD AT No 7]

Cliff and the Shadows part

IT'S the end of an era. And there will be a lot of sighs, a lot of tears to wipe away from fretting fans across the world. But it had to happen one day.

Cliff Richard is breaking away from Hank, Bruce, Brian and John—his instrumental whiz kids known as The Shadows.

There is one more film to do, possibly one more television show.

They have no stage bookings as a partnership, and I doubt whether they will record together again.

Cliff, who first hit the

Shadows: "I want to teach religion in schools. So when making your plans go ahead without me."

That's why we found The Shadows leaving London in two weeks time for their first major world tour without Cliff. They will also represent Britain in a Yugoslavian Pop festival.

At the moment Cliff and The Shadows are taking an early summer

main good and close friends. And if an opportunity to work together should crop up, we'll all take it."

The Shadows will go on tour in Spain, Japan and Australia. Cliff remains in London to start work on a new film for American evangelist Billy Graham. Some of the scenes will be shot in Soho.

Foster

Normally, Cliff gets £100,000 a picture. But this one he's doing without a fee. To foster the faith he believes in.

CLIFF RICHARD, the wild rocker of 1958 . . .   . . . and today's suave singer.

the charts — but what happened to Sue?

We never see her name there.

Very soon now, I'm glad to tell you, we just might. She's out this week with an up-beat catchy commercial sound on "Don't Go Home" (Philips) and I've a feeling it's going to sneak into the hit parade.

Says Susan: "I have had a dozen records out and although they've sold well they haven't made it. Maybe I've been too sophisticated."

Susan, she is 24, is living proof that you can still be successful without appearing in the top ten.

She is one of Britain's most heavily booked artists, making

TOP TEN CHOICE

YOUR guide to the best of this week's new releases:

1. SOMETIMES (Piccadilly) — Rockin' Berries
2. NOS DA (Page One) — Christine Campbell
3. MAKING MEMORIES (HMV) — Frankie Laine
4. LITTLE GAMES (Columbia) — Yardbirds
5. TIME ALONE WILL TELL (MGM) — Connie Francis
6. COLOURS OF LOVE (Philips) — Vicky
7. DON'T GO HOME (Philips) — Susan Maughan.
9. I CAN FLY (Fontana)—Herd
10. MA FETE FOR RAINE (Vogue) — Antoine

● CHART ANALYSIS Rockin' Berries ballad tempo; Christine-sounding lullaby ties with a theme song there's a little nostalgia in that Frankie Laine waxing.

Yardbirds have original theme and nice Francis wonderful version of the Remo song.

Vicky comes English lyrics vision and Gants give development to song.

Watch the for DAYS for

San Francisco's golden decade

ALL started simply enough — with a dance, organised by a group of people known as the Family Dog in 1965. But it led to new music: the San Francisco sound, which, when linked with the music produced by bands from the Los Angeles area, was collectively known as the West Coast Sound — the father of the rock which dominates the popular music of today.

After that first dance — important because it fixed the music as an alive sound aimed at the feet rather than the head — local groups found their playing chops and developed their individual styles. And the legends grew: Big Brother And The Holding Company, the Grateful Dead, Quicksilver Messenger Service, the Jefferson Airplane.

★ ★ ★

These bands quickly grew into national headliners, but the majority fell by the wayside: who remembers the Daily Flash, Mystery Trend or Loading Zone today?

★ ★ ★

The sound was no flash in the pan. As the superstars got bigger and better, there was an influx of musicians from all over the United States — Steve Miller and Boz Scaggs from Texas, the Youngbloods from New York, Mike Bloomfield from Chicago.

★ ★ ★

It all exploded in the summer of love in 1967: hippies, flower power and kaftans. Suddenly San Francisco became THE place to be. The media pounced, record companies signed everyone who could play (and plenty who couldn't); and the dream turned sour. With the eyes of the world turned towards them, the musicians lost their sense of fun as big business took over.

★ ★ ★

But the music stayed alive — ever absorbing new influences — with a " second generation " of bands: Santana, Creedence Clearwater Revival, It's A Beautiful Day.

★ ★ ★

There was a pause for re-grouping: then the San Franciscans worked their way back to the top, culminating this year in the gigantic-selling Number One album " Red Octopus " for a Jefferson Airplane offshoot, the Jefferson Starship. And there are new bands working their way up: Earth Quake, the Tubes and Terry And The Pirates.

★ ★ ★

TODD TOLCES in San Francisco examines the rise of the city's music, and, overleaf, takes stock of the important bands there today.

'I talked with Buddha. I talked with God. I saw myself at the age of 103.'

ERIC BURDON AS SAVAGE MESSIAH

Meditation is like a miracle cure —says Donovan

Newcastle-born Burdon was a member of the Animals in the mid-1960s, the blues-based group which had its origins in the Alan Price Combo. Burdon's rudely emotive vocals were highly distinctive.

Eventually he was drawn to the US West Coast where he found the cultural climate more conducive to his search for spriritual reality. He produced several excellent singles including San Franciscan Nights and Monterey, which eulogised the 1967 Festival.

At the beginning of the 1970s he found funk in the form of Night Shift, which later became War and for a while backed Burdon. His reminiscences of his experiments with drugs are some of the more lively on record.

Sleeve Art—the zaniest yet

BEATLES' LATEST JUMPS FROM KARL MARX TO SHIRLEY TEMPLE!

Sergeant Pepper's Lonely Hearts Club Band was the Beatles' eighth British album and was regarded as the highpoint of their career. Indeed, it has probably become the best-known album of contemporary music. The record was inspired by the Beatles' involvement in drugs and eastern mysticism. Its release in 1967 preceded a downhill period that saw among other things the Beatles receive poor notices for their television film *Magical Mystery Tour* and the first real signs of a major split in the Lennon-McCartney relationship.

For many people the best song on *Sergeant Pepper's Lonely Hearts Club Band* was *A Day in the Life*. The record sleeve's design and the inclusion of lyrics, as well as the overall album concept and the use of electronic sounds, was highly innovatory for the time and was considered 'serious art'.

Who's who in Sgt. Peppers Band

CHECK the heads against the numbers—and see if you knew who they were.

1, Guru (Indian holy man); 2, 3, 4, Aleister Crowley (The Beast 666—black magician); 5, Mae West; 6, Lenny Bruce (American comedian); 7, Stockhausen (Modern German composer); 8, W. C. Fields; 9, C. J. Jung (psychologist); 10, Edgar Allan Poe; 11, Fred Astaire; 12, Merkin (American artist); 13, Drawing of a girl; 14, Huntz Hall (Bowery Boy); 15, Simon Rodia (folk artist creator of Watts Towers); 16, Bob Dylan; 17, Aubrey Beardsley (Victorian artist); 18, Sir Robert Peel (Police pioneer); 19, Aldous Huxley (philosopher); 18, Dylan Thomas (Welsh poet); 19, Terry Southern (author).

20, Dion (American pop singer); 21, Tony Curtis; 22, Wallace Berman (Los Angeles artist); 23, Tommy Handley (wartime comedian); 24, Marilyn Monroe; 25, William Burroughs (author of "The Naked Lunch"); 26, Guru; 27, Stan Laurel; 28, Richard Lindner (New York artist); 29, Oliver Hardy; 30, Karl Marx; 31, H. G. Wells; 32, Guru; 33, Stuart Sutcliffe (former Beatle who died before group became famous); 34, Drawing of a girl; 35, Max Miller; 36, Drawing of a girl; 37, Marlon Brando; 38, Tom Mix

(cowboy film star); 39, Oscar Wilde; 40, Tyrone Power; 41, Larry Bell (modern painter); 42, Dr. Livingstone (in wax); 43, Johnny Weissmuller (former Tarzan); 44, Stephen Crane (nineteenth century American writer); 45, Issy Bonn (comedian); 46, George Bernard Shaw (in wax); 47, Albert Stubbins (Liverpool footballer); 48, Guru; 49, Einstein; 50, Lewis Carroll; 51, Sonny Liston; 52, 53, 54, 55, The Beatles (in wax); 54, Guru; 57, Marlene Dietrich; 58, Diana Dors; 59, Shirley Temple (child star); 60, Bobby Breen (singing prodigy); 61, T. E. Lawrence (Lawrence of Arabia); 62, American Legionnaire.

IT'S A NEW sort of "pop" art. At least, it's art and it's connected with pop. And leading the trend, of course, are the Beatles.

This is the sleeve of their latest long-player, "Sgt. Pepper's Lonely Hearts Club Band"—to be released on June 1—and for the first time the design is the Beatles' own.

by Judith Simons

the psychologist, and Karl Marx, philosopher founder of modern Communism, shows the moulding of adolescent thought.

Interest in the world of writers tends to be conventional, except for William Burroughs, author of "The Naked Lunch," and Terry Southern, author of "Candy."

The influence of Indian culture on George Harrison is seen through several gurus (spiritual teachers).

There is one person in the Great Parade who never made his mark on the world, though he inevitably would have done, had he lived—Stuart Sutcliffe, a member of the Beatles in their early days, died in Hamburg before their talent was recognised.

Not unexpected, and totally disarming, is the humorous egotism. For the Beatles themselves are depicted twice—in outrageous military uniforms made of luminous satin, and as wax effigies from Mme. Tussauds.

"Sgt. Pepper" itself

Nostalgia

The parade of personalities is dubbed by the Beatles simply: "People we like." And the choice gives an insight into their tastes.

There is the inevitable nostalgia for boyhood heroes—explorer Livingstone, Lawrence of Arabia; a host of film memories—Tom Mix, Mae West, Fred Astaire.

The inclusion of C. J. Jung,

reflects the new-look Beatles—a group now withdrawn from the screaming hysteria of pop world audiences and dedicated to originality and perfection.

The record took six months to make.

Mr. Peter Brown, 30-year-old assistant to Beatles boss Brian Epstein, said yesterday: "It took me weeks of telephone calls to celebrities all over the world to get the necessary permission to use their photographs.

Marathon

"Most were rather surprised, but quite happy when I approached them. Stockhausen, for instance, turned out to be quite a fan of the Beatles!"

Yesterday it was announced that the Beatles are to represent Britain in the biggest live television show ever made—a £750,000 round-the-world marathon with an audience of 500 million viewers.

The programme, "Our World," will link 31 countries, including Russia, Japan, Australia, Britain, and America, via five space satellites for two hours on the night of June 25.

HOW CYNTHIA GOT LEFT BEHIND AND MISSED OUT ON THE BACK OF THE ABSOLUTE

Express Staff Reporters

THE BEATLES went off on a pilgrimage to the Welsh mountains yesterday for some transcendental meditation.

With something humdrum to meditate about on the train.

Such as that time on British Railways waits for no woman —even John Lennon's wife Cynthia.

Which is why, as the four Beatles sped North on the 15.05 to Bangor with a bearded holy man, Cynthia, in her long flowered coat and rows of beads, was left weeping on a Euston platform.

Mind you, she wasn't the only one late.

The scramble

None of the Beatles' party arrived until six minutes after the train's scheduled departure. Fortunately, a locomotive change caused a hold-up.

So, with the help of a policeman, they managed to scramble into the last coach as the train moved off—all except Cynthia.

She burst into tears. But an hour later she was on her way by car to join the other "pilgrims" at a course being conducted at Bangor by Himalayan mystic Maharishi Mahesh Yogi.

The Beatles heard him expound his theories at London's Hilton Hotel on Thursday—and were so impressed that they dropped everything, including recording sessions, to travel with him yesterday

The thinkers

Along too to hear what more the mystic has to say went Rolling Stone Mick Jagger, in purple trousers, and Marianne Faithfull.

Explained the Beatles' city organiser

"This is

platform 3 when the train pulled in.

Someone managed to push a bunch of carnations through to the holy man who waved it like a wand, enthusiastically.

"This is wonderful. Everyone seems to meditate. It is all too beautiful."

Somehow, the Beatles and Jagger were guided safely through the crush and driven a mile to the teachers training college where they booked in for a few days —30 bob board and lodging— and sat last night at the mystic's feet for the conference's opening session.

It began with the Maharishi asking : "How many of you have been meditating ? Does anyone want clarification of any experience ?"

One man who did stood up and said : "I have seen something similar to the absolute. It vibrates and my mind seems to be on it, at the back of it, and at the side."

Nothing to worry about, he was assured.

The source

"It is the effect of the contact with self. This contact is the mark of great happiness. The source of this great happiness is there within us all the time.

"We have to make contact. It is like saying the bank has lots of money but it doesn't help us unless we contact it."

Another man asked : "Is it possible to be asleep and know you are asleep the whole night through ?"

Replied the Maharishi: "Yes, it is being asleep and awake together. This is called cosmic consciousness."

Jagger called it "intriguing." He did admit, though, th—. . . don't know an awf—. . . it."

Epstein on the Beatles: I was not their boss.. I was just their friend

THE STAR MAKER

THEY called him the Prince of Pop . . . the Napoleon of Show Business. And Brian Epstein earned his fame and his nicknames the hard way.

He once said of his struggle to the top: "It was tough. You shout and you fight and you claw and if you haven't got faith and tenacity, you give up. I kept on."

But Epstein, the Star Maker, was more modest about his greatest show business find — the Beatles. He repeatedly denied that their success was due to him.

BY BRIAN McCONNELL

Salesman

People kept asking for their records, so — in November, 1961—he went to the Cavern Club to hear them tap and

A month later, he signed them up and Epstein, the former public school boy who had been a window-dresser, salesman and auctioneer was on the way to making them

millionaires and becoming one himself in show business he

But the matter had troubled him particularly when Beatle Paul McCartney admitted to the Press that he had taken the hallucination drug LSD.

"I couldn't sleep that night and in the morning I decided to admit that I had taken LSD too," Epstein said later.

"This helped Paul. Nobody likes to be a loner. And I believe that some good has come from the publicity about drugs."

Neither Paul nor LSD—he advocated the general use of LSD—

Epstein said he had taken LSD about five times, but he didn't know when he would take it again.

Many things drove

SO HAPPY WITH CILLA

In the background . . . Epstein stands smiling on the steps of a plane as the four boys he helped to make famous greet fans after an overseas trip.

With Lionel Bart at Liverpool's Cavern Club . . where it

Even in the limelight he was lonely

the impression that he would sacrifice much of his wealth to secure a cure for his recent ill-health and an appearance in the limelight

Epstein's untimely death at the age of 32 on 27 August 1967 in the bedroom of his London flat shook both the Beatles and the general public. The Beatles were in Wales with the Maharishi Mahesh Yogi and immediately travelled back to London on hearing the news.

Epstein had previously attempted suicide. A number of possible factors leading to his death have been revealed over the years but he had certainly suffered from depression long before meeting the Beatles. Epstein's memorial service was held at the New London Synagogue, Abbey Road, St John's Wood on 17 October 1967. Obviously, many tributes were paid to his work with the Beatles but none was more notable than the three columns given in *The Times*'s obituary. At the inquest at Westminster Coroner's Court it was pronounced that his death was accidental. He had died from the cumulative effect of bromide in a drug that he had been taking over a considerable period of time.

Daily Mirror

Monday, August 28, 1967 • • • No. 19,805

EPSTEIN (The Beatle-Making Prince of Pop) DIES AT 32

NO WONDER THE MIRROR OUT-SELLS THE FIELD..'

BBC 'News-Stand' pays a remarkable tribute to the favourite daily newspaper of 15,756,000 readers

HAS any newspaper ever before been praised so highly by a completely independent commentator?

Here is a shortened version of what Mr. Brian Connell said about the Daily Mirror on the BBC's Home Service programme — News-Stand — on Friday:

"I will give you three guesses as to the source of these three extracts from this week's newspapers.

● "If Mr. Callaghan is sharply questioned about the way in which British wages and costs are rising after the freeze, he will be able to turn the question back and ask whether wages are not also going up in other countries, in America and the Continent of Europe. They are. But on the whole the Americans and the Continentals are justifying their higher pay by higher productivity. The fall in British industrial production since last year (index down from 135 to 133) suggests that the anticipated rise in wage rates this year is not being paid for by increased output. The position of the pound and the strength of the economy have improved since July last year. But it has been an improvement from near disaster. We are still precariously balanced on the tightrope."

● "September 3 is voting day in the presidential elections in South Vietnam. Or it is for those who can escape the attentions of the Vietcong guerillas long enough to get to the polls. No one supposes that the elections will be fair. The winners, both military men, are known in advance. General Thieu, chief of state, will be present Premier, Nguyen Ky, Vice-President, will be the Vice-President. But at least some kind of elections are being held. Which is more than can be said for North Vietnam, where ruthless dictatorial

CONTINUED ON PAGE TWO

BEARDED Brian Connell is the journalist who's often been called "the Richard Dimbleby of ITV."

In opposition to the formidable Dimbleby, he covered the wedding of Princess Alexandra and Mr. Angus Ogilvy at Westminster Abbey.

And it was Brian Connell who covered Sir Winston Churchill's funeral programme —which won for Independent Television the Cannes Film Festival Grand Prix Award for an outside broadcast.

For twenty-five years, Connell—who has also had several books published—worked as a journalist in Fleet-street.

Millions of TV viewers came to know him as a newscaster for ITV and for three years, as link man for the ITV current affairs programme This Week.

When he resigned from This Week in 1963 because of a dispute with Associated Rediffusion, he said: The disagreement was over the manner in which I can best continue to contribute to the programme as a professional journalist with an established reputation to maintain."

Mr. Connell joined Anglia Television four years ago as a programme advisor.

By TOM TULLETT and DAVID WRIGHT

BRIAN EPSTEIN, the man who made The Beatles, is dead.

The Quiet Prince of Pop, who built up a fantastic multi-million-pound show business empire, was found dead in bed at his £31,000 London home yesterday afternoon.

He was just thirty-two.

And last night Paul McCartney, one of the four Liverpool lads who made Epstein their friend, said:

"This is a great shock. I'm very upset."

Epstein, who always managed to ride the crest of the Liverpool pop wave, was found about 2.45 p.m. by his Spanish butler.

Knock

The butler went to wake him in his second-floor bedroom at the three-storey terrace house in Chapel-street, Belgravia.

He knocked . . . and knocked again. There was no reply. So the butler went inside.

The room was in semi-darkness. The curtains were drawn. And Epstein was in bed.

The butler said later: "Mr. Epstein was alone in the house last night. He appeared to be quite well."

Commander John Lawler, head of the No. 1 district, Metropolitan Police, said: "We are treating this as a sudden death.

"There will probably be a post-mortem examination, but this is a matter for the coroner."

And a spokesman for NEMS Enterprises Epstein's firm that managed The Beatles, Cilla Black, Billy J. Kramer

Cause of death is still a mystery

and other big pop names, said:

"The reason for his death is unknown, but there were no untoward circumstances."

Epstein's body left the house in a coffin about 5 p.m. And soon tributes from pop stars and fans began to flow in from all over the world.

Plans

The Beatles—who are in Bangor, North Wales, for the mass rally of a meditation society—made immediate plans to return to London.

Actress Jane Asher, who is with them, held Paul's hand and wept.

Beatle John Lennon said: "Our meditation has given us confidence to withstand such a shock.

George Harrison said: "You cannot pay tribute in words. There is no such thing as death only in the physical sense. Life goes on. The important thing is that he is O K now."

Ringo said: "We owe a lot to Brian.

"Only a month ago, Epstein admitted being high on the drug marijuana.

The Star Maker—See Centre Pages.

THE QUIET MAN FROM LIVERPOOL WHO RAN A 'STABLE' OF STARS

P.M. MAKES MOVE

MR. HAROLD WILSON is suing members of pop group, The Move, for alleged libel. The ca.. is over a postcard sent through the p.. publicising a new record.

It shows a drawing of the Prime Minister sitting on a bed in the nude.

Mr. Wilson's decision to take legal action was revealed yesterday in a statement from a firm of solicitors acting for him.

The statement said :

"In the Vacation Court this afternoon Mr. Quintin Hogg, QC, applied *ex-parte* on behalf of the Prime Minister for an injunction to restrain Anthony Secunda, Bev Bevan, Trevor Burton, Christopher Kefford, Carl Wayne and Roy Wood from printing, publishing, circulating or distributing a card alleged to be libellous of the Prime Minister.

"The injunction was granted until September 6 when a further hearing will take place."

Last night copies of the postcard were handed out at the Locarno Ballroom, Basildon, Essex, where The Move were appearing.

One member of the group autographed a copy after it had been handed to him.

But it was not until they left the stage that the group .... the writ. Carl Wayne

said : "We always send a card when we release a record. We honestly did not intend to slur his (Mr. Wilson's) name."

Mr. Wilson was not directly involved in the choice of Mr. Hogg—the Tory Shadow Minister for Home Affairs—to represent him.

Mr. Hogg was given the brief by the firm of solicitors, which is headed by Lord Goodman, the Labour life peer and a personal friend of Mr. Wilson.

The postcard advertises The Move's latest record, *Flowers In The Rain*.

Risque

Two thous and copies of the card were posted to TV companies, promoters, other pop stars and friends of The Move. One arrived at 10 Downing Street.

The group's manager, Mr. Tony Secunda, said : "I got the idea some time ago.

"I asked a cartoonist to draw the card and sent copies to people in the pop world. I suppose it is a bit risque. But it captures the atmosphere of the moment."

Mr. Secunda said the cards were not in envelopes when they were posted.

He added : "The total cost of the whole operation, including printing, was about £10."

The Move, whose hits include *Night of Fear* and *I Can Hear the Grass Grow*,

specialise in #..
music.

The five membe.. Birmingham, sma.. vision sets, fur.. effigies of Adol.. stage.

The Rank banned the gro.. theatres earlier.. because the a.. violent.

And six we.. Move was sack.. sario Larry Pa.. hired them fo.. night concerts .. at Great Yarm.. fused his reque.. their volume.

The groupe.. £1,000 in a ge..

Trevor Bu.. group's rhyth.. publicity bro.. ambition as .. and live in ..

Roy Woo.. ist, was once.. wants to .. block of fla..

Fe..

Chris .. ambition, .. lionaire, .. Bev B.. lists his .. as "A lo.. Carl .. "It's o.. start a .. violence.

Of th.. he said .. doing .. audience.. Afterw.. pletely .. trans..

He .. a mo.. the bi.. do in ..

"I .. expe.. abou.. the .. as .. stud..

M.. Prim.. yea..

Ge.. pa.. Cl.. an.. 19..

Prime Minister Harold Wilson may have given the Beatles MBEs but he didn't feel so benevolent when a publicity leaflet for the Move's *Flowers in the Rain* depicted him sitting in bed in the nude. However, the Move were amply rewarded for their loss of royalties by the accompanying publicity that made them household names.

Stand-ins made our record say the Love Affair

By DON SHORT

THE Love Affair pop group made a startling admission last night.

They admitted that professional musicians played their instruments during their recording of *Everlasting Love*, the record which is now top of the hit parade.

Only one of the five members of the group, 17-year-old lead singer Steve Ellis, took part in the recording.

On the ITV pro-

gramme, Good Evening, Jonathan King quizzed the group about the recording.

Drummer Maurice Bacon said: "Only Steve is on the actual record."

The other members of the group were not prepared in time to make the record, but had since had sufficient rehearsal

to be able to play the song on television, he added.

A spokesman for the group said last night: "When the record was made the group was newly formed, so professional musicians stood in at the recording session.

"But the group will be on all future recordings."

If pop stars kept their romances quiet so also did some their musical ability. Anonymous session men played for the comparatively incompetent. Record companies hunted for the right face and personality to front the sound on television and in the Press. But the group Love Affair blurted out that, apart from their talented vocalist, Steve Ellis, they hadn't taken part in the recording of their hit. The public was amazed and the industry hoped no one else would tell the truth.

DAILY MIRROR, Wednesday, February 7, 1968   PAGE 23

Love Affair came a cropper on Eros

THE five members of the Love Affair pop group, who climbed on the Eros statue in London's Piccadilly, were warned by a magistrate yesterday:

"There are limits beyond which you cannot go in your desire to obtain publicity for yourselves."

The magistrate, Mr. Geraint Bees, fined the five £7 each at Bow-street court.

He ordered them to pay £.. 5s. costs and bound them over for a year. They had denied insulting behaviour and

obstruction. The youths were said to have been posing for publicity photographs linking their hit record "Everlasting Love," with Eros, god of Love.

Three of the five— Stephen Ellis, 17, Rex Brayley, 19, and Lynton Guest, 17—had climbed to the top of the statue.

The other two — Michael Jackson, 18, and Maurice Bacon, 15— stopped climbing when they were asked to.

Mr. Colin Ross-Munro, defending, said that the youths had not meant to cause obstruction.

CREAM

BACKGROUND TO A BREAK-UP

EXCLUSIVE BY CHRIS WELCH

CREAM are breaking up. The world-famous trio that features Eric Clapton, Ginger Baker and Jack Bruce are to go separate ways in the Autumn.

Said Eric at his Chelsea home this week: "I've been on the road seven years and I'm going on a big holiday."

It was two years ago, in July 1966, that three of Britain's most outstanding instrumentalists electrified the blues world by joining forces.

It was two years ago that Ginger Baker rang me to say: "Me and Jack are forming a group with Eric."

Then came the denials. Eric was the star of John Mayall's Bluesbreakers, Jack was with Manfred Mann and Ginger was with Graham Bond. Nobody wanted to lose their keyman.

But Cream were not going to be turned off. Soon they were rehearsing together in a London church hall, a thunder of blues startling their first audience — some Brownies, a caretaker, and manager Robert Stigwood.

They made a sensational debut at the sixth National Jazz and Blues Festival — in pouring rain at Windsor.

They had their first hit with "Wrapping Paper" in November 1966, then came "I Feel Free," con-

certs at the late lamented Saville Theatre, and this year they conquered America and became Superstars.

They had their successes — and failures. Eric got hung up on the pop scene for ...

Eric told me last May that the Cream were breaking up. But it was to be kept secret until business problems had been sorted out.

At the time Eric said: "I went off to a ... feren[t] ...

"They were recorded in his basement with friends at Wood stock."

time, before Cream started.

"That is a big ba... We want ...

NEW YORK was whipped into a fifth dimensional frenzy by the arrival of Britain's Cream and the Who, for a week of concerts.

Eric Clapton, blues guitar king back in London this week, reports that their show was a "smashing" success ending in a cream cake battle and Pete Townshend swimming in his dressing room while the hapless promoter clutched his head and reportedly lost £27,000.

Popular myth has it that Cream were the first of the 1960s' 'super-groups'. Ostensibly super-group meant a collection of revered musicians who had already found fame elsewhere. In reality, only Eric Clapton of Cream had a highly-rated musical pedigree, having previously played with the Yardbirds and John Mayall's Bluesbreakers. While some musical encyclopedia writers have acknowledged Cream's excellence there is a feeling that they have been overrated when measured against their total record output. But they are remembered more than most.

A frenzy of whipped Cream in New York

How Eric Clapton kicked the demon

Triumph: Cured actor Clapton (left) with writer Steve Turner.

Eric Clapton, who was born in Ripley, Yorkshire on 30 March 1945, is one of rock's greatest guitarists. In the latter half of the 1960s and the first half of the 1970s he was a member of various legendary groups including: the Yardbirds, John Mayall's Bluesbreakers, Cream, Blind Faith, Delaney and Bonnie and Derek and the Dominoes.

During the early 1970s he gradually became a heroin addict but, partly due to the advice and help of Pete Townshend of the Who, he managed to fight off his drug dependence. After leading a reclusive life style in 1971 and 1972 due to his drug problems, he staged a come-back concert at London's

ERIC CLAPTON climbed out of the depths of his drug torment.

He was a superstar when he got hooked. But 31-year-old Clapton, Britain's top rock guitarist, took the cure.

One man who witnessed his struggle was writer Steve Turner. "Eric always attributed his great musical ability to being a junkie," says Turner.

"He never thought he could do it once he was straight. But he has."

'I told one of the roadies to sell my guitars for whatever price they could get'

Rainbow Theatre in 1973. The release of *461 Ocean Boulevard* in 1974 marked the end of his heroin addiction and the start of an impressive solo career. He married George Harrison's first wife, Patti Boyd, in 1979.

TWO OF ROY ORBISON'S SONS KILLED IN A BLAZE

A knock on the door of room 242.. then he hears of the tragedy

DAILY MIRROR, Monday, September 16, 1968

By DON SHORT in London and BRIAN HITCHEN in New York

THE world of singing star Roy Orbison disintegrated with the thunder of yesterday's dawn. There were knocks on the door of his hotel room. He awoke. And gentle voices told him: Two of your sons are dead.

Slowly, the sad-eyed American whose soulmate is unhappiness, heard how tragedy had called on him yet again.

Fire had swept his £100,000 lakeside home in America. One son was dragged to safety.

The two other youngsters got as far as the front door . . . and disappeared when an explosion ripped open the basement.

One boy is saved by grandfather

The other two boys disappeared.

Thompson said that thick smoke from the fire could be seen seventeen miles away.

"The fire was so intense — there is absolutely nothing left of the house," he said.

"The grandfather is hysterical with grief.

"The blast from the ex-

Collapsed

Roy Orbison, millionaire and international celebrity, in his room

attention—so he called in a doctor.

Together, they went to Room 242 at 5 a.m. They knocked on the door and went inside.

Orbison, 32, was grief-stricken. The doctor gave him sedatives. After about fifteen minutes, he left.

The singer was led to a car outside the hotel. Soon he was on his way through the New Forest in Hamp-

shire to the airport and the 10 a.m. flight to New York

THE TRAGEDY was the second to hit the pop and country and western singer from Vernon, Texas, in two years.

In 1966, his wife Claudette—who inspired his song "Oh, Pretty Woman"—was killed in a motor-cycle crash.

Even during his marriage, though unhappiness was not far away.

He and his wife, whom he married in 1957, parted for a short time about four years ago.

When she died, Orbison concentrated his love on his sons. On their happiness.

Only a few nights ago he told friends: "I can't wait until Monday, when I'll be home with the kids."

Last night his concert at Bournemouth was scrapped. "Cancelled" notices were put up.

But still on sale is Orbison's latest record, released three days ago. Its title: "Heartache."

The singer . . in happier days

A day when unhappiness stayed away. . . It is S..... 1964, Roy Orbison and his wife Claudette romp with...

THE BRIDE'S

Roy Orbison's wife dies in motor-cycle crash

JUNE 66

From Daily Mail Reporter : New York, Tuesday

POP singer Roy Orbison's 26-year-old wife, Claudette, mother of three young sons, was killed last night.

She died when her motor-cycle was in collision with a truck a few miles from their new home near Nashville, Tennessee.

The 29-year-old singer and his wife, both keen racing fans, were returning from a drag race meeting on separate motor-cycles.

Mr. Orbison was riding 100 yards ahead of his wife when the crash happened.

Roy Orbison with his wife Claudette and Roy, one of their three sons.

Orbison surfaced as a rockabilly singer in the mid-1950s but his greatest success came during the first half of the 1960s when he had regular hits on both sides of the Atlantic. He had one of pop's most distinctive voices and brought an element of drama to his ballad compositions. He toured Britain frequently and his popularity in the UK outlasted that in his native United States. He continued to have hits in Britain until the end of the decade. Somehow he managed to carry on his career in spite of almost overwhelming personal tragedy.

I'm proud, says Mick Jagger of Marianne's baby

Express Staff Reporter

ROLLING STONE Mick Jagger, whose 21-year-old girl friend Marianne Faithfull is expecting a child, said yesterday :—

"I don't care for convention. I am very proud and it's great to be having a baby."

HE was speaking in London at the new home the couple have bought in fashionable Cheyne Walk.

SHE was in Ireland in a 100-guineas-a-week rented mansion—confined to bed by a gynaecologist flown out there because of difficulties with the baby she is expecting.

Said 23-year-old Jagger, who expects to move into the Cheyne Walk house this week : "Marianne is having a hard time, but she will be all right, we have been told."

NO MARRIAGE

The baby is due in March—but though plans are in hand for the end of Marianne's marriage to 25-year-old John Dunbar, whom she met when only 17 and still at a Reading convent school, she and Jagger do not plan to marry.

Marianne said yesterday : "We are not the marrying sort of people. It works out well as it is, so why risk spoiling it.

"We are both very glad about the baby, and neither of us really cares what people say."

For the past two months Rolling Stone Jagger has flown every weekend to Ireland.

With Marianne in Ireland is her mother, and her son Nicholas, now almost three, the only child of her marriage to art dealer John Dunbar.

ON CAMERA

Herbert
Buckingham
Khaury
... being of
sound mind

Tiny Tim and his bride . . . "As many children
as the good Lord sends."

Tim leaves

WEDDING No. 2 FOR CILLA .. IN WHITE

JUDGING by the laughter at the church door, weddings are fun for pop star Cilla Black.

She and her manager, Bobby Willis, had just had their second wedding in six weeks.

The first was at a London register office.

Yesterday's was in Cilla's home city of Liverpool—at St Mary's Roman Catholic church, Woolton.

The 25-year-old singer received a special dispensation for the ten-minute ceremony, because Bobby, 27, is a Protestant.

And this time it was a white wedding for Cilla, who wore red at the register office ceremony. She walked down the aisle in a white minidress and white boots.

Picture by CHARLES OWENS

Gravel-voiced Cash from the deep American South has run the potentially lethal effects of amphetamines and alcohol and survived. He has consistently championed the causes of improvements in the American prison system and Indian rights. His album *San Quentin* was occasioned by his appearance at the famous prison. Cash married into a famous US country music family when he took June Carter as his second wife.

The story behind the smash show at San Quentin prison...

JAILHOUSE ROCK

by PETER JONES

WE'VE seen the television show, via Granada earlier this week. We've heard the album. The memories linger on about "Johnny Cash In San Quentin", when the folk-singer took his guitar and his talent "inside" for one thousand convicts.

That song "San Quentin" was written by Johnny only the day before. He told the cons: "I think I understand a little bit how you feel about some things . . ."

And: "I tried to put myself in your place and this is the way that I feel about San Quentin."

"San Quentin, may you rot 'n burn in hell . . . San Quentin, you bin livin' hell to me . . ." The prisoners packed in the dining hall. Maximum-security men held in their cells, but with the music piped through. "San Quentin, you bin livin' hell to me . . ."

As one American reporter reported: "He finished his song of San Quentin. There was a moment's pause. Then the inmates stood on their chairs and tables and screamed their applause.

45

Daily Mirror

5d. Thursday, March 13, 1969   No. 20,283

Arrests — on Paul's wedding night

BEATLE GEORGE AND PATTI ON A DRUGS CHARGE

George...drov

Family of four shot dead in bungalow

By MIRROR REPORTER

FOUR people were found shot dead yesterday at a riverside boatyard.

Police named them last night as Mr. and Mrs. Walter Beecham, the owners of the yard, and Mrs. Beecham's parents, Mr. Frank Bourton, 76, and his wife Ruth, 77.

Their bodies were found in the Beechams' bungalow at the boatyard —in Bredon-road, Tewkesbury, Gloucestershire.

Bedroom

Police were called to the yard by a window cleaner who made his usual weekly call at the bungalow, in a built-up area of Tewkesbury, yesterday afternoon.

He saw Mr. and Mrs. Bourton, of Gravel-walk, Tewkesbury, lying on the floor of a bedroom.

Police broke into the bungalow and found the bodies of Mr. Beecham, 54, and his 50-year-old wife, Margaret.

Last night a pathologist was examining the bodies.

Gloucestershire police said in a statement that they were anxious to trace the Beechams' 26-year-old son Paul, of Grayston-close, Mitton, Tewkesbury.

They believe he may be able to help them with their inquiries.

Alerted

They issued a description of Paul, who was said to have light brown curly hair, and of a green three-litre Rover saloon car he was believed to be driving.

Police throughout the Midlands were alerted. Later the car was found at Pershore, near Evesham, Worcs.

Chief Superintendent Richard ——ry, head of Gloucestershire CID, is leading the inquiry.

By MIRROR REPORTER

BEATLE George Harrison and his wife were arrested by Drug Squad detectives last night— only hours after the wedding of Beatle Paul McCartney.

They were charged with being in illegal possession of the drug cannabis.

They were given £200 bail each and are due to appear in Esher magistrates' court, Surrey, next Tuesday.

Their arrest came after eight Scotland Yard Drug Squad officers drove up to their £40,000 bungalow on the exclusive Claremont Park estate at Esher.

Warrant

The Beatle's wife, 24-year-old Patti Boyd, was alone in the bungalow at the time.

Detective-Sergeant Norman Pilcher, who led the police team, told her that they had a search warrant.

She let them in, then phoned her 25-year-old husband, who was in London.

He immediately drove home in his white Mercedes, stopping on the way to pick up a lawyer.

A few minutes after he arrived, he and his wife walked out of the front door, flanked by detectives.

Police said they had taken possession of a substance in the house.

The couple were driven off in a police Jaguar to Esher police station and charged.

They left the police station shortly after 11 p.m. with their solicitor.

As he walked to a chauffeur-driven Ford Zodiac, George said: "I've nothing to say except that I'm going home for a good night's kip."

News of the arrests was given to the other Beatles —including Paul McCartney and his bride—shortly after the police swoop.

PAUL McCARTNEY, the last bachelor Beatle, hugs the instant family he acquired yesterday. He married 27-year-old American photographer Linda Eastman—and got a daughter, too. Heather, Linda's six-year-old daughter by a previous marriage, attended the wedding at Marylebone Register Office, London.

TOGETHERNESS!

The ceremony began after a 55-minute wait for the best man. He was Paul's younger brother Mike McGear, of The Scaffold pop group, who was late because his train from Birmingham broke down. When he finally arrived, Mike crawled into the register office on his hands and knees, pleading "Forgive me, it wasn't my fault."

Picture by JOHN KELLY. Full story—See Centre Pages.

Diana Ross, Florence Ballard and Mary Wilson were the original members of one of music's best known and loved women groups, the Supremes. They sowed the seeds of their musical partnership as they sang their way to school and were signed by Berry Gordy for Motown after graduating from school in 1961. Their tenth release, Where Did Our Love Go took them out of R&B and into the national Top 20 listings.

Ballard left the Supremes amid great controversy in 1967. It was said that there was much rivalry between Ross and her and that Berry Gordy fired her. Lead artist Ross left at the end of the 1960s after they had appeared on the famous Ed Sullivan television show and played a season in Las Vegas. The Supremes have had various line-ups but, save for a brief solo career, Mary Wilson has remained a member. Diana Ross is one of the few women pop stars to have become a personality in her own right and to have found success in other areas of showbusiness, notably films.

Page 38—MELODY MAKER, November 11, 1972

Michael Watts in New York reviews the film Lady Sings The Blues

Diana triumphs as Billie

We'll never split —Supremes

DIANA ROSS, leader of the Supremes, will never go solo — unless the group breaks up.

Diana told the MM this week: "I have never thought about singing solo. Lot's of people have put this question to me, but I don't think that I would ever leave the girls.

WONDERFUL

"They love me and I love them so much, and if we broke up, it would only be... us got mar... sing on m...

AP 65

After the traumas and triumphs, Mary Wilson talks about the secret of her success . . .

THE SUPREMES are still the world's most successful girl vocal group. Still the most glittering, the most polished, the most professional.

And the girl who has been with them through all the triumphs and traumas of stardom is Mary Wilson. Twelve years after those first hits like Baby Love, she is the only original member of the group. She is the Supreme survivor.

Mary, 32 and beautiful, is as professional dealing with the Press and all that goes with stardom off stage as she is the Queen Supreme on stage. Chatty, and fun to be with, as I found when I talked to her in London.

Mary was in town during the group's European tour. With her was manager-husband Pedro Ferrer and one - year - old daughter, Turlese—and the other two Supremes, Scherrie Payne and Susaye Greene.

Singing

"In this business," sai... Mary, clothes a... immacul...

The Supreme survivor

MY 6

POP

by MANDY BRUCE

people manipulating you to make you a big star.
"Yet I don't think r... become harden... have sel...

claimed th... me...

certain standard of living— then it's very difficult to go back, I know I couldn't go back."

...Florence's replacement in the Supremes was the ...vishing Cindy Birdsong. The next break from the ...oup was in 1967. ...the exquisite Diana R... ...ly then the trio's est... ...ed leader bid a te... ...well to the Supreme... ...alone, which she... ...doing successfully

...n Cindy Birdso... ...e a baby. Sh... ...o the group tw...

...a February ...again. ...eason ?

DIANA ROSS QUITS!

DIANA Ross has split from the Supremes to go-it-alone as a solo artiste, RM understands. The other two girls in the Supremes, Mary Wilson and Cindy Birdsong, are set to continue with that name with Jean Terrell coming in as replacement for Diana Ross.

A debut solo disc is expected from Diana in February or March.

"I Second That Emotion" recorded by Diana and the Supremes with the Temptations is currently in RM's charts.

oc 9

EX-SUPREME FLORENCE DEAD

FLORENCE BALLARD

IRONICALLY, IN the week the Diana Ross Tour was announced, came the news that one of the original Supremes, 32 year old Florence Ballard, died as a result of a heart attack. She was admitted to the Mount Carmel hospital on Saturday, in Detroit, and was found to have taken a mixture of drink and drugs. She died on Sunday.

Florence left the Supremes amid much

controversy in 1967. Shortly before she was due to appear with Diana Ross and Mary Wilson at the Hollywood Bowl, she was told she would not be going on. She was replaced that night by Cindy Birdsong. Miss Ballard claimed she was

offered a million dollars to leave the group, but says she never received any of the money. She also lost a law suit against Tamla Motown and the Supremes when she later filed a claim against them.

Florence's marriage broke up in 1973 and she was since reported to be living with her three daughters on welfare handouts. Florence, who was reported to have been trying to make a comeback, was the one who named the Supremes, by choosing the name out of a hat. She sang on all of the groups' hits and contributed to eight gold records.

F 28 0

Daily Mirror

No. 20,379

5d. Friday, July 4, 1969

The paper with ...

ANNA, THE GIRL WHO TRIED TO SAVE BRIAN JONES

A BLONDE in dark glasses . . . her name is Anna Vohlin.

And in the humid darkness beside a swimming pool early yesterday she tried to breathe life back into pop star Brian Jones. She failed.

Jones, the controversial guitarist who helped to launch the Rolling Stones, was dead.

Minutes earlier Anna, a 22-year-old Swedish student, had been swimming with 25-year-old Jones in the pool at his farmhouse in Sussex.

Swimmer

For a few minutes she had gone inside, She returned . . . to find him unconscious

Vainly Anna and another friend of Jones, who quit the Stones last month tried the "kiss of life."

Tom Keylock, his road manager, said last night: "We don't know how it happened. He was a strong swimmer."

Later, a post-mortem examination was held. An inquest was provisionally for Monday.

Sad Anna was pictured at the house last night. Later she went hiding.

Brian Jones's cash—Back Page
Don Short—Page Seven

DAILY EXPRESS Friday July 4 1969

Life and death of a Rolling Stone

Mick Jagger : Met him at a London club

Charlie Watts : Joined group in 1963

Keith Richard : Shared flat with Jones

Bill Wyman : More of a conformist

He had never been happier...

by JUDITH SIMONS

LEWIS BRIAN JONES. Born 28.2.43. Died 3.7.69. Profession : self - taught musician. Occupation : Rolling Stone. Height: 5ft. 8in. Weight: 9st. 4lb. Hair : Blond. Eyes : Grey - green. First public appearance : baby show at West Gloucestershire Women's Institute Annual Show.

From childhood Brian Jones was at odds with his environment. Born in Cheltenham, he grew up with an intense devotion to the tortured blues music of the American Negro.

The mournful sounds seem to suit his own teenage frustration as an English boy.

a competent guitarist, pianist, and saxophonist, educated by records of Chuck Berry, Muddy Waters, Bo Diddley, and Jimmy Reed.

After a brief spell of trying to conform—he was a junior architect with a Cheltenham council—he left home; stayed in London, sleeping on the floor at the home of blues guitarist Alexis Korner.

In 1962 he found the path to recognition. He formed a group, booked to play once a week at an Ealing, London, club where Jagger and art student Keith Richard were among the patrons.

were joined by the more conformist Charlie Watts and Bill Wyman. They acquired a team of managers.

Early in 1964 they were established : their record " Not Fade Away " reached Number 3 in the hit parade, and their stage image, forceful, untidy, apparently undisciplined, like their music, had become an alternative teenage rage to the " lovable " Beatles.

But as the popularity of their music grew, through hits like " Satisfaction," " 19th Nervous Breakdown," " Jumpin' Jack Flash," and their bank balances grew accordingly (Jones's personal fortune is in the region of ... confused.

Saga of the Rolling Stones—CONTINUED

SUNDAY MIRROR, July 13, 1969 PAGE 5

ANITA'S BABY IS MINE SAYS KEITH

PLANE DASH BY JAGGER TO BE NEAR MARIANNE

Marianne ... in a coma

ROLLING Stone Keith Richard is the father of a baby expected by German actress Anita Pallenberg, it was revealed last night.

Miss Pallenberg, 22, was at

Sunday Mirror Reporter

one time the girl friend of another Stone, the late Brian Jones.

And she co-starred with Mick Jagger, the pop group's leader. A

spokesman for the Stones, Mr. Leslie Perrins, said:

" Because of a number of inquiries from newspapermen I have been requested by Miss Pallenberg to state that she is expecting a child in August.

" Mr. Keith Richard states that he is the father "

Miss Pallenberg makes this statement in the hope that she may be allowed to continue her pregnancy in peace and quiet.

" Neither she nor Mr Richard has any further comment to make at this time—or in the foreseeable future.

It is understood that the couple, who are not married, have not discussed marriage plans.

Festival

Miss Pallenberg's friendship with Brian Jones—the ex-Stone who drowned eleven days ago while under the influence of drink and drugs—started in 1965. She visited him in ...

Miss Pallenberg's film, A Degree of Murder, was a German entry at the festival.

While in Cannes, Jones said: "We do not consider that marriage is necessarily the most logical step in our relationship at this time."

Dating

When it was later announced that Miss Pallenberg's romance with Jones was over, this girl never said—"I dig, this girl very much. Brian's romance with Anita was all over when I started dating her.

There is no rift between Brian and me.

Last month, Miss Pallenberg broke a collar bone when a car driven by Richard crashed near Chichester, Sussex.

Richard, 25, escaped unhurt. After the accident, Miss Pallenberg rejoined him at his country home in nearby West Wittering.

The news of her expected baby is the latest sensation in the long Rolling Stones saga of controversy.

Rushed

Last month, Jones split with the group and was replaced by Mick Taylor. Then, a few days later, Jones was found dead in his £25,000 Sussex home.

Sunday Mirror Reporter, Saturday.

MICK JAGGER finished filming a hanging scene for his Ned Kelly film in Melbourne today and flew to Marianne Faithfull's hospital bedside.

Marianne was still in a coma in the intensive care unit at St. Vincent's Hospital, Sydney. Doctors said the 22-year-old actress was maintaining her slight improvement.

Special prayers are being said for her by the hospital nurses, who belong to the Sisters of Charity order.

A hospital spokesman said: "She is alone in a strange country and her dear little Marianne."

Hundreds of bouquets and thousands of phone calls from fans around the world have been received at the hospital for Marianne.

The spokesman said the unit was "stripped for action." But he would not add anything to

the routine bulletin on Marianne's condition.

Tonight the Sydney Sunday Mirror had a front-page picture of the singer in her hospital bed.

It showed oxygen tubes leading from an artificial respirator to her mouth.

Marianne collapsed in Sydney's Chevron Hotel on Wednesday, the day after she arrived with Jagger to begin work on the Ned Kelly film.

Detectives and customs men are now waiting to interview her.

They want to know if drugs found in her hotel room were brought into the country within the regulations.

Police took possession of two bottles of sodium amytal—one suspended, The Sunday Mirror doctor says: Drugs interfere with the essential supplies of the blood to the brain. This leads to a loss of functioning power of the brain, and the effects could be permanent.

To all who run shops ...businesses

THE SHOW MUST GO ON

250,000 roll up for the Stones

SUNDAY MIRROR, July 6, 1969

IT was a show that attracted a quarter of a million fans ... the show that the Rolling Stones put on at Hyde Park yesterday. It was a show that went on despite the recent death of founder Stones member Brian Jones—because the other Stones believed it that way. It was a show that started sadly when Stones leader Mick Jagger paid tribute to Brian by reading a poem on death by Shelley. And it was a show that ended, inevitably perhaps, in hysteria ... with a young girl being carried off screaming after trying to throw herself at Jagger.

Stones leader Mick Jagger in action at the show

Hats off to teenage fashion the eye-catching sequins worn by Pamela Donaldson, of Tooting and the two Hell's Angels below who helped to keep the crowd in order

Actress Miranda Hampton cools it with a drink

BRIAN JONES: A STAR 'ON THE DOWN ROAD'

Jones—sense of doom

Way out in the sun ... a pretty girl takes a watery stroll—in the Serpentine.

Marianne Faithfull—Mick Jagger's friend—and her son, at the concert.

Although there were numerous one-day events that drew huge crowds, such as this one at Hyde Park, the late 1960s were dominated by festivals which ran over several days. The first rock festival was held at Monterey, California in 1967. It included some of the most talented artists and groups of the time and was a celebration of the hippie culture of the mid-1960s. Some 30 festivals were held in the United States before the decade finished. Whereas 30,000 attended Monterey, the Woodstock Festival of 1969 attracted an audience of 450,000, which was a figure exceeded only in rock history by the 600,000 at Watkins Glen Summer Jam in Indiana in 1973.

However, the rock world did not invent festivals for these were very much a part of jazz and folk music culture long before the advent of the electric guitar. In the United States the Newport Jazz and Folk Festival at Rhode Island had been started in 1954. In Britain the first proper festival was a two-day jazz event at Beaulieu in 1958. The first National Jazz Festival was at Richmond, Surrey in 1961. It became the National Jazz and Blues Festival in 1964. The Rolling Stones played there in both 1963 and 1964 and in 1965 a number of contemporary artists from blues backgrounds were billed. As the decade progressed jazz and blues were less strictly interpreted. The first Isle of Wight Festival was at Godshill in 1968 when 8,000 people heard the likes of Jefferson Airplane, the Pretty Things and Tyrannosaurus Rex. In 1969 80,000 attended and by 1970 the figure had risen to 200,000.

A part of the huge crowd in Hyde Park yesterday for the Rolling Stones' great free show.

The Washington Post
Times Herald

SUNDAY, AUGUST 17, 1969

© 1969, The Washington Post Co.

No. 255

Phone 223-6000

Today — Cloudy, warm, humid,
chance of showers; high in upper
80s. Monday—Cloudy, warm, humid,
chance of rain. Probability of rain
30%. Temp. range: Today, 75-88;
Yesterday, 76-88. Details, page D11.

A4   Sunday, Aug. 17, 1969   THE WASHINGTON POST

400,000 Jam N.Y. Rock Festival

FREE POP - BUT SOMEONE PAID

WOODSTOCK, which deposited an under 30 population the size of Liverpool into an area the size of Stonehenge (with appropriate facilities) is over. The festival of love and peace (and incidentally music that went unheard by the great majority) ended as usual with the promoters less than friends with each other, lawyers being visited and all the rest of it that goes with large festivals these days.

Woodstock, of course, was phenomenal in terms of crowds —half a million all sitting on Max Yasgur's dairy farm in Sullivan County. It was also incredible in the amount of money it lost—truly the promoters put principles before money when they made it open house, and started asking for donations.

Such is the life style of the peaceloving rock fans that no donations were forthcoming from the avid diggers of peace-through-rock.

And the expenses went up and up: 500 dollars an hour for helicopters with more brought in to act as hovering ambulances, extra security guards, more garbage trucks. Expenses began to increase early Friday morning, hours before festival - start, when 30,000 fans were already in the concert area. When asked to leave they didn't. The fence had been trampled down and from then on, with the police guards being pulled out at the last minute, the question of tickets for the festival was a laugh. A short, bitter one from the promoters who found themselves halfway through facing debts of one and a half million dollars.

Thousands Rolling in for Woodstock Rock

FRIDAY, AUGUST 15, 1969

By B. J. Phillips

BETHEL, N.Y., Aug. 14—It's not exactly the classic way to hitch a ride.

The hitchhikers who dot the Thruway leading upstate from New York City don't "thumb." They stick out two fingers in the V peace sign.

It is considered a more effective way of getting a ride to An Aquarian Exposition, Three Days of Peace and Music, The Woodstock Pop Festival.

The "V," like the hair and the bellbottoms, is the first visible symbol that a culture is gathering. By to-night, most of the 200,000 who have bought advance tickets will be here.

Two hundred thousand people — by mid-week a license-plate tour of the parking lot produced a roll call of states—drawn to this small, confused, curious, resigned-to-it town in the Catskills.

Americana

What brought them to Bethel is rock music — their common denominator, the distillation of the finest, the worst, the angriest, the most gentle, the happiest, the saddest things that youth believe is in their lives.

"Face it, that's their music and their way of life," said Jerry Amatucci, Bethel's town supervisor and chief of police.

Their music is at Woodstock in the form of nearly 25 of the biggest names in rock and folk music.

Their way of life is spreading out over 600 acres. It's people with pamphlets, calling for violent revolution, and a sunbather who looked at one pamphlet and said, "Leave me alone with the sun."

That Rocky Road

". . . so they broke out guitars and drums and tambourines, sat on the hoods, trunks and roofs of cars and tried to make the best of it."

BEATLES, STONES & FAITH MAY JOIN DYLAN

SUNDAY night at the Isle of Wight could well be one of the biggest jam sessions in the history of music. After the programmed appearance of Bob Dylan, the concert may not end, said a spokesman for Fiery Creations who are promoting the event.

A wire from George Harrison has expressed the Beatles desire to make an appearance with Dylan in a free-style stage escapade which would run long after the scheduled close. As well as the Beatles, messages have been received from Blind Faith, Jack Bruce and the Rolling Stones. The Bee Gees are flying to the festival site in their own private aircraft and there is a possibility that they too are interested in joining the epic line-up.

The last word appears to be in the hands of the evasive Bob Dylan himself.

Dylan arrived last night at Heathrow Airport and was greeted by about 200 fans. Then he drove straight down to the Isle of Wight where he is staying in a manor house. The Band had already arrived.

The idea of a monumental jam session involving some or all of the world's top groups has been virtually approved by the festival organisers and they are expecting Dylan to welcome the prospect.

A spokesman for the Beatles enterprise, Apple, said the four were at present putting the finishing touches to their as yet unnamed LP. It is likely that the LP will be held back for release in December instead of the September date. They are considering the appearance with Dylan at the Festival, but no absolute statement could be made as to whether this event would mark their first live stage presentation in 4 years.

record mirror

AFTERMATH

- **One person murdered**
- **Three others dead**
- **Singer knocked unconscious on stage**
- **Mass Beatings**

NOW THE AMERICAN GOVERNMENT IS INVESTIGATING THE ROLLING STONES CONCERT WHICH TURNED INTO A BLOOD BATH – page 5

Price 1/- Every Friday

Altamont was a 'raceway' in Alameda County, California, which provided the location for a free concert on 6 December 1969 starring the Rolling Stones and the Grateful Dead. There was considerable violence during the concert and, while the Stones were playing *Sympathy for the Devil*, a young black man was stabbed to death. The murder could be clearly seen on the film made of Altamont.

The 'love, peace and freedom' of Woodstock became a thing of the past as many commentators latched onto the event as symbolising the condition of contemporary youth. Altamont suggested that violence rather than love was the more potent force in society.

ALTAMONT
-the day the Stones stopped smiling

THE OPENING shots of "Gimme Shelter", before the credits, show Mick and Charlie, with a donkey in tow, prancing around on a motorway under construction, flourishing the starred and striped top hat.

They're laughing and it looks like they're having a good time. You can see that from the still on the sleeve of "Get Your Ya-Yas Out", which was from that photographic session.

The top hat recurs at all the Stones' concerts on that tour – this time on Jagger's head – as a typically half-matey, if insulting gesture, but it's last time you really see the Stones smiling.

The hustle of being the biggest rock band in the world – a block busting tour doesn't leave much time over for that. The film of the American tour of late 1969, appropriately entitled "Gimme Shelter", is really just a long lead-in to that biggest event, the free concert at Altamont Speedway.

HOPELESS

Is the biggest disaster in the short history of rock and roll just because a guy was murdered, but...

MARTIN HAYMAN
reviews GIMME SHELTER: the Rolling Stones. Directors: David Maysles, Albert Maysles, Charlotte Zwerin. Distributors: 20th Century-Fox. The film opens at the Rialto, Coventry Street, London, this Thursday.

Park, San Francisco. What nobody had foreseen was even San Francisco's inability to deal with the colossal influx of people, flying, driving, hitching rides in from as far as New York, to see the great rock and roll...

ing for a substitute would have been intolerable.

So on it went, regardless. There are some tense and gripping scenes of telephone conversations where the Stones' legal representation, advised by the speedway owner, discusses the organisation with public officials.

It emerges immediately that the logistics of the event were impossible, in terms of parking alone. The speedway owner, whether out of stupidity or sheer honesty, admits during the discussions that he's only in it "for the publicity". But that's taking it from the end.

SELF-CONSCIOUS

The whole film...

● ALTAMONT: Hells' Angels policing the Festival

certs, is all image, no substance; his personality is reduced to the external manifestations of the supreme star, the gestures, the dancing, the drawl: all composite parts of Jumping Jack Flash, prancing alone and oblivious in the vacuum of 300,000 pairs of eyes.

NIGHTMARE

By contrast, we immediately pull back to Jagger and Charlie Watts sitting around the video-tape machine, watching the playback of...

you know ... I mean, the way they cleared a path for us through the crowd ... such a shame ..." Altamont is over; all that's left is a record of it on celluloid and the accusations and counter-accusations that followed.

The chronological layering is confusing at times but mostly extremely effective. It puts the Altamont event at one remove, as though it were just a celluloid nightmare that might occur as fiction in other guise.

get to the crucial point: as a black guy in a pale green suit leaps to the front of the stage, Jagger raps out: "Let's see that again" and we're treated to a slow-motion action replay of the stabbing from which the young black was later to die.

DISTRAUGHT

At this point...

EVENING STANDARD, FRIDAY MAY 1971

LEXANDER WALKER puts the question that is fascinating the Cannes Festival

Did this moment of murder set Jagger on road to marriage?

WAKE UP!

John's message is to shock you into awakening, says a reader

...ONDMAN...

'I never have known how long we're going to go on. We won't go on ...ever' MICK JAGGE...

...AS THE OSMOND...

Rolling in health wealth and happiness

Kinky of

Saturday Interview

THIS has very
...efinitely been the
...est week of David
...owie's life.'
...His picture is on the
...nt of Gay News. His
...album is top of the
...ts.

...all 18,000 tickets for
...oncert at Earls Court
...were sold within
...of the box office

..., the most outrageous
...er of them all, is for
...ent moment the king
...in's rock 'n' roll
...The hottest, most
...loved and hated

...turned when he
...to the bar of the
...venor House Hotel
...for the only inter-
...given in his

around us was
the way we
...
about ...
our er...
environ...
there.
Both

...I'm not worried that I...
...ght upset young...
...way offer...

Long-established groups continued to be successful. The Beach Boys made a strong come-back with an album entitled *Surf's Up*. McCartney, after an uncertain start, formed Wings with his wife Linda, Denny Seiwell and former Moody Blues guitarist Denny Laine, which found success on both sides of the Atlantic. Lennon produced a series of albums, of which *Imagine* received the most attention. However, it was criticised by some who were tiring of what they called Lennon's platitudes even though it was not long before that they had been praising his work. There was little appreciation of Yoko's musical ability either with or without Lennon. Harrison came out of his semi-reclusion and persuaded Dylan to perform at the concert for Bangladesh, which took place at Madison Square Gardens, New York in 1971.

The Stones continued in much the same way as they always had, defying critics who predicted their end and, of course, running foul of the law. This period also finally gave Carole King the recognition she deserved, despite her previous successes as the songwriter of many classics for others. Her album *Tapestry* reflected the contemplative mood of much American music which was a reaction to the turbulent, Vietnam-conscious 1960s. *Time* magazine hailed James Taylor as the voice of the new music. Bob Dylan and the Grateful Dead reverted to a country style while others, like Dory Previn and Joni Mitchell, examined the problems of forming and keeping relationships.

Introspective and reflective songs, however, were a comparatively small part of the music scene that also encompassed hard rock. The end of the previous decade saw the emergence of such superstars as Pink Floyd, the Moody Blues, Yes and Emerson, Lake and Palmer. Three British rock groups, Led Zeppelin, Deep Purple and Black Sabbath, were also in the process of ensuring their place in rock history. There were other outfits like Hawkwind, Free, Mountain, Jethro Tull, Status Quo, Focus, and the Faces, and the loudest of them all, Grand Funk Railroad, finding enormous followings.

A solo Rod Stewart would become hugely popular as would Elton John, the Electric Light Orchestra, the Mahavishnu Orchestra, Santana, an infamous artist called Alice Cooper, and David Bowie. Not all of these well-known names merited press headlines. As many of them were album-orientated, they did not receive the kind of media prominence that a singles' group receives though naturally the more outrageous and downright decadent were noticed.

The mid-1970s were the period of the honeyed Philadelphia sound. Two Philadelphia producers, Kenny Gamble and Leon Huff, were writing songs and bringing a number of groups who appeared on their Philadelphia International (Philly) label to the notice of the public. The O'Jays were arguably the best known from this stable. Another producer, Thom Bell, saw his group the Stylistics go way beyond their soul following to achieve a much wider audience. Marvin Gaye released *What's Going on* in 1971 which contained statements on Vietnam and pollution and was disappointed that, though it was successful, it never received the critical praise of a *Tommy* or a *Sgt Pepper*.

However, for headlines and media coverage there was nothing to touch yet another teen-pop hysteria boom as one youthful act succeeded another. For once, many of these acts had considerable talent when they were allowed to express it within the narrow demands of their market. The Osmonds, the Jackson 5, David Cassidy, and the Bay City Rollers caused the most hysteria but the likes of Slade, Sweet, Marc Bolan, David Essex and a few others were not far behind.

But not even the best music can remove one dark element of this period. Between 1970 and 1974 the rock world lost Jim Morrison, Janis Joplin, Jimi Hendrix, Les Harvey of Stone the Crows, Duane Allman, Tami Terrell, Al Wilson of Canned Heat and Gene Vincent. And there were numerous others.

Well, Well!

Once more John and Yoko display themselves and their love to the world. This time it's through a set of of 14 lithographs. Pictured below one of the printable ones.

OUTRAGE. OUTRAGE. John Lennon has dared to do it once again.

He and Yoko take off their clothes again, so to speak, in an exhibition of lithographs called 'Bag One' at the London Arts Gallery. What's so different is that for the first time, they have sprung into action with their nude poses and presumable that's why the Sunday newspapers are full of comment about insulting the world.

WAKE UP!

John's message is to shock you into awakening, says a reader

John Lennon and his second wife, Yoko Ono, kept saying the world should be at peace and they conducted several lengthy 'bed-ins' to show they were serious. Their first was at the Amsterdam Hilton and followed their 20th March 1969 wedding. The second began on the 25th of May in Montreal, Canada. While in bed they, with the help of many famous visitors, recorded the eventual hit *Give Peace a Chance*. Lennon also coined the phrase 'War is over, if you want it', which became the slogan of many peace movements.

The couple arranged for peace posters to be put up in 11 cities but missed out on Tel Aviv, Moscow and Saigon. Lennon, Yoko and the Plastic Ono Band played a special peace concert in Toronto as the decade drew to its close. It was Lennon's first performance since the Beatles stopped playing live in mid-1966.

A week in bed .. the great Lennon protest

HAIR PEACE.

BED PEACE.

BUT THEY WON'T MAKE LOVE IN PUBLIC

From DON SHORT in Amsterdam

BEATLE John Lennon and Yoko Ono, his bride of five days, took to their bed yesterday for the "special happening" which they had promised would surprise the world.

And that, really, was that. For the only surprise was that they did practically nothing at all, except clutch a tulip each.

They plan to stay that way for seven days. Just sitting around in bed "as a protest against war and violence in the world."

Many of the 200 reporters

and photographers who filed through their £20-a-day suite at the Hilton Hotel in Amsterdam were puzzled at first by the lack of action.

Winked

John — reading their thoughts, — perhaps — winked and said: "I hope it's not a let-down. We wouldn't make love in public—that's an emotionally personal thing.

In his white pyjamas, 28-year-old Beatle said: "This

is our protest against all the suffering and violence in the world." Yoko, 34, wearing a high - necked, old-fashioned nightie, said: "We want to tell the youth of the world that we are with them. She added: "We will be in bed for seven days and we hope to conceive a baby."

John said: "We're happy to be called a couple of freaks as long as we are happy and can make other people happy."

Picture by CHARLES LEY

BILLY COTTO DIES A THE FIG

—See B

PAUL IS QUITTING THE BEATLES

5d. Friday, April 10, 1970

No. 20,616

Some say Lennon's attachment to Yoko Ono and her constant presence in the studio while the Beatles were recording hastened the break-up. The Beatles' financial affairs were in a mess and McCartney was alone in objecting to Allen Klein being brought in to sort them out. Paul preferred the possible help of his father-in-law, who was a prominent American lawyer. Whatever the reasons for the Beatle split-up, it was McCartney who publicly announced his intentions of going solo, who said the Beatles had died and who took legal action to ensure that this was so.

BY DON SHORT

PAUL McCARTNEY has quit the Beatles. The shock news must mean the end of Britain's most famous pop group, which has been idolised by millions the world over for nearly ten years.

Today 27-year-old McCartney will announce his decision, and the reasons for it, in a no-holds-barred statement.

It follows months of strife over policy in Apple, the Beatles' controlling organisation, and an ever-growing rift between McCartney and his song-writing partner, John Lennon.

In his statement, which consists of a series of answers to questions, McCartney says:

"I have no future plans to record or appear with the Beatles again. Or to write any more music with John."

Last night the statement was locked up in a safe at Apple headquarters in Savile-row, Mayfair—in the very rooms where the Beatles' break-up began.

The Beatles decided to appoint a business adviser." Eventually they settled for American Allen Klein.

His appointment was strongly resisted by Paul, who sought the job for his father-in-law, American attorney Lee Eastman.

After a meeting in London Paul was out-voted 3 to 1—John, and the other Beatles, George Harrison and Ringo Starr.

Since the Klein appointment Paul has refused to go to the Apple offices daily.

He kept silent and stayed at his St. John's Wood home with his photo-

Clash over the running of Apple

grapher wife Linda, her daughter Heather, and their own baby, Mary, to

McCartney . . . a policy deadlock.

John Peel hits out at Lennon 'in sincerity'

by Lon Goddard

JOHN PEEL yesterday hit out at the sincerity of John and Yoko Lennon's campaign for peace. He said: "They spend a lot of time flying around the world and spending weeks in big hotels.

"This week they bought another big expensive car. Is that for peace too? I could buy a new telly for peace.

"They don't appear to be really sincere in what they are doing," Peel's outburst—he himself is a known advocate of world peace—came after Lennon appeared to ignore telephoned pleas to Apple to support the Campaign for Nuclear Disarmament.

CND asked Lennon in a letter to support their march from Crawley to the West End at Easter and the Easter Sunday festival at Victoria Park Bethnal Green.

But there was no reply to the letter.

"We have tried for many weeks to get in touch with John Lennon, but Apple always says come back later or next week", said a spokesman for the organisation. "We have phoned and I have written a letter to Apple, but received no reply. John Peel has phoned twice for us and got the same answer. I have had two appointments with John arranged through his assistant, Tony Bramwell, but each time he was out or forgot.

"Apple say they can't do anything and it is possible that John does not even know. We did have one interview with him some time ago where we discussed the aims of the CND and he told us he would do as much as possible."

"We know it is difficult to get in touch with these people, as they have so much to do, but we have not asked until now. We have our Easter march and festival coming up on Easter Sunday, so we would like to get in touch with them."

John Peel said, "If they can't get in touch with the CND, then I have my doubts about how serious they are about working for peace. The CND exists solely for the pursuit of peace, so I think they could spare the time to see them."

Apple replied that, "John hasn't been available for the last two or three weeks, because he is in the studio editing some films. He hasn't even been into the office for the last two weeks. Sometimes it is difficult to get information to John when he is involved with something. If they could ring Diane here, I'm sure she will pass on the message."

JIMI BANNED

JIMI HENDRIX Experience's new album, "Electric Ladyland," has been banned from a number of record shops in Britain. The shops are in various provincial towns, including Hull and Bristol.

The album, which features a colour photograph of 21 nude girls, was released last week and has sold over £80,000 of records since the release.

Other leading record stockists, including Boots and W. H. Smith, have said they will stock the album but will not display it and will sell it in a brown paper cover.

The cover for the album was taken by photographer David Montgomery.

This week, Jimi Hendrix commented from California: "I don't know anything about it. I don't decide which pictures will be used on my records. In the States, this album had photographs of Noel, Mitch and me on the cover." (See page six).

55

Al Aronowitz on the death of Jim Morrison

JIM MORRISON, the handsome Irish giant who blazed to pop glory as the lead singer of the Doors, is dead in Paris. He was only 27.

According to his manager, he died of natural causes, either a heart attack or pneumonia. Morrison was not known to be a heavy drug user, but he drank a lot, and he catapulted to stardom out of the same cauldron that cooked up Jimi Hendrix and Janis Joplin.

Notoriety

His manager, William Siddons, said that Morrison died on Saturday, July 3.

"This is the end, beautiful friend"

from "The End," by The Doors, 1967

UST 15, 1970. Vol. 17 No. 32 1/-

MIKE (DC5) SMITH BALLS!!!!! p13 p3 p12

BEATLES — Page 4

FLASH RAP: JIM LETS FLY!

DOOR'S LEAD singer Jim Morrison went on trial this week on charges of indecent exposure.

The incident occurred last September at a Miami concert where witnesses claimed that Morrison had exposed himself on stage during the Doors' act. Many people said at the time that nothing was seen, but enough complaints led the Florida police to arrest Morrison. A spokesman for the Doors said:

◄ JIM MORRISON

"Normally, Jim does not wear underpants on stage, but on this occasion, he did. That makes the charge even less believable. Whatever the outcome of the proceedings, the Doors will definitely appear at the Isle of Wight Festival. If convicted, Jim would be released on bail to appear. None of the tracks on their forthcoming album (released at the end of August) "Absolutely Live" were recorded at the Miami concert."

"I just hope Nixon keeps his mouth shut during this trial," the spokesman added.

AKER REPORTERS COVER MUSIC WORLD IN THE USA

Morrison leaves $3 million

from COSMO DONAHUE in San Francisco

JIM MORRISON, the 27-year-old rock hero and lead singer of the Doors, who died recently in Paris, left an estate consisting of practically no cold cash at all, but nevertheless valued at more than $3,000,000 (three million dollars) due from the inevitable profits of his various enterprises and other assets.

Morrison's common-law wife Pam will get it all thanks to an iron-clad will in San Francisco last month is now in Toronto, Canada, with his touring band. Kris who was recently in New York and the subject of a Look

Girls throw away bras as the big festival gets under way

POLICE 'INVADE' POP SHOW ..BUT FIND ONLY LOVE

By KENELM JENOUR

POLICE praised the "pop" generation for their good behaviour yesterday.

Five hundred constables and detectives drafted on to the Isle of Wight for the mammoth five-day pop festival found themselves with little to do.

After the near-riots and drug troubles of last year's show the police were expecting all kinds of problems.

But instead they found themselves mingling among a good-natured — if half-naked — crowd who had nothing but music, peace and love on their minds.

Attraction

Chief Inspector George Cutcliffe, of Hampshire county police, said: "I must say we have all had a pleasant surprise.

"Most of the kids are behaving themselves."

Special squads of officers from Hampshire, Sussex, Dorset and the Thames Valley are already on the island and a reserve force is standing by on the mainland in the event of future trouble.

Up to last night, Drug Squad detectives had made ten arrests.

With the live music starting four hours late, the topless girls at the festival — and there were dozens of them—were the star attraction on the opening day.

They actually queued to have their breasts painted by a Belgian body artist called William.

And there were more fans watching William's art work than there were listening to rock records in the vast arena.

Dressed

First in the queue to test William's work was pretty Frances Pickles, 21, of Lonsdale-drive, Enfield, Middlesex.

"It's just like being dressed really," she said, surveying her orange, green and blue painted body.

"Boobs are back in again this year, so a girl may as well show them off."

Then she strolled off among the crowd—leaving her bra behind.

Even all the bare breasts on view failed to disturb the police.

"As long as no one else is offended it certainly

It's all so peaceful as thousands stream in

doesn't bother us," said Mr. Cutcliffe.

Two hundred priests and clergymen moved on to the site to offer help to anyone who needed it.

They set up a marquee which offered communal sleeping to fans — but strictly no sex.

Miss Caroline Coon, of the Release Organisation, arrived with a team of thirty — including three doctors and three solicitors — to help anyone in trouble, particularly over drugs.

Miss Coon, 24, said: "Our doctors will be dealing with 'bad trips' at the festival.

"We are particularly keen to see that no 'instant justice' is carried out on people arrested on drugs charges."

The peaceful image

ended for a brief spell last night when a live wartime hand-grenade was found.

A bomb disposal squad was flown over by helicopter from the mainland to explode it.

But police said there was no cause for alarm and sabotage was not suspected.

Mr. Cutcliffe said:

"The grenade was probably left behind by troops who held manoeuvres here and came to the surface during the erection of the festival arena."

More than 200,000 people are expected at the climax of the event, which stars American folk singer Joan Baez.

Christopher Ward at the pop show—Page Nine.

The bare facts

With flowers painted on their bodies, a topless girl and her boyfriend stroll round the festival site.

SUNDAY MIRROR, September 20, 1970   PAGE 3

JIMI WAS TOO FULL OF LIFE

.. says the girl who found him dying

By GEORGE MARTIN

IT was revealed last night that Monika Dannemann, the girl in whose hotel room pop star Jimi Hendrix died, is a top West German ice skater.

Monika had been a friend of the world famous guitarist for some time, her brother said in Dusseldorf.

It was the 23-year-old German girl — who is now with friends suffering from shock—who found Jimi unconscious on Friday

morning, apparently because of an overdose of sleeping pills.

Monika took part in a world ice-skating championship at Richmond in 1964, but had dropped out of top-class skating in recent years.

She is now being cared for in a secret hideout.

A friend said: "She has to rest . . . and try to forget."

When she found the pop star unconscious on Friday, she called frantically for help. But when the ambulance reached St. Mary Abbotts Hospital, Kensington, the wild man of pop was found to be dead.

Jimi Hendrix once said he had grown out of drugs.

But it is believed he finally fell victim to an overdose.

A police theory is that a freak accident led to his death.

Waking in Monika's suite on Friday after an all-night party, he groped for some pep pills.

Instead, by mistake, he grabbed extra-strong German sleeping pills.

And, it is thought, he took nine.

Monika is certain it was a terrible mistake.

Yesterday, Monika's brother said: "My sister

rang half an hour ago. She said Jimi only took nine tablets and no one would die from so few. Apparently he became sick and was asphyxiated."

He added: "She said Jimi was too full of life to kill himself."

Hendrix certainly had plans for the future. Monika told her brother that Jimi was looking forward to going to America to finish an LP.

Mystery

But the last few days in his life were clouded in mystery.

Hendrix was to meet a man last Tuesday who recorded some of his earliest work, Ed Chaplin of New York.

"He never showed up. First time I've known Jimi break an important date," said Mr. Chaplin.

"Nobody could contact Jimi in the last few days," he added.

Jimi Hendrix was the most enigmatic person in showbusiness today.

ON STAGE his 'freak-out' could have been mistaken for a sex-maniac with D.T.s.

OFF STAGE, he was quiet, intelligent, well-mannered.

But he seemed to have reached a crossroads, and was even thinking of quitting the showbiz rat race.

He told freelance writer Stephen Clackson at the Isle of Wight pop festival last month.

"I am all alone and I say 'What are you doing here dressed up in satin shirts and pants?'

"I've got this feeling to have a proper home.

"I like the idea of getting married. Just someone who I could love."

RELUCTANT HEROES

A MAJOR recruiting drive by the Argyll and Sutherland Highlanders—saved by the Conservative Government from extinction—has ended its first week without a single new recruit.

Monika Dannemann is helped from her hotel.

The mo.. ..eliable name in... hot..   ESTABLISHED 1794

KAYS is ren...
Value, Sele...
Service. Ov...
half millio...
customers...
how we're...
ing for new...
running a...
SHOPPIN...
easier and...
ful. We'...
in this s...
many y...
why pe...
home s...
more".
Prove...
Everyt...
know...
by p...

Seattle, Washington-born Hendrix first found his fame in Britain thanks to being brought over by Chas Chandler of Animals and Slade association. Hendrix played psychedelic blues and heavy rock. His guitar virtuosity drew huge audiences. Shortly before his death his career had met obstacles. His group the Experience broke up. He was busted for drugs. He was constantly hassled by police. The official cause of his death was inhalation of vomit following barbiturate intoxication. Hendrix was one of rock's greatest guitarists.

The American magazine *Rolling Stone* called Janis Joplin the 'high priestess of rock'. It was the Monterey Festival in 1967 and the accompanying film that brought her overworked whisky voice to the notice of many. The late Lilian Roxon, the United States's most revered rock chronicler, saw Joplin's whole act as a frantic, sweating, passionate, demanding sexual affair.

Real-life Quincy opens his casebook

PURE POISON KILLED THE ROCK QUEEN

■ THOMAS NOGUCHI is the real-life forensic expert on whom the TV series Quincy is based.

■ As Los Angeles County Medical Examiner his beat was Hollywood and he was nicknamed the "Coroner to the Stars".

■ Today we conclude his inside stories with two more of his celebrated investigations.

SHE was the hard-drinking wild woman —the Queen of Rock, worshipped by millions of fans.

Janis Joplin was addicted to the excitement of her frenzied stage performances. But she was also hooked on drugs.

And on October 4, 1970, in a Hollywood hotel room, she plunged a needle into her arm for the last time. Janis crumpled dying to the floor in her nightgown. She was just 27.

Tragically, according to friends, Janis was fighting her addiction and had managed to stay off drugs for several weeks.

It appeared that she had not injected a large amount of heroin that night—no more than a normal dose.

Why, then, did Janis Joplin die?

● Series adapted by ROY STOCKDILL from Coroner to the Stars, by Thomas Noguchi and Joseph Di Monga, to be published by Corgi next year.

Puncture

I supervised the autopsy. We found many old punctures in the veins of her arms and one fresh one.

We sent her blood to t...

word that no drugs had been found in her room.

So there arose the possibility of an accomplice. Could it even have been murder?

I went to take a look at the hotel room. A detective told me a needle and syringe had been found but no heroin.

However, when I looked in...

JOPLIN: Tried to fight her deadly addiction

...ciates, had looked in to check her belongings. The th...

...many different ways. On the east coast of Americ...

Daily Mail, Friday, May 7, 1971

DICKIE

The 'oldie' crooner who survived a new age of pop

DICKIE VALENTINE was Britain's top pop star in the mid-fifties, when singers wore hair cream and were called crooners, groups had never been heard of, and girl fans tended to 'swoon.'

By MICHAEL CABLE

From 1952 until 1958 he won virtually every pop poll conducted to find Britain's No. 1 male singer.

His records—like *All the Time and Everywhere, A Blossom Fell, Christmas Alphabet* and *Finger of Suspicion* were ... hits.

Inevit... generatic... idols a... name di... the Top... he adjuste... his act... cabaret ca... just as rew...

Sp...

In his hey... once hired... Albert Hall... special 'thank... to members o... —he earned... a week.

In recent years he commanded between £500 and £1,000 a week for his appearance...

... London 'night spot, where he made one of his first appearances as a singer at the age of 18.

In 1949 he joined the Ted Heath Band and it was during his five years with it that he made his name. He went solo in 1954.

...d wife, Wendy, three years ago

...s is how it ended ... the burned-out car in which...

LIKE countless thousands of youngsters, Janis Joplin left home, a dumpy, plain-faced nobody, to seek fame in the bright lights.

When she first went to San Francisco to join the hippy "flower children," she wandered the streets like a waif.

She dressed like a down-and-out, seldom had a bath, ran with a wild mob—and suffered what was to her the ultimate humiliation and degradation.

Desperate for money, she decided to sell her favours on the street to anyone who would buy.

She offered herself for five dollars a time—and found no takers.

That changed rapidly when she virtually exploded at a Californian pop festival in 1967. That was the occasion that Janis Joplin, according to the critics, "Blew the rock..."

Search for love drove superstar to destruction

SOFTLY, Dickie Valentine crooned the fateful words. But the heart-throb of the fifties didn't know it was to be his very last song.

"And now the end is near and so I face the final curtain"—the lyrics from the hit song "My Way" held a tragic irony for 41-year-old Dickie.

Hours after singing the wistful lines at the end of his act at a club in Caerphilly, South Wales, he was dead, the victim of a road crash.

Dickie, his pianist Sidney Boatman, and drummer Dave Pearson were all killed when their car hit a bridge as they were driving away from the club early yesterday.

Tour

His death came just few years...

By CLIFFORD DAVIS and KEN RODGERS

charts in the fifties after starting his career as a page boy at the Palladium.

The son of a London lorry driver, he couldn't read a note of music.

He made his name singing with the big Ted Heath band, then switched to being a performer...

A Billboard Publication

record mirror

1s/5NP

December 19, 1970

Mr and Mrs Lennon doing their LP thing — page five

EQUALS v ENOCH RACE DEBATE

by Bill McAllister

THE Equals have challenged Enoch Powell to a debate on the race problem. Lead guitarist Eddie Grant, composer of the group's controversial latest single, "Black Skin Blue Eyed Boy", which emphasies the point of racial equality, has written to the Tory M.P. and asked him to join a proposed debate on David Frost's TV programme about race.

Grant, who recently discarded his blonde wig for a natural Afro hairstyle, said, "Enoch Powell is saying things that the young people of today do not believe in."

With the release of "Black Skin Blue Eyed Boy" some weeks ago, Grant also declared that the Equals would from now on finish with purely commercial efforts and direct their work to the furtherance of tolerance and racial equality.

Bitter

If the proposed venue of the David Frost programme falls through — no reply has yet been received from Frost — then Grant has offered Powell the alternative to name his time and place.

The debate's theme would be based upon the following words from the Equals' single — "It's a brand new world with brand new people/In one big world we're just one people."

'Name the time and place . . .'

Grant is also bitter about the exposure his group get and the lack of exposure given to other talented coloured people.

"You pick up a magazine and there are always pictures of white stars," he said, "but never black ones, like Sidney Poitier or James Brown.

No comment

"I also believe inter-racial marria White girls scream at Equals, but don't h the chance to admire beauty of other b people.

"T h e bl population of country has a potential as at managers or an else that the whit does. They can be asset to Britain.

No commen available and fi from Mr Powell withdrawn London te numbers.

FACES: BIG PUSH SET FOR JANUARY

Faces album set for January release

FACES second Warner Bros. album is scheduled for January 22 release and is tentatively titled, "Long Player".

Featured among the album tracks are two 'live' numbers, McCartney's "Maybe I'm Amazed" and "Feel So Good", recorded during their last US tour.

This month the band complete recording of the album and take a two week holiday prior to a non-stop list of New Year bookings here — their first real intensive concentration of personal appearances in Britain since they emerged from the ashes of the old Small Faces over a year ago with the addition of Rod Stewart and Ronnie Wood. More on the Faces see P10.

record mirror

3

Kinks — a major tour set

KINKS undertake their first British tour for nearly six months, guitarist Dave Davies plans to make solo discs again and the group returns to the States in March to further promote the hit single, "Apeman"' and album, "Kinks Part One: Lola Versus Powerman and the Moneygoround."

Kinks have set aside February in order to cover the country and dates confirmed so far are at Luton College of Technology on February 5, Sheffield University on February 19, Nottingham Trent Polytechnic on February 20 and Leicester Top Rank Suite on February 27.

Further dates are anticipated within the next few weeks. Reason for Kinks lay-off from British appearances has been completion of the score for the Hwyel Bennett film, "Percy," by Ray Davies.

Dave Davies, who first released a solo disc, "Death Of A Clown", in 1967, and scored a big hit, is to re-enter as a solo artist. But it does not mean he is splitting from the group, and he is unlikely to accept solo dates. Dave is currently preparing material.

RAY DAVIES

WHY PAUL SAID — END IT ALL

Comfort sign for Harvest

SOUTHERN Comfort's singles and albums will in future be released through the Harvest label, but ex-leader and group founder, Ian Matthews is still uncommitted to a recording deal.

Comfort's three year contract with Harvest is for six figures and ends all speculation concerning the band's future.

They are already recording — at EMI's Abbey [studios] — and hope to [have] a single out within the [month] as a follow-up to their No. 1, "Woodstock", and an album by March.

Much of the band's material will be written by rhythm guitarist Carl Barnwell and bassist Andy Leigh. There will be no one specific lead singer, as was the case before Matthews quit, with most members of the group sharing vocals.

Rumours that Matthews, who is still trying to form a new band, was to join Elton John's label, DJM, are unfounded, the singer's managers commented this week. It is known, however, that Matthews is negotiating with several major companies and a signing is [expec]ted very shortly.

DUTCH TOP TEN

FOLLOWING on from his British chart success Dave Edmunds enters this week's Radio Veronica Dutch Top 10 at number eight with "I Hear You Knocking." At number one is "My Sweet Lord" by George Harrison off his "All Things Must Pass" album. The rest of the positions are: 2. She Likes Weeds, Tee-Set; 3. Lonely Days, Bee Gees; 4. Yesterday When I Was Young, Charles Aznavour; 5. Voodoo Chile, [Ji]mi Hendrix Experience; 6. [T]ears In The Morning, Beach [B]oys; 7. See Me, Feel Me, [T]he Who; 9. Peace Planet, [K]seption; 10 The Witch, [R]attles.

THE Beatles are dead. The final swift move in the dying throes of pop's greatest phenomenon, came when Paul McCartney applied for, and was granted a "statement of motion."

Intention of McCartney's writ is to extract himself financially and legally from The Beatles, thus putting paid to the constant stream of rumours over the past year that the group would reform for either concerts or recording.

There has also been a complete denial from the group of the rumour that a replacement for McCartney is being sought — yet another nail in the Beatles' coffin.

Since the matter of McCartney's writ is "sub judice" until after the hearing on January 19, there was no comment from the group, but a spokesman said they were all "reviewing their own individual efforts."

Break-up of The Beatles began almost 18 months ago when John Lennon began preparation of his controversial "Two Virgins" album. Alienation between McCartney and Lennon had already begun and affected the other two members, George Harrison and Ringo Starr.

There has followed, over the interim period, a consecutive series of Beatle solo efforts ... Lennon with the Plastic Ono Band, which not only undertook concerts, but has issued several albums; Harrison making 'guest' appearances with such acts as Delaney and Bonnie and now releasing his giant-selling three album set; Ringo taking on session work and making his two solo albums.

Of all the Beatles McCartney has, until now, been the one least in the limelight. Only his solo album, "McCartney," has indicated what he has been doing this year.

To all intents and purposes, it seems, the Beatles are dead. In a just-published American interview, John Lennon refuted the old viewpoint that they were inseparable and stated emphatically that they all had to learn to exist as individuals. He also

JOHN LENNON

disclaimed the Beatles as a "myth."

There is no heart left now by the individual Beatle members of The Beatles. It's all over.

In next week's RM there will be a "Beatles Special."

Footnote: There are no plans to issue any of the "golden oldie" rock numbers recorded by The Beatles some time ago. And no plans for any "Greatest Hits" compilations have been made.

Shack disband

STAN WEBB has disbanded Chicken Shack. After four years together, the news comes as a shock to the large following Shack had built up as one of the country's staunchest blues bands. Webb declared he hadn't satisfied himself for the last 18 months with the current lineup, and will retain the group name when he reforms the band.

Magna Carta

MAGNA Carta have been invited to perform in concert at London's Royal Albert Hall with the Royal Philharmonic Orchestra on June 23.

It is understood that Magna Carta will be featuring some original work.

And Magna Carta's next single — "Time For Leaving", written by group member Chris Simpson — will be released here some time in February.

Grant out

EQUALS lead guitarist and composer, Eddie Grant, is out of action for a month — at least — after collapsing late last week with an "inflammation of the heart."

Grant was rushed to Northwick Hospital, where he is still being treated, and his condition is reported as being "pretty serious". A spokesman for the group said: "This has come about through overstrain and overwork. The band is meeting this week to discuss the situation as there are a lot of commitments."

Equals may take on a deputy for Grant if they can find someone suitable, but if no-one is found it will mean the cancellation of a heavy date schedule and TV and radio commitments.

Their new LP, "Black Skin Blue Eyed Boys", is set for release within the next month.

Tamla visit

THE double billed star Tamla package featuring Stevie Wonder and Martha Reeves and the Vandellas now begins its British tour on January 22 at the Astoria, Finsbury Park, London.

The acts arrive here on January 18, play the Astoria, and continue their itinerary with (23) City Hall, Sheffield; (24) Odeon, Lewisham; (28) Odeon, Manchester; (29 Odeon, Birmingham; (30) Odeon, Hammersmith; (Feb. 5) Capitol, Cardiff; (6) Winter Gardens, Bournemouth.

PAUL McCARTNEY WITH LINDA

JOE DROPS HIS BRITISH TOUR

COUNTRY Joe McDonald has pulled out of his British tour with Keef Hartley, due to begin on January 21.

Reason is the cancellation of his Scandanavian dates which makes the visit impractical. The tour, however, is still on and a replacement to co-star with Hartley's group is now being sought. It is not known whether it will be a British or American act.

Dates are: (Jan 21) Royal Albert Hall, London; (22) Town Hall, Birmingham; (26) Guildhall, Portsmouth; (29) Free Trade Hall, Manchester; (30) Colston Hall, Bristol; (Feb 1) Dome, Brighton.

Meanwhile, Sacha Distel is set for his first major tour, and his first appearances in this country for 18 months.

The French singer's date-list kicks off with a concert at Croydon's Fairfield Halls on March 14. Other dates are: (March 16)

Wakefield Theatre; (17) ABC Peterborough; (18) ABC Hull; (19) ABC Stockton; (20) Odeon, Manchester; (21) Coventry Theatre; (24) ABC Gloucester; (25) Guildhall Portsmouth; (26) Capitol, Cardiff; (27) Odeon, Birmingham; (28) Granada, Shrewsbury.

Appearing with Distel at the venues will be Ted Rogers, Stefan Grappelly and Los Tontos.

Lyceum concerts

SUNDAY concerts begin again at London's Lyceum from January 10 when Southern Comfort top the bill and are joined by Brinsley Schwarz, Patto and Molesto, a South American band, rumoured to be one of the first signings to the Rolling Stones new record label.

Big names set for Int. Country Festival

RM can exclusively reveal this week the full star-studded line-up of the Third International Country & Western Festival to be held at Wembley on April 10 and 11.

Promoter Mervyn Conn has booked the cream of America's Country talent and plans to add the top British names, too.

Loretta Lynn, who triumphed at last year's Festival, returns again and is joined by other Country stars like Waylon Jennings, George Hamilton IV, Bobby Bare, Hank Williams Jnr., Hank Snow, Roy Acuff, Tompall & The Glazer Bros., Tommy Cash, brother of Johnny, and Australian Country artist Lee Conway.

The two-day event will attract Country fans from all over Britain and in addition to being a showcase for the artists performing talents, also provides a focal point for other areas of Country music interest such as magazines and records.

St. Tropez with girl friend,

Mystery of the new girl in Mick's life

It would seem that MICK JAGGER's latest girl friend, whom many people in France label as his future wife, is not quite the "wealthy South American society girl" she is portrayed to be in the Continental Press.

BIANCA PEREZ MORENA DE MACIAS is an attractive young lady, as Mick well knows, but it is now clear she has not always moved in such opulent circles as the Rolling Stones.

Bianca was apparently born in Nicaragua, but she left there at a very early age and her knowledge of Spanish is rudimentary, to say the least.

. . . speaks English far

. . . yesterday that . . . only twenty. . . . ars ago she was . . . as a hostess at . . . eat producers' . . . and at one . . . lived in a . . . id's room in . . . y Rue de . . . a Paris

. . . ed about . . . exclusive . . . in St. . . . she is . . . Mick . . . "I'm . . . but I . . . ber."

Stones sue Klein for £12m

PHILIP FINN

NEW YORK, Tuesday.
THE Rolling Stones filed a £12 million damages claim today against their former manager Allen Klein.

The action is by Mick Jagger, Charlie Watts, Bill Wyman, Keith Richard, and Louis Jones, father of the former Stones guitarist Brian Jones.

. . . was set down in the . . . preme Court in . . . Klein

Jagger and his four letter words, by Pan Am girl

PAULINE LOUGH, a Pan Am ground stewardess at Heathrow, has spoken for the first time about her row with Mick Jagger aboard a jumbo jet.

Jagger grabbed her by the arm and used four letter words to her, claims 24-year-old Pauline.

"I've never met a passenger quite as rude as this," she told the Evening Mail.

First Jagger and his party of eight pushed past a queue of passengers and walked on to the aircraft. "They would not queue up to be checked off", she said.

When Pauline went aboard she found them sprawled over the wrong seats in a first class compartment. She asked them to move and Jagger told her to 'Shut up', said Pauline, whose home is at Surbiton, "He started saying 'bloody this and bloody that'.

☐

"I said if be continued to use language like that he would have to leave the aircraft."

"He grabbed my arm and said 'If you don't shut up I'll kick you up your ——'.

"I said, 'The first movement you will be making will be

getting off this aircraft'."

Pauline said a woman passenger told her "I've never heard anybody spoken to like that".

Pauline reported the incident to Captain Charles King who said he would not have abusive language on the flight.

Jagger, according to reports, has denied grabbing Pauline and using bad language. He said he was told by a stewardess she wished he could be dropped from 30,000 ft.

☐

Pauline said she did not tel . . . him this and can only imag . . . he must have overheard . . . private conversation.

In Jagger's party bound . . . Paris via Heathrow to . . . Angeles were his wife an . . . and some friends. Later . . . submitted a written . . . Pan Am about the . . . which happened as . . . was waiting to take . . . Would Pauline . . . deal with Jagger . . . said: "If it come . . . my job, I'm . . . person who w . . . considered I' . . . head and I . . . My reaction . . . A spok . . . said: "W . . . — this . . . dent".

Jagger names wedding day

Standard Reporter

MICK JAGGER has name . . . the day for his wedding . . . South American beaut . . . Bianca Morena di Macias.

And the trendy Frenc . . . Riviera resort of St. Tropez— . . . where the couple have bee . . . staying—is eagerly looking for . . . ward to Wednesday this week.

Members of the town's jet se . . . are convinced the marriage wil . . . take place then in the old town . . . hall.

But Jagger's friends are not . . . so sure

Said one, society photographer . . . the Earl of Lichfield, today: "He . . . has changed his mind lots of . . . times.

"The wedding was to have . . . been two weeks ago, but it was . . . called off.

Gave lift

"The tip is Wednesday . . . but who knows?"

Jagger gave the Earl a lift . . . on Saturday as he drove to Nice . . . airport. It was thought he was . . . en route for Paris to pick up . . . "Les alliances" . . twin wed- . . . ding rings for a traditional . . . French ceremony.

A friend of Bianca's said in St. . . . Tropez today: "It will definitely . . . be on Wednesday but if there is . . . too much activity from the press . . . he could call it off.

"With the special dispensation . . . he has he can get married vir- . . . tually anytime . . . in secret."

Jagger has chartered an aero- . . . plane to take guests from Lon- . . . don to St. Tropez for the wed- . . . ding party. But people he is . . . almost sure to invite claimed not . . . to know the departure date.

His Press agent Mr. Leslie Per- . . . rin said: "I know there will be . . . an aeroplane going. But no-one . . . has told me when.

Mick weds in church!

THE wedding of Mick Jagger and Bianca Macias in St. Tropez is history now. But we feel we must show the many, many Mick Jagger fans just how the knot was tied in a little church high above the French holiday resort. Mick looks quite calm, but Bianca seems to be disturbed by something at least at the moment the photographer took his picture.

The reception later was in an almost disused hall next to the Cafe des Arts and was a bit rough, but soon the reggae music was blaring out and the champagne was flowing and everyone was having a great time. Mick even sang a bit with Doris Troy, and Terry Reid is said to have entertained as well. Three of the Beatles were there, and two of the Faces were Ringo and Paul, plus wives. It was a big day, too, for Mary McCartney, aged 2, flying to

and from Nice within 24 hours and going to the wedding party — but that's show business!

And in a smaller room, for his dad and mum and family, Mick and Bianca had a "wedding breakfast" meal, with speeches, just like they do at weddings in East London.

MICK and BIANCA say their 'I-do-s' in a little church on a hill overlooking St. Tropez. From left are: MRS. EVE JAGGER, Mick's mother; AHMET ERTEGUN, head of Atlantic Records who distribute Rolling Stones Records; brother CHRIS JAGGER, MICK (in fourth row) who looks after the Stones office; JO BERG-LENBERG after the Stones; seen MARLON; actress NATHALIE DELON and KEITH RICHARD (with film producer ROGER VADIM); (witnesses).

Sentimental Mick, after all! Mick and Bianca sailed away in a luxury yacht for a cruising honeymoon, leaving behind a worried manager of the Byblos hotel where many wedding guests had occupied rooms and left, through a misunderstand- ing, without paying their bills the next morning!

This could be the last time

THE STONES BEGIN THEIR LONG-AWAITED—AND POSSIBLY FINAL—TOUR OF BRITAIN. MICHAEL WATTS REPORTS . .

MELODY MAKER, March 13,

'I never have known how long we're going to go on. We won't go on *forever*'

MICK JAGGER

THE JAGGERS . . . unconventional as usual

The Jaggers put a new name on the scene

THE Jaggers, Mick and Bianca, have decided to call their baby daughter Jade . . . a name you don't hear every day of the week, and one that is certainly new on the French.

Under French law there are limits to the imaginative rein given to parents in the naming of their children. Only certain names of saints and figures from ancient French history are allowed.

To go beyond these bounds—and Jade does—special permission has to be obtained from the civil authorities. Mick and Bianca, being French residents these days, found the authorities most accommodating. After all, they hardly expected the couple to conform to convention.

On sale Friday, week ending July 3, 1971

NEW MUSICAL EXPRESS

4

WHICH WAY POP?

TALKING POINT

AMERICAN JOURNALIST JOHN STIRN HAS PROBED THE QUESTION AND FINDS THE JAMES TAYLOR ERA IS IN AND THAT THE

EAR BASHERS ARE OUT

THERE are possibly some people who are not aware of the significance of Andy Warhol doing the cover art for "Sticky Fingers." It means rock music is dead. Not the term rock music. That is alive and well and somehow applies to folk singer James Taylor. But the music known as rock has become a ghost and the remains are gentle, reflective and calm.

Hippie expert Dr Lewis Yablonsky (sociology, San Fernando Valley State College) has written: "Music is the backdrop. It served, as in all cultures, to validate, reinforce and illuminate the culture. In other words, if the backdrop is changing, the culture is changing.

Warhol and the Rolling Stones symbolised a point of view that spread tentacles beyond their respective arts. Andy was the leader of the pop school of fine art located in New York City but has since drifted off to Holland and San Francisco. The rolling Stones are a rock music group dominated by Mick Jagger, the super music star of the 1960's.

Creative

Don Hackman has written in "The New York Times" that both realised that the creative stuff of the sixties came from the bloodied spirits of a society that had little interest in ivory tower art. It was a decade when art was raw and offensive, full of discoveries and nonsense, when a quarter of a million kids sat in the mud and sang "give peace a chance" while thousands of sociologists sat on their academic hilltops and

youth cult has gone on to something else. Warhol and the Stones remain symbolic. Warhol is thinking about changing his name so he can start fresh, and the Stones have moved their operations to the quiet in the south of France and married Mick Jagger says he doesn't buy the idea of a youth revolution.

Writer Stanley Booth, who is working on a book about the Stones, says the group has "always realised that their evolutionary heroism is a pose, that it changes nothing, that rock and roll is only a little paprika on the nuclear television dinner."

And Jagger himself says: "I think a lot of young people have started something and we're never going thing and we're never going

their faith in it (rock music). They expected it to be everything, to express all they feel and do."

Rock music has come to mean a lot of things. So when it is stated that rock is dead it means that superamplified music associated with the Beatles, Jefferson Airplane, Canned Heat, Cream and the Stones is gone. And so are most of the groups that played it. For clarity, call this music acid rock.

John Mayall, father of British blues-rock, says acid rock was associated with "lack of discipline, stumbling, enormous volume. I never did like it."

Eric Clapton, who used to chip plaster half a block away with the sheer power of his amps when he was with the Cream, now is with a group called Derek and the Dominoes. When Clapton plays

these days a listener can even talk to his neighbour if he cares to.

The Grateful Dead is also typical. Their producer, Bob Matthews, says: "The Dead are now inclined toward country and western. Turning the amps way up doesn't just make it louder — it distorts. Here in San Francisco there's a new, more sophisticated sound evolving.

"You find a lot of interplay between musicians from different groups who come together on a higher level of creativity. Right now it's about communication, education and purification.

Bill Graham

A few people have attempted to stand up and announce why all this is happening. One of them is Bill Graham, who owned Fillmore East and West, once bad to rock music what Marienbad is to bath takers. Graham announced this spring that rock was finished and so was he; his halls will shut down.

"It was the inability to cope with success that killed rock music and the musically refined form of lyric and tune that combines the

IN?

JAMES TAYLOR is named as the leader of the new wave of pop favourites who are easier to listen to and have something to say.

OUT?

Personified by MICK JAGGER, the combination of the Rolling Stones and Andy Warhol is symbolic of the Sixties, but their coming together via an album sleeve could mean the end of an era.

The wave of the future is suggested by James Taylor, the 1971 country folk parallel to Bob Dylan. "The simple fact," says Taylor's producer, Peter Asher, "is that people like Jimmy (Taylor), Joni Mitchell, John Sebastian and Randy Newman are so much easier to listen to than Grand Funk. Sensitivity and subtlety are coming back."

"Newsweek" agrees: "The new direction is toward contemplation, appreciation, celebration, a self-effacing harmony and poise seeking to refocus on a utopian vision that had become fuzzy — a getting "back to the garden," as Joni Mitchell sings.

Critic Leonard Feather notes music has become varied, splintered, going in several directions at once. But the unifying note is that the anger is gone.

Barometer

"Music has served lately as a kind of barometer of what is going on with young people," Feather writes. "If what I hear on the air nowadays is any indication, maybe we have turned the corner and reached a point where we have had it with anger and are going into something more constructive."

LENNONS
AT HOME
Page 14

GEORGE-RINGO RAVE-UP

● GEORGE: took most of the vocal work

Dylan, Clapton, Leon, Shankar watched by 18,000 crowd

FROM JACK HUTTON, NEW YORK, MONDAY

BOB DYLAN, Leon Russell, George Harrison and Ringo Starr sang and played on stage before 18,000 people at New York's Madison Square Gardens yesterday and I could hear every note, every word. That is the difference between U.S. music audiences now and in 1964 when I saw, but never heard, the Beatles play their first American date at Carnegie Hall.

Ear-shattering

Then, they were screened by police and drowned by a continuous ear-shattering howl.

On Sunday, the multi-million dollar band, including two Beatles, played to 36,000 people at two shows and the multitude loved them and listened. Just look at the line-up of George and Ringo's rave-up. Apart from them — Leon Russell, Eric Clapton, Bob Dylan, Klaus Voorman, Billy Preston, Jim Keltner, Badfinger, a brass section and a choir. Money could not buy it and they all played for free. The proceeds — 250,000 dollars from the concert plus film and record royalties — went to the United Nations Children's Fund to aid Bangla Desh refugees.

Air-cooled

Ticket touts were said to be h...
one was selling as far as...
into the huge, air-cool...
Giant balloons were gen...
of the crowd to another. ...
about tons of equipment o...
drum kits, instruments and ...

CONTINUE...

BOB DYLAN FOR BRITAIN

•

BRITISH CONCERT DATES FOR MOODIES

SEE PAGE 2

THE WHO...

Harrison was rather overshadowed by the Lennon-McCartney partnership during the Beatle years. However, his first post-Beatle album *All Things Must Pass* received much critical acclaim when it was released in November 1970. Of all the Beatles, Harrison was the most involved in Indian culture and music.

He was a sincere humanitarian as was illustrated when he organised the Concert for Bangladesh. Twenty thousand people attended the August 1971 concert at New York's Madison Square Gardens. It was Dylan's first live performance since the Isle of Wight Festival two years before and one of Eric Clapton's few stage appearances during this period.

Chaos as fans make a grab for their idol

GARY GLITTERS FOR THE GIRLS.

FOR this happy chap all that glitters is pure gold.

He is, as any weeny-bopper will tell you, the fantabulous singer Gary Glitter.

Yesterday, Gary was the centre of a touching scene.

He has become famous for his catch-phrase: "Do you want to touch me?"

But it was nearly his undoing when he signed autographs at a West End store.

There was chaos as fans, aged from fourteen to forty, fought to grab a handful of their idol's clothes.

Mr. Glitter, who spends about £300 a week on his dazzling outfits, was forced to escape through the tradesmen's entrance.

"They suddenly went berserk," Gary said later. "There were clothes flying everywhere and all my sequins were pulled off. Luckily I managed to hang on to my trousers."

A store spokesman said: "It was one big glittering mess. They tried to pull the man's trousers off and we had to call extra security."

Story DEBORAH THOM...
Picture BELA ZOLA

Disc and Music Echo—November 20, 197...

McCARTNEY:
'I know I'm good. If I'm in the right mood I can write a solid gold hit.'

WINGS (left to right): Denny Seiwell, Linda, [...] and Denny Laine

ONE of the members of Wings has been through the hassles of being in a media group and all that goes with it: flash bulbs and interviews, screamers and critics, the trouble, the strife the lack of privacy.

That was Paul McCartney, of course, and the band were the Beatles.

Now McCartney has successfully gained a new band, Wings, as well as gaining privacy and freedom, both for himself and the group. His only hang-up now revolves round the band he loved—the Beatles.

Wings have successfully and quite deliberately manipulated publicity that any band needs, to work just the way they want to.

At the "do" for Wings in London's Majestic Ballroom last week, security was so tight that guests carrying bags big enough to carry even a box Brownie camera had them confiscated until after the ball.

So when a [...]
from [...]

by GAVIN PETRIE

limiting to a band adopting that beat. There is mild uproar amongst the band and Paul protests: [...] course not. Reggae [...] and best [...]

WINGS TAKE OFF . . . . .

"WINGS—Wild Life" on one hearing imm[...] through and is an appealing mix[...] excitement.

MUMBO [...]

[...]king. Paul's screaming vocals some-[...]ice. Linda on electric piano also en-

[...]R KNOW—An acoustic introduc-[...]beat. It builds up to a sliding (but [...]guitar instrumental break and ends

[...]—Yes! Linda is more than Mrs. [...] and takes lead vocal in this roll-[...] a strong melody line. [...]uitar break, that you feel you [...]nger before the next track. [...]artney ballad with string and [...]rd Hewson. A giant dramatic

YOUR FAVOURITES
... THE BIG SCREEN!

FILM

[...]DERTON

[...]ASE [...]R!"

[...]K GUYLER
[...]SANDER[...]
[...] HOWLET[...]

NO2

GUARDS KICKED AND BITTEN

By ROBERT HART

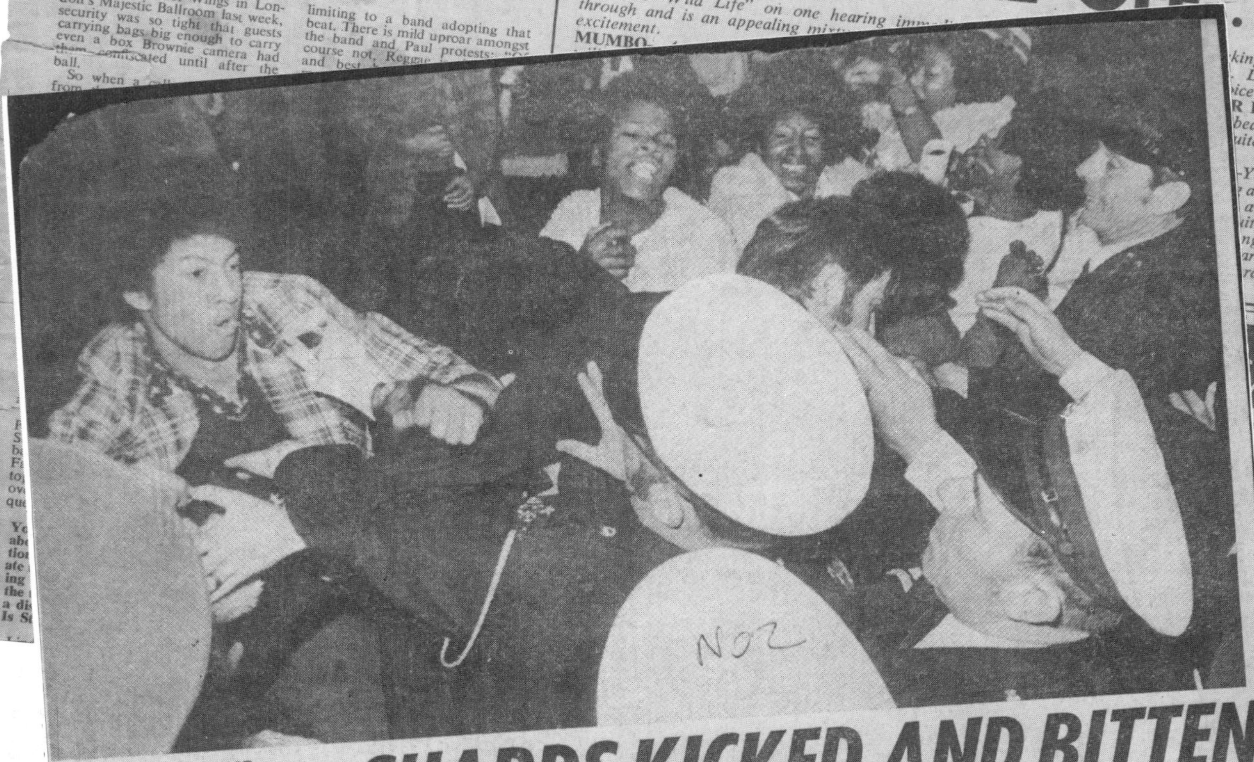

POP concert security guards battled with an avalanche of rioting teenyboppers last night.

Guards were punched, kicked and bitten as hundreds of hysterical girls stormed the backstage dressing rooms at Empire, Pool, Wembley.

The American pop group, Jackson Five, went behind locked doors after their first performance made 8,500 fans go wild.

The teenyboppers—mostly black

teenage girls—made a frenzied dash to get backstage.

Several security men were almost flattened in the crush. Reinforcements managed to force back the screaming fans with a hastily-rigged barricade of tables and seats.

After the second show, the Jack-

son Five dashed from the stage into a chauffeur-driven Rolls-Royce waiting to whisk them back to their London hotel.

But crowds of screaming fans continuing to besiege the stage doors, chanting "We want the Jacksons."

They kicked in glass door panels

and yelled abuse at guards who tried to tell them that the group had left.

A number of scuffles broke out as the girls were forced into the car park, where they finally dispersed. One exhausted security officer said later: "It looked really bad for a while."

On the eve of the [...]

OBVIOUSLY I had the market on teen magazine heart throbs cornered. I was sitting in my Las Vegas hotel room in front of fuzzy textured wallpaper picturing a romantic vision of the Roman ruins and I was chatting with the Jackson 5 on the telephone.

When I finished with them it was in an elevator next a statue of Julius Caesar to zip upstairs to talk to the Osmonds. If David Cassidy had knocked on my door the teenybop vibrate would have been complete.

The Jackson 5 had spent a hectic [...] in Motown's Los [...] recording

[...]ongs

[...] were record-[...] of songs," [...] Jackie told [...] the [...] the Jacksons' [...] California, [...]they could [...]ing on at [...]at we do is [...] songs and [...]cers and [...]town pick [...]m having [...] pool and [...] 16 track [...] use it to [...]s," ex-[...],14-year-[...]Sun-[...]ther.

[...]thing in [...]ife now [...] Eng-[...] kind of ex-[...]t to sightsee [...]ever miss doing the [...] normal kids do [...] told me.

growing up in the limelight, Michael said that he doesn't [...] about three miles a[...]

I want to sightsee some in England, says Michael. Which place is Napoleon in?

JACKSON FIVE talk to MM in New York

MELODY MAKER, October 28, 1972—Page 53

things." Marlon's aim is acting in a cowboy film.

THE BOYS' FATHER, who back home in Indiana played guitar as a hobby, inspired them to become musicians. Onstage Tito plays guitar and Jermaine plays bass while Randy joins in on the congas as well as sings and dances. "Nobody ever took lessons," Jackie pointed out. "Music was just a family thing and we used to come home from school and rehearse. There was just nothing else to do."

Tito, however, has decided to start going to music school. "There's a lot to music and a lot to learn," he explained. "Nobody knows all there is to be learned."

Jermaine and Michael have been writing some songs together. "There wrote several songs for a special person," said Jermaine. "One is a soft song that I'm doing for Glen Campbell to record. It's not finished yet and I'm fixing it up now. Eventually I'd like to make an album containing all my own original songs.

New stuff

Marlon, who can't wait until he gets to England, said the group will be doing some new material for their shows there. "I don't know what is yet," he told me. "They haven't told us yet but we'll be rehearsing some new stuff."

The "they" who haven't told them refers to Motown's staff of writers, choreographers, costumers, conductors and producers who keep a close watch on every aspect of each group. It's been that way from the beginning at Motown where very little is left to chance. Even interviews are closely watched with definite time limits laid out and even one often [...] answers [...]

[Sidebar text, right column:]

Among the many hyped family groups and male pin-ups mainly launched for under-16 girls from the early 1970s onwards, the Jackson 5 managed to add genuine talent to the razzmatazz. The brothers were led by a remarkable vocalist in Michael, who was only 10 by the time this group from Indiana hit the charts with *I Want You Back*. Some of the brothers also made solo recordings. Michael in particular had hits in the early 1970s with *Got to be There*, *Ben* and *Rockin Robin*.

Once their 'teen-solo' days were over they became just 'The Jacksons' and, after a period of little activity, they made a successful come-back in the disco boom of the second half of the 1970s. Michael stayed with the group but deservedly also found superstardom in his own right.

Melody Maker

EMBER 27, 1971   7p weekly   USA 30 cents

Hawkwind take off
SEE PAGE NINE

DYLAN GETS BACK TO PROTEST

by MICHAEL WATTS

A NEW Bob Dylan single, recounting the death of George Jackson, one of the Soledad Brothers killed a few months ago, is to be released in Britain in two weeks.

The single, out in the States on Monday, is a return to Dylan's protest or "finger pointing" days — and in terms of its stark simplicity and emotional bite is one of the best tracks he has cut in years.

An interesting feature is that the song is the same both sides. I heard a tape on Monday of the two cuts. The A-side has Bob singing in a voice that re...

New Musical Express

EVERY FRIDAY 5p

THE KEITH MOON FILE
exclusive

No. 1289
Week ending October 9 1971

LONDON EDITION
Seven day guide to gigs — every week

SANDY DENNY: N. E. Poly. Waltham Forest, October 8.
EVERLY BROTHERS: Albert Hall, October 12.
MAGGIE BELL (STONE THE CROWS) with Canned Heat: Albert Hall, October 11.

8 EXTRA PAGES

ROD CHART SENSATION

First time ever: No 1 in British and American Singles & Albums charts

AMAZING Rod. In what has to be the first time it's ever been achieved with the same single and album, Faces vocalist Rod Stewart has this week pulled off a remarkable chart triumph. His "Every Picture Tells A Story" album is No 1 LP and the track from it, "Maggie May," the No 1 single in both Britain and America.

For Rod and the Faces, it caps a two months period during which they have climbed from respected but minority-interest band to an overwhelming international acceptance. Stewart, when NME spoke to him this week, ventured that the success of the album was more rewarding to him than the single. "The single is a freak, a one in a million chance," said Rod, "but the album has permanence and a lasting value.

"Even so," he added candidly, "I still cannot see how the single is such a big hit. It has no melody. It's got plenty of character and some nice chords but there's no melody to it. Rod's single, and Melodious or not. Rod's single, and the album gloriously crown what in the past has been a sometimes frustrating career for the one-time apprentice footballer turned rock singer.

WHO LAUNCH LONDON
ROCK

I AM not by nature a gambler. However, I am ready to stick my neck out and lay odds on David Essex becoming one of the most sought-after young men of show business in 1973.

Already he has received rave notices for his portrayal of Jesus Christ in the London theatre production of "Godspell", an American rock musical based on St. Matthew's Gospel.

He plays Christ almost as a clown, with red nose and white face.

"Before I started on the part I read the New Testament all the way through," said David. "I wanted to find out what Jesus was like, because I couldn't visualise him as a long-haired, bearded person.

"To me, He seemed a bit of a joker, a complete contemporary of his day. Something of a revolutionary who was anti-establishment.

David Essex—THE actor of 1973

Wild gear

"His qualities were warmth, humility, truth and a deep love of humanity. Well, to me that makes a person a happy person who might put on some wild kind of gear. Which is what I did."

We met on the Isle of Wight, where David was on location for the film, "That'll Be The Day". He was given time off from appearing in 'Godspell', but returns to that production as soon as the film is finished.

He says the story of the film is a bit like his own. It tells of the problems of a teenager growing up after a rough childhood.

Tough

His own early years were tough. He was born in the East End of London, the only child of a gipsy mother and a docker father.

"Well, my mother is a long-way-back gipsy. I think she is the great-niece of the original Gipsy Rose Lee."

David, 25, tall and slender with dark hair and warm brown eyes — he is bound to be labelled a "smasher" — says his schooldays were pretty violent.

Weapons

"The police used to come round the classrooms at the end of each term to search us for weapons. I

was a real tearaway, always nearly expelled, but not quite.

"I set fire to the science laboratory once. Then, another time, a couple of us gassed the biology master's bees. I was sorry afterwards, but I got paid back for it with a real whacking from the master. Very hairy, that was."

Rotten school

He disliked school — it was a rotten one, anyway — but was considered very intelligent. That made little difference in his surroundings.

"The thought of even going to a university was a great big laugh."

He worked in street markets in his spare time. I can remember it ne

DAVID GETS THE GODSPELL MESSAGE

Two song writers, Andrew Lloyd Webber and Tim Rice, saw the musical of their semi-rock double album *Jesus Christ Superstar*, which had been released a year earlier, become a major hit on Broadway. Although they had planned that it would be turned into a musical, they had hardly envisaged the $1.2 million advance ticket sales on Broadway. The United States had just come through the Jesus Movement and in any case 50 per cent of the country's population was churchgoing.

Jesus Christ Superstar received a lukewarm reception in the writers' British homeland but once the United States became smitten and the commercial machine was well oiled, there followed a rather belated reappraisal.

Naturally, a film was made and this together with the saga of record and stage play led the American magazine *Rolling Stone* to call the event: 'Jesus Christ, star of stage, screen and hullabaloo'. Another musical with a religious theme entitled *Godspell* was staged in its wake. An aspiring young British pop singer of undoubted charm and looks called David Essex was cast in the role of Jesus in London's West End. Both musicals had long runs and seem destined for revivals from time to time.

TIME

Jesus Christ Superstar Rocks Broadway

10

Rock-music's answer to the X-cert movie
SABBATH, BLOODY SABBATH

WHEN the streets and clubs of Liverpool had been ravaged by a horde of marauding record company talent scouts in the wake of a tidal wave created by The Beatles, and every buttie-chomping Scouse who could say ''Fab'' and ''Gear'' and carry a guitar had been taken away to the big city to charm the world with his funny accent, the telescopic eyes settled on Birmingham.

Provincial rock was in, they figured, and Birmingham was bigger than Liverpool, and an easier route down to the pulsating, throbbing, twanging heart of the music industry. So Brumbeat it was, or was supposed to be, except that the great Midland hunt unearthed a few hit singles and that was that.

But look at it now — how many groups can you think of that come from Liverpool? But you have got The Move, or at least its offshoots, the ELO and Roy Wood's Wizzard, Led Zeppelin, The Moody Blues, Ten Years After, Traffic, Savoy Brown, Blackfoot Sue, and (stretching the geographical boundaries just a little bit) there are Slade.

There are also the oft-forgotten, gigantic-selling Black Sabbath, prophets of doom, collectors of gold records and purveyors of their own brand of black (country) magic through the medium of heavy riffs and overwhelming wattage.

DEEP PURPLE FANS FEVER

THE DEEP PURPLE LINE-UP

POLICE authorities in Scotland were this week still counting the cost of Deep Purple's flying visit to Glasgow, Aberdeen and other centres. And they said: ''We've seen nothing like this since the heyday of the Beatles''.

Glasgow, the group, ntly high in the singles' charts with 'Black Night', were originally booked into the Electric Garden, which holds about 600. The gig was switched to Tiffanys, which can hold more than 1400.

And even then there were 3,000 fans from all over Scotland locked out in Sauciehall Street. Five were arrested and later appeared in court. Several more were removed from the roof of the hall where they were trying to dig t gh the slates.

e group more than lidated on their su ess in Scotland earlier this year. And left a trail of damage caused by irate fans who couldn't gain admission.

Meanwhile the tour goes on. This weekend (October 25) Deep Purple go to France for 10 days — and their date at the Olympia Theatre in Paris was sold out within hours of the box office opening.

They then go Scandinavia and back to Britain for a short series of dates: November 18, St George's Hall, Liverpool; 19, Belle Vue, Manchester; 20, Hull University; 21, Deep Purple visit to University College, London; 22, Fairfield Hall, Croydon. And then to Germany for two weeks, with stablemates Ashton, Gardner and Dyke. German police are making special plans. On the last special plans. On the last

Dusseldorf, shut-out fans tried to burn their way into the auditorium with petrol blazers.

Though work has started on the group's sixth album, it is unlikely to be on sale before Christmas due to touring pressures. It is more likely to coincide with their 14-day, 14-venue tour of Britain in January — which includes one appearance at London's Royal Albert Hall. But meanwhile, organist Jon Lord is collaborating

with Tony Ashton on the score for the movie 'The Last Rebel'.

A new single? Say Deep Purple: ''We just can't say. Really it is a matter of luck whether we come up with something both good enough

and short enough to release in single form. In any case, 'Black Night' was something of an accident — just something that happened in the throes of recording studio haze helped along by the odd drop of alcohol!''

Most amazing though, is the in-person drawing power of the group. As they say: ''We're getting one week off at Christmas. We'll

INSIDE: TONY BENNETT SPECIAL

MELODY MAKER, December 9, 1972—Page 3

Y LLINGWORTH ports as Led eppelin open heir giant British tour ...

ITY HALL, New- castle - upon - Tyne : Lordy what a beauti- l, beautiful band.

One has to own up. If you anna dance, if you REAL- Y wanna hear a rock 'n' oll band, wipe off that loody silly make-up and o see Led Zeppelin

Of course, if you haven't got a ticket now, you'll never get one because they've sold out all the British dates. No hype, and no mean achievement. Hell, let's stop dollying around, Zeppelin are the most exciting, most hard-hitting horniest hell-raisers sideways of the Stones.

Newcastle — a lovely little city — proved to be a pretty amazing first stop-off.

One usually experiences a fairly strange time on first night- nerves, and cobwebs, leery equip- ment and all that. Zep kicked off at a volume that to say the least, was outrageous with its intensity. It hurt, it really hurt.

If you REALLY wanna hear a rock 'n' roll band, wipe off that bloody silly make-up and go see Zeppelin

a pace that most bands would pee themselves over if they managed to attain it once in their lives, for 30 seconds during an encore. Three hours of one extraordinary level.

Zeppelin threw what seemed everything into two-and-a-half hours, and then, with the threat of the City Hall being torn down, they came back on for two encores.

The first was stag- gering, and the second, well, it was just amaz- ing. They were off the stage for fully eight minutes while the au- dience displayed the sort of doings that bring a bit of a lump to yer throat. For eight solid minutes they roared, and growled, and thumped and stamped for an encore.

The balcony of the Hall was literally shak- ing, and the level of shouting was insane.

Lights kept pan- ning the stage, and while those lights panned there was hope that they would return. The shouting, and stamping went on, and on.

No, there was just no way this audience wa going to go hom without one more. N way.

Just when it seeme that voices were abo to crack — or t balcony was going give in, the fig emerged — and were on stage again.

For a REAL enc You know, a RI one.

Looking back on last time I saw band — several mo back at Nassau seum, Long Island extraordinary nig feel in no way they give less in land. The gigs smaller, sure, there's less about the whole But give Zep stage, no matte big, no matter

ROBERT PLANT: no need to make comparisons

Page 4—MELODY MAKER, January 4, 1975

Damage, lovely damage

Status Quo may not be a critic's band—but they've got a huge, dedicated following that's not above smashing up a few seats at concerts. But it doesn't worry the riff-rock kings—they need that direct contact with their audience. ALLAN JONES reports

HURRICANE ALICE!

3p Saturday, November 11, 1972   No. 24,020

Alice Cooper with his snake called Yvonne.

He's a riot..and 3000 frenzied fans join in

ALL the pop frenzy that hit Glasgow last night is mirrored in the face of one girl fan as, arms outstretched, she reaches towards a hurricane called Alice.

The scene is Green's Playhouse, where Alice Cooper and his group gave 3000 fans a show like they've never seen or heard before.

Hundreds of girls rushed a cordon of police surrounding the stage and three rows of seats collapsed under the crush.

Dozens of girls fainted and two were taken to the Royal Infirmary for treatment. They had bruised ribs and shock.

Alice Cooper, eyes smeared with black make-up, strutted the stage holding a snake called Yvonne. The fans loved it.

Hysteria grew as the group's act went on, larding the music with mock torture scenes, a sha[...] knife fight, a hanging.

In the auditorium, the[...] was a scuffle—for real. T[...] youths were arrested a[...] charged with breach of [...] peace.

Story : ART GRAH[...]
Pictures : DAVID ROBERT[...]

MELODY MAKER, July 15, 1972

● Alice Cooper simply reflects to what lengths a group must go to tickle the jaded palate of an American youth dulled with cheap wine and downers... the gross product of a rancid teenage sub-culture ●

I have fingernails now, you see

SAYS MARIANNE FAITHFULL, THE GIRL WHO BEAT HEROIN

SUNDAY MIRROR, October 1, 1972

SUDDENLY the whole world is in her hands.

The hands of shattered pop star Marianne Faithfull.

Now she can gaze at them and know she is cured of a terrible addiction . . . heroin.

For Marianne's dream of a new life lies, quite literally, at her fingertips, writes Ronald Max...

"I'm cured," she said. "I'm really cured.

"And now I'm going to build my life piece by ..."

... her fingernails started growing ...

... tiny cosmetic detail ... someone so beautiful, ... for Marianne they ... the proof that a ... dful battle has ...

... se healthy fingernails are a vital part of ... re from the dread-diction.

... last night, the girl on whom life ... topped smiling ...

talked about how she fought the curse of heroin . . . and won.

Marianne, a pop star at the age of sixteen, seemed to have everything that life could offer.

But three months ago life had become so desperate that she registered as a heroin addict and went into Bexley Hospital, Kent, in the hope that she could be cured.

"I reached the point when I thought I was Cain's child, cursed and depraved. But now I am cured in every way," she told me.

"Doctor Willis, who treated me at the hospital pointed out that you cannot be cured until you admit you are an addict.

"But once I took the step of registering so

that I could get heroin on the National Health. I had taken the first step towards being cured.

"Now everything is all right. Just look at my fingernails. I've got fingernails now, you see."

She went on happily: "You remember the way I used to bite my nails?

"Well, Dr. Willis said to me 'Stop biting your nails. You are not going to behave like ...

"So ... part of ...

F...

"But I ... talk ab ... Everything ... everyth ... means to ... the future ...

Marianne ... heroin ... living with ...

introduced her to the drug.

That was when she finally turned into an addict.

Just six months ago, Marianne told me: "I had been thinking of registering — but not any more.

"I have had a per-

sonal shock and it put me off heroin. I haven't had any for ten days.

"I don't need it, I don't need treatment, and I don't need to register."

But soon she was taking heroin again regularly. And then came the cure ...

Now she looks fitter and healthier than at the start of the year. Her skin and hair, then dull and lifeless, are back to normal.

She told me: "My mother has been fantastic about it.

"Most parents who find out that their son or daughter is a heroin addict would say: 'Get out.'

"My mother didn't. She came to see me and has helped to cure me.

"Now I'm going off ... holiday, whi...

Daily Mail, Thursday, October 25, 1973

Drugs

Fined Rolling Stone: Friends had left them

By TIM EWBANK

ROLLING STONE Keith Richard was in his four-poster bed with his girl-friend Anita Pallenberg when detectives arrived.

Under the bed they found a strongbox. There were drugs inside.

Inside a bedside cabinet they discovered a revolver, a ·38 Smith and Wesson; inside a wardrobe 110 rounds of ·22 ammunition; on top of the lavatory cistern traces of Chinese heroin in two spoons; downstairs, near the grand piano, a shotgun.

Richard, a 29-year-old guitarist, and Anita, who is 31, were just waking up when men from the Drug Squad made their early morning raid on his house in Cheyne Walk, Chelsea.

Yesterday the couple appeared in Marlborough Street Court, London.

EVENING NEWS, Wednesday, October 18, 1972   C

AUSTRALIA ORDERS JOE COCKER TO GET OUT

From STEPHEN CLAYPOLE

SYDNEY, Wednesday.

ENGLISH pop singer Joe Cocker has been ordered to leave Australia before noon on Friday. The order also applies to six members of his party.

Immigration Minister Dr. Alexander Forbes said that Cocker will be taken into custody and deported if he has not left on his own accord by then.

He signed the deportation orders after considering the circumstances that led to the seven being fined on drug offences in an Adelaide court.

Dr. Forbes said these offences carried sentences of up to two years' imprisonment and so they had been deported under section 13 of the Migration Act.

"I have done this because this Government takes a very serious view of such offences, especially when committed by persons who are in a position to have a profound influence on many young Australians," he added.

Seven fined

Cocker was due to give three concerts in Melbourne, two in Brisbane and one in Perth between Friday and his original departure date of October 27.

Cocker and five members of his group were each fined £140 for having marijuana.

A sixth member was fined a total of £280 for possessing heroin and a syringe.

Cocker was not available for comment at his hotel in Melbourne today.

But talking about the fines yesterday, he said: "It's the same all round the world—in Europe, America, anywhere."

Kinky King of Rock

Saturday Interview EXCLUSIVE by John Blake

THIS has very definitely been the best week of David Bowie's life.

His picture is on the front of Gay News. His new album is top of the charts.

And all 18,000 tickets for his concert at Earls Court tonight were sold within hours of the box office opening.

Bowie, the most outrageous performer of them all, is for a transient moment the king of Britain's rock 'n' roll castle. The hottest, most despised, loved and hated star of all.

All heads turned when he minced in to the bar of the staid Grosvenor House Hotel to meet me for the only interview he has given in his week of triumph.

He is very tall, thin as a blade of grass, and his tinselled, sequinned, sparkling outfit is topped by a bony, angular face and a brush of tangerine, obviously dyed hair.

The fact that he is bisexual, despite being a husband and father, is now common knowledge.

[...] that telling the [...] orthodox around us was very much the way we were.

"It just put us on a much larger area when I was asked about it all. It didn't affect our environment because our environment was already there.

Both Bowie and his wife lead fairly independent lives. She often flies out to watch his concerts but they are apart for long spells.

He has just spent a couple of months travelling across Russia and Europe by train with two male friends after a concert tour of the USA and Japan.

Japan particularly excited him and he plans to wear exotic costumes of Kabuki—the traditional Japanese theatre, at Earls Court.

I asked if he was going to clean his act up a bit. He replied :

"My act has never been obscene in any way, shape or form.

"I'm not worried that I might upset young children. I may offend their mothers —or more probably their fathers—but certainly not the kids."

Child psychology is a problem that I expect is going to occupy him a fair bit when his two-year-old son Zowie grows curious enough to ask: "Daddy, what's a bisexual?"

"I love him, he's a great kid," he says. "But I wouldn't tell him how to live or what he should become.

"All I aim to do is to make sure he can speak three or four languages because that will give him a very good start in anything he wants to do."

AMAZED

Just then we were interrupted by a uniformed porter, aged about 50, who asked: "I'm terribly sorry to bother you, Mr. Bowie, but do you think I might have your autograph for my daughter?"

The kinky king of rock put his name on the paper and the porter added : "And I hope Zowie is well, sir."

Bowie smiled and said : "My God, I'm still amazed when people recognise me— but when they start asking kids by name [...]

DAVID BOWIE: "My wife didn't mind my talking about it. Our environment has always been one in which we could move . . ."

TOP TEN

1. Tie A Yellow Ribbon, [...]own (Bell)
[...]aiser, Sweet
7. Brother Louie, Hot Chocolate (RAK)
8. Drive-In Saturday, David Bowie (RCA)
9. My Love, McCartney's [...]
[...] Guy,

David Bowie is undoubtedly one of rock's greatest talents. His career has spanned three decades. Image has always been his forte and in the glam-rock period of the 1970s his androgynous persona gave rise to a cult following. His futuristic costumes, stage performance and album concepts led the field. Other glitter performers struggled to find an audience outside Britain but not Bowie.

He may have gained headlines because he sometimes wore dresses, used make-up and played bi-sexuality to the hilt, but he was far too talented to become the mere hyped product of Press reporting.

ALL DRESSED UP TO DIG DAVID

David Bowie at Earls Court some say, could have been the musical event of the year. Be that as it may, it provided a fascinating insight into the followers of Bowiemania. Julie Welch reports on the events inside Earls Court, while photographer Mick Gold looked at the people who had come to pay homage.

Why does David Bowie like dressing up in ladies' clothes?

SO there was this geezer dressed up in ladies' clothes, and I fought, "cor blimey," I fought.

But it turned out, he was quite a straight geezer, know what I mean like?

Frankly, it is somewhat difficult to know what David Bowie means. You see, he is tasting the fruits of life, not unlike the Prophet Ezekial whom you will recall spoke in his sermon at the vinyards of the tribe of Ishgosh: "Go forth and have ye a good laugh."

David Bowie means no harm when he poses in a gorgeous gown on the cover of his latest LP recording. "It's a pretty dress," he says simply. "I

just want to be an all round entertainer."

David laughed.

Just what happened after Bowie's hit, and why did he sink into renewed obscurity?

"It's very weird. My father died and a week later I had a hit record. The juxtaposition was like a pantomime, a comic tragedy. Since that time I have had a complete change of management and have started writing again.

"My new LP is actually a year and a half old. But I've got my next one in the can and another half completed. I went to America a few weeks ago to promote this one, and as I knew I was going to Texas, I wore a dress. One guy pulled out a gun and called me a fag. But I thought the dress was beautiful.

David revealed that at one time he was in danger of becoming bitter and twisted. "But I'm definitely happy now. I'm very content which is worrying. I've become optimistic about things and I never used to be.

Terrified

"My writing was schizold, but it's much more simple now. I've been working with Terry Cox of Pentangle and getting a group together to go [...] and [...] haven't [...] done [...]

Evening Standard

46,244

London: Thursday March 15 1973

David Cassidy Special

5   4p

THE NEW IDOL
—he's here to send Wembley crazy!

A cheery wave from David as he steps down from his green and white Caravelle airliner.

Evening Standard: John Minihan

How David Cassidy became the face on a million bedroom walls

by ANDREW BAILEY

J CAN COUNT them on fingers. The Big Ones: Beatles, Elvis, the g Stones, the onds, the Jackson and above all at this in time — David dy.

phenomenon David is o do four shows at the e Pool, Wembley (Fri-8 p.m. and Saturday 4 p.m. and 8 p.m.), was on David's last London that the

message came across loud and clear that the pop scene had a new idol.

Yet people laughed at his record company when they drew up plans to control the crowds of admirers they confidently expected would faithfully follow David around London. They were saying that that type of fan fever had long since gone out of fashion.

But the fans besieged David when he paid a lightning visit to the BBC. They surrounded his car as he tried to get away. They banged on the roof and sta

---

After the pop stampede the big question: What went wrong?

THE SUN, Tuesday, May 28, 1974   7

London shows ban as probe starts

By JOHN HISCOCK

AN inquiry starts to-day into the question everyone is asking: What went wrong at the Cassidy concert?

London licensing chief, Mr Frank Cooper, said yesterday: The full machinery of London's County Hall will be involved.

And until the probe is finished there will be no more big pop shows in London.

Hundreds of young girl fans were trampled and crushed at the White City Stadium on Sunday night as they surged towards Cassidy.

Details

Mr Cooper, whose committee licensed the show for the Greater London Council, said: We want to know the full details of what happened and why.

It is a terrible tragedy that these girls were injured, but at the moment we cannot apportion blame.

Everyone involved with the concert, including promoter Mel Bush, will be asked to provide

THE GIRL WHO 'DIED' FOR DAVID CASSIDY

By COLIN MYLER

SCHOOLGIRL pop fan Bernadette Whelan lived for her idol, David Cassidy. And she nearly died for him.

Last night doctors were fighting to save 14-year-old Bernadette after her heart stopped in the frenzy of Cassidy's London farewell concert.

Before the concert her mother, Mrs Bridget Whelan, warned her not to go because of the risk of being crushed in a hysterical crowd of fans.

But Bernadette pleaded: I'll be all right Mummy. Please let me go—it will make me very happy.

She queued for 12 hours to get a spot near the front of the 35,000 crowd . . . a spot where the pressure of the stampede was at its worst when the fans went wild.

About 800 girls needed treatment and many were taken for hospital check-ups.

After Bernadette fell unconscious a St. John Ambulance officer got her heart going again. But she was still very serious at Hammersmith Hospital last night.

Dangerous

Mrs Whelan was in tears at her home in Stockwell Park, South London, as she said: The doctors have told us to fear the worst.

She went on: I didn't want her to go, but what

Mrs Whelan . . . tears

' I'll be all right Mummy. Please let me go . . it will make me very happy '

Amazing

DIRECT
LINE FOR
CLASSIFIEDS
01-353 2345
9 a.m.-6.30 p.m.

46,272

Evening Standard

London: Tuesday April 17 1973   5

SOUV

WILD, WILD, WILD —THIS FOUR-MAN STEAMROLLER CALLED SLADE

THERE were at least 150,000 disappointed fans in Britain a few weeks ago when Slade played at the Wembley Empire Pool. They were the unlucky ones whose ticket applications arrived too late.

What they missed was a concert that had the excitement of a Cup Final and the hysteria of a Beatles show. Just one more demonstration for the few remaining doubting Thomases that Slade are the most magnetic British group on the scene today.

Though the fractured English of their song titles may make headmasters gnash their teeth, there is no denying the hit statistics of records like Take Me Bak 'Ome, Look Wot You Dun and Mama Weer All Crazee Now.

Slade's sledgehammer drive to the top has confounded some of the pop prophets. Just when it seemed that the soft, easier-listening approach was taking a firm commercial grip, along came this foursome from the Midlands.

As gritty as the industrial Black Country, Slade have got audiences once more off their rumps and dancing in the aisles. When the blast of Slade hits you, it's straight into a sort of "rock knees-up." When Noddy tells you to stand up, you stand up. And you can look around and see that not just most of the audience but every single one of them is doing the same.

But Noddy doesn't have to tell the fans to buy their records. They do that anyway, and with such fervour that Slade have shot up the charts with every single and album they've released.

The way the group is going it's being said

cut, puts it like this : "What's the point of aiming for anything but the top. If you set your sights any lower, you can only achieve something smaller."

"You just look at what sort of figures the champions have set and go for a World Record. They way we're moving, I personally can't see us missing."

Like the Beatles in the early days, the success of Slade has had little to do with the members' individual virtuosity and more to do with the way they reflect the mood of the fans. At the moment, assert Slade, their music should not be analysed or interpreted to be anything more than fun.

In an interview in New Musical Express, shortly after Slade had won the magazine's Live Group of the Year award, Dave explained the group's inner workings.

"The four guys are really a very good cross-section of what our audience are like. We're a good mix of working, middle and upper class. There's always an element of young people who want to dress up and be exhibitionists—I'm just one of them."

One of the most tangible signs of the fan fever that Slade stimulate is the way that hundreds of youngsters turn up to their concerts wearing Slade-styled top hats, complete with mirrors.

Noddy was amazed the first time he saw them. "They must have spent hours and hours making them," he com-

Ripe

In the future, though, Slade plan to broaden their musical outlook. Already some rather more "clever" recordings have been made but not released because the time isn't ripe.

Slade works so well because, according to Dave, they have achieved a balance among themselves. Dave himself decided long ago that he wasn't going to be another Eric Clapton and that there was no point in aiming for that class.

Don Powell, Jimmy Lea, Dave Hill and Noddy Holder—they have a command over an audience : the dynamic rocking sounds and dazzling visual act ensure that every show is an all-action, everyone-get-involved occasion.

in a box at home. You should see what's written on them . . ."

If identification is the name of the game, then Slade are in tune with their following more than anyone else around. It hasn't been a matter of them working out which is the most commercial angle and then making their image appear to be natural.

The boys really are just an extension of themselves when on stage. They have been on the road for five years, first through the skinhead phase, which they now prefer to forget, before emerging as themselves.

Sometimes the group still finds it hard to accept the power of their following. On

The group are currently being sent via their fan club, more than 10,000 letters a week. Many come from young people who feel that Slade understand their problems because they come from the same background and share the same attitude to life.

But when it is suggested that the group have a large degree of genuine control over their fans the idea is dismissed. Proof of this Slade will say, is the way in which You'll Never Walk Alone, the national anthem of football supporters, found its way into the act.

"One night," recalled Noddy, "the audience just started singing it, all together. We hadn't said a thing. We just stood back and let them take over."

Noddy calculates that at least 75 per cent of their fans are also football fanatics. They get letters saying things like "All we live for is Slade and Liverpool Football Club."

Not surprisingly this type of reaction has put them in the gallery of "working class heroes" along with Rod Stewart and the Faces. Miles away, in fact, from those other teen idols, the Osmonds.

Noddy met the Osmonds at their recent Rainbow date. He told one reporter: "They seemed like nice, ordinary blokes. I didn't take any inter-

est in their records because it's not the stuff I listen to. I think they appeal to a much younger set than we do."

"Our image is as different from their's as chalk from cheese. But everybody has their own niche. The Osmonds, the Jackson, Cassidy, Gary Glitter, Bolan, Bowie, the Strawbs, everybody has their own little thing. He's aware that the competition is tough. "Unless you're good in your field, you won't survive. There is always somebody ready to take your place. If you have a limited amount of money to spend on records and you can't afford to be complacent."

Aura

Slade are aware that what it boils down to is having an aura, a command over an audience. In their case the dynamic rocking sounds and dazzling visual act make sure that every show is an all-action, everybody-get-involved occasion. Mass appeal at its most effective.

Or, as Dave Hill puts it : "We're not really interested as a band in improving our own stature as musicians. We're only interested in entertaining and giving our audiences a good time. We don't feel the need to educate them."

Tape

Sometimes the group still finds it hard to accept the power of their following. On

Rover safety

OSMONDMANIA

AS THE OSMONDS BEGIN THEIR LONG-AWAITED BRITISH TOUR THIS WEEK, LAURA DENI, IN AN EXCLUSIVE INTERVIEW FROM LAS VEGAS, GIVES THE LATEST INSTALMENT IN THE BEHIND-THE-SCENES STORY OF THIS EXTRAORDINARY FAMILY NOW IN ENGLAND FOR THE THIRD TIME.

"OSMONDMANIA" is spreading throughout England again as the Osmonds make their third trip to London.

"We love London because London has been so nice to us. We now consider London our second home," they said while appearing at Caesars Palace in Las Vegas.

What makes this trip so extra special for the Osmonds? It's the fact that it is a honeymoon for newlywed Merrill, who has just got married to Mary Carlson.

Honeymoon

"Mary has never been to London before. This is part of the honeymoon. This is one of the reasons I was anxious to get married," said the friendly, self-assured, hazel-blue eyed lead singer about his bride.

Merrill met lovely Mary Carlson this summer. She was a schoolteacher at American Folk High School in Heber City, Utah.

The Osmonds' mother was looking for a tutor for Jimmy and Marie because "everybody studies on the road", they explained. "That is really what got them together. It was a summer romance which developed. They fell in love and on September 5 the smiling couple got engaged.

"One of the most frequent questions we get is 'Why did they get married so soon?' The answer is Merrill wanted to take her to Europe. From Vegas on it's all work. There

is more to the tour than England, so Merrill said 'it's a real opportunity to have a great honeymoon," they explained.

Theatre

"The difficult part of it is that we won't be able to sightsee," complained Merrill about his well-known face. "We may be able to get to the theatre. I love the theatre. In the daytime Mary is going to be pretty much on her own, or with other members of the family."

The entire Osmond brood will travel on the tour. Mary has retired as a schoolteacher. But she will give Jimmy and Marie lessons.

And so, on Monday, September 17, at the Jesus Chris[t] of the Latter-day Saint (Mormon) temple in Salt Lak[e] City, Utah, Miss Carlson, 22, daughter of Mrs. Vel[da] Carlson of Heber City and the late Roy Carlson marri[ed] Merrill Osmond, third oldest of the performing Osmo[nd] group, in church rites conducted before the immed[iate] family. A private reception for family members [and] friends followed.

For their reception the new Mrs. Osmond wore a [full] lace wedding gown and veil. Virl Osmond, one of t[he] non-performing brothers in the family of nine ch[ildren] took the official wedding photographs.

The couple began their honeymoon in Las Vega[s as]

the Osmonds opened their fourth headline engagement at Caesars Palace three days after the wedding.

Mom and Dad Osmond were in a booth with their new daughter-in-law as Mary watched Merrill, on stage for the first time. His gold wedding band caught the spotlights and teeny boppers yelled out "Congratulations, Merrill" as his brothers shook his hand.

During the show his brothers kidded him about being on his honeymoon, telling the SRO crowd that they were lucky to have Merrill on stage at all — and promising Mary to hurry up the show, getting him back to her as soon as possible.

Reception

[...] 12, at the Beverly Hills, California, [...] Records President, Mike Curb, [...] Curb and the Osmonds [...] for friends and

The first half of the 1970s saw record companies once again hurrying to find new groups for the teenage girl market. Although it had always been part of company policy, it was conducted with even more unseemly haste than usual. The advent of such acts as Slade, David Essex, the Osmonds, Mud, Jackson 5, Marc Bolan, David Cassidy, Sweet, Gary Glitter, the Wombles and the Bay City Rollers was accompanied by high teenage music magazine sales and overall media frenzy. Newspapers and magazines have never had it so good and, apart from the remarkable sales of *Smash Hits* in the 1980s, this period is not likely to be repeated.

JOANIE

"I LOVE Gabriel so much. That's my son. I went to Hanoi and saw the bombing of the city by people of my nation. I was frightened. I had never really before faced the possibility of death.

"I was frightened not only for those around me but passionately so for Gabriel." Joan Baez talking about her trip last year to Vietnam.

"The children listen for the alerts and then they run to the nearest shelter and for a time stay near the entrance. They laugh and play. It seemed so strange.

"For the moment, perhaps for ever, the bombing is over. What cannot be changed is the damage done to people." Joan talks about a girl whose age must have been about 12. "She had a sleeveless blouse. Both arms ended in fire-blackened stumps, at the shoulder."

'Why I love my son . . . Why I love the world'

JOHN LENNON—ordered out by September 10.

Lennon to fight order to quit

WASHINGTON, Thursday FORMER Beatle John Lennon, who has been ordered out of the United States within 60 days or face deportation, is to appeal against the decision and, says his lawyer, it would take a "number of years" for the appeal to be resolved.

The lawyer, Leon Wildes, said an appeal against the Justice Department decision would be filed with the U.S. Court of Appeals in New York "as soon as we study the immigration ruling and outline our grounds of appeal.

"I would say if he (Lennon) tells me he is interested in staying on, he will be here a number of years until it's resolved," Wildes said.

Lennon, 34, has been in the United States since August, 1971, on a non-immigrant visa which expired in February 1972. The government refused to extend that authorisation because in 1968 Lennon had pleaded guilty to a marijuana possession charge after a quantity of the drug was found in a binocular case in his home.

He has been fighting the charge since; and supporters said the government was trying to get him out of the country because of his strong anti-war views. (UPI)

JOAN PAYS THE PRICE OF PEACE

POP PAGE by PAULINE McLEOD

IF Joan Baez had listened to the sweet-talking wheeler-dealers who wanted to run her life, she'd be a multi-million-airess by now.

As it is, the dark-eyed, mellow-voiced singer went her own way. And she made money but then lost money—and now she's just about breaking even.

The high priestess of peace has given away thousands of dollars to her anti-violence charities, has missed out on thousands more through mis-management and has given countless benefit concerts to promote her political beliefs.

JOAN BAEZ: A slice of the good life.

It was said that if Dylan was the 'king' of folk-rock and protest during the 1960s then Joan Baez was his 'queen'. Baez was certainly influential in gaining Dylan an initial hearing. For a while they were romantically involved. Baez was very beautiful with a captivating voice and many of the song lyrics on her high-selling albums were full of social and political observations.

Her most controversial record was *Where are you now, My Son?*, which was the result of a visit to Hanoi. One side of the album contained a quasi-documentary account of a US bombing raid on that city. That record, her views and her founding of the Institute for the Study of Non-violence in Carmel, California, hardly endeared her to Americans of the political right. She has continued to fight for human rights and shown particular concern for the turmoil of Latin America. She is herself of Mexican-Spanish blood on her father's side.

British invasion ~second time around

Who would believe, in this year of Outrage and Heavy Metal, that 13,000 New Yorkers would flock to a show featuring Herman's Hermits, Gerry and the Pacemakers, The Searchers, Billy J. Kramer and Wayne Fontana? It was a crazy, time-warp situation . . . but amazingly it worked, as MICHAEL WATTS reports.

AH, the sixties, the fabulous sixties! Who can remember them?

Drugs, for one thing. Wasn't that the time everyone was taking acid so they could see their veins light up all fluorescent, and smoking grass, and actually **giggling** on it?

Let's see, the sixties: hard rock and soft rock, and psychedelia, and someone handing you flowers on the street, and signing letters "love and peace", and Kenny Everett **first** time around, and Afro hairstyles on white kids — boy, they had really long hair back then when you come to think of it. They thought mankind was going to be averted from its collision course by 1970.

Well, here it is — 1973! The guys on the street are still putting paint on their faces, only they're applying it more skilfully and it's more likely to be in pursuance of Alice Cooper's S and M trip than Portobello Road hippiedom. And Lou Reed now gets letters from boys asking whether they should become full-time gay, while Paul McCartney has to go out on the road and prove himself all over again. What's happened? We're what's happened. The fabulous seventies!

Naturally, it hasn't always been like this. It had to have a beginning somewhere, this hydra-headed pop monster. You won't believe this kids, but there was a time, in fact, when John Lennon was considered something of an "'ardcase," when the Moody Blues used to do "Bye Bye Birdie" with balls and when bands generally only had three small amps, but that was okay because nobody listened too much, anyway. I guess you saw a re-run of the Shea Stadium concert. Yeah, it really was that bad. Listen, a lot of the time it was a good deal worse.

You can't tell people that, though. They just don't want to know. You point out to them that the Swinging Blue Jeans, the Remo Four and the Fourmosts, that

them sounds so fabulous. These are the punks of the seventies, kids who bought Beatle records in their preteens, grew up with Led Zeppelin and Grand Funk, realised they

generally hung in the air like an all-pervasive mist of exotica.

New York promoter Ron Delsener was the first to realise and act upon it earlier this year. "Everybody had this ideal!" he said, "every body!" He was positively lyrical. "Promoters, the street, the hustler

Wayne Fontana they then found, but he was in hospital with an ulcer. Pretty soon the other acts fell into place: Gerry and the Pacemakers, Billy J. Kramer and the Dakotas, and the Searchers. It was going to be bannered: "The 1960s. British Rock Invasion (Revisited)"; yes, rock, not beat music. It was funny, but still, the

and heavy, brown features, Nader's richly entrepreneurial presence can be felt imposing itself on the evening of June 25 in an upstairs room of the English Pub, which stands at 57th and Seventh Avenue. The room is full of journalists, and though several of them are punk writers there are a lot of straights, too, most of them from the

still there.

They'd come straight from the airport; booze was still on the breath of some of them. They trooped in as if they owned the joint and made right for the bar, with the exception of Wayne Fontana in his black shades, curling his cocky Northern lip, who sat down on a table; Wayne has taken the pledge for the tour. He was still

eased himself in. Click click. One for posterity. Count the originals who aren't there. None of the Pacemakers, none of the Dakotas, none of the Mindbenders — the flame that burns quickly.

"I don't believe this!" murmurs one of the photographers for an American teenybop mag. "This is the funniest thing I've ever been to."

Herman / Peter poses with his French wife, Mireille. Twenty-one gold hits to his credit. He looks expensive; the years haven't done anything but improve him. The face of a teenybop angel, it's nevertheless hard to imagine him now without his guest spot image of the Cilla Black and Cliff Richard shows.

He and Gerry, who had a long run in "Charlie Girl" with Anna Neagle, haven't done too badly . . . Herman/Peter finally answers the questions as to why he'd come. "You see," he says almost reprovingly, " there are still people here who haven't seen us."

Old Hermit freak Toby vigorously nods his head, with its heavy halo of fuzz and round-rimmed glasses, and for an instant there can't be two more dissimilar yet sympathetic people in New York.

THERE were 13,000 people at Madison Square Gardens last Wednesday, and this meant moms and dads and old biddies, reformed grease, pure English music nuts, Englishpeople resident in New York, 25-year-old secretaries who remembered it all from way back then and a lot of young teenyboppers who wouldn't have known Billy J. Kramer and the Dakotas from the Young Rascals.

It wasn't a Led Zeppelin audience, and it wasn't a bunch of screamers for David Cassidy. Who knows why the chicklets were there? Possibly they'd seen a picture of Herman in Sixteen or Fave, maybe there was some unexplained stirring in the collective sub-conscious. They knew it was English. That meant it must be old, didn't it? That meant it must be fab gear.

There were passes on the door for Dave Mason and Richard Starkey plus one. George Harrison was in town. No one saw any of them. Lennon was in Washington, attending the Watergate hearings. He most probably wouldn't have come anyway. They say he has no particular fondness for the days of the other Liverpool groups he originated with it. No nostalgia there. Brian Epstein long dead, his stable had been dissipated to various corners of the world. The pool has settled back into what it was before the fuss. Somewhere up there Tommy Quickly and all the others are probably still kicking around. No one remembers, or part

HERMAN'S HERMITS: this is one hell of a cute kid.

& POPSWOP MIRROR DECEMBER 7, 1974

7

Queen, Queen, Queen, Queen, Queen, Queen, Queen

The Scourge Of Europe?
. . . being an instrument or manifestation of divine wrath

Killer Queen slay America!

Rolling in health wealth and happiness

RECORD MIRROR, MAY 10, 1975

RECORD MIRROR NEWSDESK 01-607 6411

O'BOY HITS DUBLIN

MUD STAR in a special show at Dublin Stadium

U.S. GOES ROLLER-CRAZY

Shea booked for '76

THE BAY City Rollers are to play New York's Shea Stadium in the biggest promotion of a British band since the Beatles sent America crazy back in the Sixties.

Ace U.S. promoter Sidney Bernstein has booked the giant 55,000 capacity venue for a summer '76 concert following a "Rollers crazy" media reaction throughout America's teeny Press.

BCR STORM NYC?
AT LEAST THEY GOT THERE SAFELY

SO THEY CAME, they saw, but as far as actually having conquered anything this remains to be seen. The Bay City Rollers arrived at JFK Airport from London on Tuesday last week and were greeted with more press here than . . . oh, well let's just say that not since Elliot Murphy has there been so much written about so little.

RECORD MIRROR, JUNE 7,

6

ON TUESDAY evening one of the biggest tours Britain's seen in a long time ended. Biggest in terms of audience, screams, hysteria and press coverage. It's been a long time since you could count on opening practically any daily newspaper and finding continuous coverage of a group. Amidst the stories of Alan Longmuir's possible split from the Rollers, the near-prison like existence of the boys in their hotel rooms and police guards round theatres, the Bay City Rollers themselves have kept pretty much to themselves and said little about what's really been going on. Last week, though, Record Mirror travelled with the group for three days around the country, and spoke at length with them about every aspect of Roller - manta.

ROLLING ROUND BRITAIN!

THE scenes outside the Civic Hall were typical of the scenes that everywhere the Rollers have played during jackets, rolled

McKEOWN FINED AND COULD GO TO JAIL

McKEOWN lead singer with the Bay City Rollers has been fined £1,100 and been given a three month prison sentence, suspended for two years.

Judge Kenneth Mynett warned McKeown at Oxford Crown Court that if he commits another criminal act in that period, he could go to jail.

McKeown must face another court appearance at Edinburgh at the end of this month, where he is accused of causing the death of a 76 - year - old woman by reckless and dangerous driving.

At Oxford, the judge said that McKeown made "an unprovoked, violent and deliberate attack" on two photographers at a concert.

Afterwards, McKeown said: "I'm very relieved it's over. It's a great weight off my mind."

LES McKEOWN: 'I'm very relieved it's over"

Mama Cass, alias Cass Elliot, was a member of the West Coast vocal harmony group, the Mamas and the Papas. They were among the first flower-power bands, wearing hippie clothes and singing about its free living philosophy and the accompanying overused word 'love'. The group's leader, John Phillips, organised, along with John Adler, the Monterey Pop Festival. As a result of the Mamas and Papas playing there, they became much more widely known but by mid-1968 they had broken up.

Mama Cass went solo and had several early hits before becoming part of the Mamas and Papas' short-lived reunion which produced the 1971 album *People Like Us*.

Her own career then progressed rather slowly. In July 1974 she played a two-week show at the London Palladium, but sadly on 29 July, she had a heart attack and died at the age of 33.

Daily Mirror

EUROPE'S BIGGEST DAILY SALE

4p Tuesday, July 30, 1974

No. 21,934

Mama Cass dead

By SIDNEY WILLIAMS and JACK McEACHRAN

CASS ELLIOT, the cheery thirty-three-year-old fourteen-stone American pop star, known to fans as "Mama Cass," was found dead in her luxury flat last night.

She was discovered, half-slumped in a divan bed, by her road manager who called at the flat in Mayfair's Curzon Place. Her clothes were draped over her bare body.

The former lead singer with the Mamas and Papas group, who rose to fame with such songs as "Dedicated to the One I Love" and "California Dreaming," was last seen alive on Sunday night. Crime is not suspected.

It is believed she died when she inhaled her own vomit.

She had just finished a two-week booking at the London Palladium—playing to sellout audiences every night.

Truth

On the first night, she stunned the audience with an admission that seven years ago, she stole blankets from the Kensington Hotel while in London for a show.

She was charged with the theft when her boat docked at Southampton. But the charge was dismissed two days later when no evidence was offered by police.

She was innocent—until she told the truth at the Palladium. And she kept on telling it at every performance from then on.

Lately, the twice-divorced star wanted to be known simply as Cass Elliot.

● Death also came early to pop stars guitarist Jimi Hendrix and singer Jani Joplin, both of whom died in 1970 aged twenty-seven—both from drug overdoses.

HOW they remember her—Mama Cass in London at the start of her tour.

Elton John rocked his way through the Iron Curtain

DAILY MIRROR, Saturday, May 26, 1979   PAGE 9

in rock

?!★!

s yesterday—new
ation, same hopes

FILTH AND THE FURY!

A REVOLUTION

PARTY'S OVER

ell-raiser Keith Moon the night before tragedy

Girlfriend finds pop idol dead in his Mayfair flat

Moon's last night out ... with party hosts Paul and Linda McCartney

phones

In the many articles that have been written about this period from the vantage point of the 1980s, it seems as if the whole of the second half of the decade was dominated by 'punk', which can be loosely defined as anti-Establishment, anti-fashion and anti-music industry.

Certainly the punk movement provided the music industry in Britain with its biggest upheaval since Presley and the other rock-'n'-rollers had created a musical form that separated parents and kids. And the punk period is arguably one of the music industry's most exciting eras. However, there were many other non-punk groups who sold records and allowed the major record companies, who were feeling threatened by the advent of punk, to continue as if it were 'business as usual'.

There was still art, style and glamour in the sophisticated form of, say, Roxy Music and the suave, intelligent lead man Bryan Ferry. There was also the new pop formation from Sweden called Abba. The foursome had won the Eurovision Song Contest in 1974 but the rather lacklustre singles that followed failed to live up to their initial promise. Neither *Ring Ring* nor *I do I do I do* made the top 20 but from 1975 onwards there was a succession of instant top three singles. Another group who competed with Abba for chart success was Boney M, whose members had been gathered together from the West German studio recording world. To complete a trio of rival acts was Blondie, a group better known for its lead singer Debbie Harry. Solo artist Donna Summer collected a mass of hits in another major market of the time, disco.

The old faithfuls, such as Wings, Cliff Richard, Elton John and Dylan, continued to collect headlines. Other famous names died, none of which was more notable or dramatic than Elvis Presley. The deaths of Keith Moon and Marc Bolan also claimed shocking headlines.

But it was punk, chiefly in the form of the Sex Pistols, that everyone was talking about. The Pistols were the brainchild of Malcolm McLaren who had had a brief association with the seamy American outfit New York Dolls and who ran an 'anti-fashion' clothing boutique in London's King's Road. McLaren ensured that the Pistols were totally objectionable and offensive. It was hardly a new ruse but, as with the Rolling Stones in the 1960s, it was successful in making the Pistols the most newsworthy act in contemporary music. Their singles like *God Save the Queen*, *Anarchy in the UK*, *Pretty Vacant*, *No One is Innocent* and *Holidays in the Sun* had a basic and driving, if discordant, rhythm and were delivered with great verve by Johnny Rotten, despite the fact that, in common with many punk bands, he had no previous musical experience. McLaren's astute hyping paid off, people either loved or hated the group and their lyrics. The nation was aghast as it seemed as if the group was attacking everything that it held sacred. Even dancing had been reduced to mindless pogoing and an audience's appreciation was shown not by applause but by spitting.

Endless groups arrived to shock and dull the senses: some would survive, such as the Dammed, Clash, Siouxsie and the Banshees, and the Fall while many others fell by the wayside. Among the latter are the Adverts, Slaughter and the Dogs, Generation X, X-Ray Spex and the list goes on and on just like the one that can be compiled of groups that came out of San Francisco in the late 1960s. Those remembered with particular affection include: Paul Weller's Jam, the Buzzcocks, London SS, Subway Sect, UK Subs, the Stranglers and Magazine. Among the many influential American punk groups were Patti Smith and the Ramones. In the fashion world no one was more significant than Vivienne Westwood.

Punk rid everyone of the idea that records, recording and club work were the sole domain of the established record companies. The punk ethos was 'anyone can do it' and many did. But punk bands did not necessarily avoid the major record concerns; EMI had signed the Sex Pistols before dropping them when scandalised by the Pistols' behaviour on the Bill Grundy televison show. A&M briefly signed them but it was Branson's Virgin label which gave them sanctuary. Polydor added Siouxsie and the Banshees and the Jam to their stable while CBS had the Stranglers, Clash and, less successfully, the Only Ones.

It was the era of Abba and the Pistols and of extraordinary sales for the albums and films *Grease* and *Saturday Night Fever*. It was certainly interesting.

EVENING STANDARD, THURSDAY, MARCH 27,

Tommy brings out the pop swoppers

MARCH 75

THE TOMMY of th
title . . . Roger Dal

's new girl friend. A model.

NEWS ON CAMERA

Pictures: GRAHAM WOOD
Story: JAMES JOHNSON

ROD STEWART and Britt
Ekland were among many
pop swop couples on show at
the premiere of Ken Russell's
film Tommy last night.

Britt is the latest girl to
capture the heart of Rod.

She now takes the place of
his fiancee, model Dee Harrington, in his home in
Windsor.

As they kissed and hugged
at the Leicester Square
Theatre last night, Britt said:

BRITT AND ROD . . . She takes the place of his fiancee Dee Harrington.

"Your pictures will tell the
story," Rod said: "It's the
real thing."

Meanwhile, at a sumptuous
party after the film, other pop
romances were on display.

Guitarist Eric Clapton was
with Beatle wife Patti Harrison; Ringo Starr arrived
with his new American girl-

friend Nancy Andrews; and
Kim Moon, the estranged wife
of The Who's drummer Keith
Moon, was escorted by Ian
Maclagan of The Faces.

And the queue of Rolls-
Royces and Daimlers around
Leicester Square proved that
whatever the country's economic troubles there is still
plenty of money in pop.

The cars were there to
deliver the conveyor belt
stars who were cheered by
about 200 fans who stood outside the theatre in the rain.

An unshaven David Esse
drew the most screams from
the crowd.

● Alexander Walker review
the film—Page 16.

ERIC CLAPTON turns up in cloth cap and raincoat, accompanied by Beatle wife Patti Harrison.

TURDAY, MARCH 22, 1975

SATURDAY SPOTLIGHT ON TH[E] ROCK OPERA

WHEN The Who re-
leased a rock album
about a boy called
Tommy they unleashed
a pop legend.

The record has
been hailed as "the
finest pop record ever
made."

It has earned a for-
tune for the four pop
stars from London's
Shepherd's Bush.

Now, controversial
director Ken Russell
has made a film of
Tommy which is pre-
miered in London next
week.

Exclusively in the

Evening News, Pete
Townshend—leader of
The Who and author
of Tommy—tells how
and why he wrote it.

Frankly, he reveals
that bullying in his
childhood and a hor-
rifying drug experi-
ence, led to Tommy's
painful birth.

TOMMY the birth of a monster

EXCLUSIVE by PETE TOWNSHEND

PEOPLE ask me if Tommy is auto-
biographical? In a sense it is.
Tommy is made deaf, dumb and
blind in the story after seeing his
father killed. I am deaf, dumb and
blind in another
sense. Closed up
and alone in the
belief that what
I see and hear
is all that exists,
unless it can be
proved that it
didn't happen.

Tommy suffers
from the experi-
ences of drugs
administered in the
story by the Acid
Queen.

She is played in

the film by Tina
Turner in a way that
makes my own more
horrifying drug ex-
perience look mild.

The scene was really,
in a way, a comment to
say that "acid" or drugs
are terrible, that LSD is
terrible and they do ter-
rible things to people;
but that the most ter-
rible thing about it all
is a society which almost
forces it on people and
then condemns them for
using it.

Drugs provide a mind-
opener but without pro-
viding anything to fill

up the cavern they open
in your head.

Tommy is also bullied
in his childhood, as I
was, and his suffering is
made worse by his
afflictions.

Later in the story he
is assaulted by his
homosexual uncle (that
part definitely isn't auto-
biographical) and he
actually enjoys it.

Famous

The thing is that in
his deaf, dumb and
blind state, Tommy is
quite protected.

In this way, Uncle
Ernie's perverted ap-

This is really where
the story crosses right
over my own life then
takes off at a tangent.

Tommy doesn't remain
just a hero to his fans,
because his mother dis-
covers a way to crack
the shell he has built
around himself.

She does this by liter-
ally cracking the mirror
in which he loved to gaze
. . . despite his blindness.

Tommy, though deaf,
dumb and blind, seemed
to see himself when he
looked in a mirror. I
think that somewhere
deep down I can see
myself too— my real self.

When he discovers that
the vision he has been
staring at in the mirror
is actually himself he

seems as if it might
help them along a bit
quicker.

They all want the
short cuts, the easy way
out. Nobody is prepared
to admit that life has a
purpose, as such.

to be like you, how did
you do it?'

And Tommy says:
"Well, it's quite simple
really. I was deaf, dumb,
and blind from the age
of six until now, around
twenty years later.

the triumph of ordinary
people over exploitation
and the decadence of
the "Temple."

So for the ultimate
parallel to my own life,
I still sit and wait."

Tommy is, in a sense,
really more auto-bio-
graphical of The Who,

● Drugs provide a mind-opener, but without providing
anything to fill the cavern they open up in your head.

WHAT A GAS! THE GREATEST SHOW ON EARTH COMES ROLLING BACK

STONED!
17,000 Londoners get high on Jagger's carnival of rock

By JOHN BLAKE
Pictures DAVID THORPE

THE Rolling Stones hit London like World War III.

Their concert at Earl's Court—the most exciting yet, as they promised—began with the sound of cannon fire, a military bugle and wartime-like searchlights.

The Stones turned Earl's Court into a flag-draped, dazzling magical place for the first London concert in a British tour which is costing £1 million to produce.

The probing searchlights picked out an 80ft multi-coloured silk dragon suspended over the 17,000 fans.

Then they focused on the five petals of a giant 30ft.-high, 100ft.-wide black, gold and silver lotus flower that stood where the stage should have been.

Slowly the petals lowered and Mick Jagger was revealed in a skin-tight turquoise suit.

Then Keith Richard, Ronnie Wood, Bill Wyman and Charlie Watts, backed by Billy Preston and Ollie Brown came into view, and the unmistakable chords of Honky Tonk Woman hit the air like rifle fire.

The Stones built up a super-powered wall of sound with It You Don't Rock Me and Get Off My Cloud and then played a couple of numbers from their new album Black and Blue.

The whole night had a sensational carnival atmosphere.

The concert proved once again—if proof were needed—that the Stones are the greatest show business act in the world and London was glad to have them back for the first time in three years.

HIGH SPOT

They thundered through their hits and strongest album tracks until Can't Always Get What You Want when Mick Jagger persuaded the overawed audience to join him in singing the choruses.

Keith Richard, in skin-tight leather jeans and white T-shirt, was in better form than I have seen him for years, and his singing of Happy was one of the night's high spots.

Mick Jagger swung on his Tarzan rope further and higher than before.

And, after Midnight Rambler, Brown Sugar and other classics that have turned the Stones into living legends, they pumped confetti over the audience and threw buckets of water over the heads of those nearest the stage.

TIPPED OUT

Then Mick—by this time naked to the waist—emptied a bucket of water over his own head.

The stamping, dancing audience dragged the Stones back for the first encore I've seen them give.

They chose Sympathy for the Devil and as they sang, people dressed as carnival characters like Humpty Dumpty, sex goddesses and gorillas, danced on to the stage.

And finally the petals of the lotus flower were lifted as the Stones played on, and it really was over.

Later all the Stones except Keith sipped Coke with stars including Lulu, Susan Hampshire and Patrick Mower, at the Cockney Pride Tavern, Piccadilly Circus, until dawn came up over London.

What a night!

John Blake's exclusive interview with bad Keith. — Page FIFTEEN

Mick Jagger showing the form that had fans roaring for more

... *ger and Keith Richard.*

ENTERTAINMENT

Harrison: The £3 million problem about writing a hit . . .

FROM PHILIP FINN, NEW YORK

FORMER Beatle George Harrison revealed this week that he had become paranoid for a time over recurring threats of legal action.

His biggest worry was facing possible litigation over his new compositions, on the grounds that someone might come forward and say they were stolen.

There are so many songs that are similar to some degree,' George said in New York.

'I started to get really worried about writing songs after I testified in court earlier this year.

'I'd pick up a guitar and say, "Well, I can't use those chords, those chords have already been used. And I can't use those words because I've heard those words before."

'Before you know, it becomes a problem and you start to get really paranoid about it. In the end I thought, "Oh, I'm not going to get hung up about this".'

George said his fears started shortly after the gruelling three days he spent in court, testifying about a charge of plagiarism involving his best-ever solo hit, My Sweet Lord.

He lost the action, which is now being appealed.

But since then there has been another legal hassle, involving a £6 million claim for damages by a record company who alleged 'non-delivery of product'.

George said this had now been settled, with an agreement reached between Warner Brothers Records and the firm suing George. Nearly £3 million was involved in the settlement.

George, who says he is still recovering from the severe attack of hepatitis which kept him bedbound for 2½ months at the beginning of the year, can now laugh at the 'Sue Me, Sue You Blues.'

He makes light of these troubles in his latest record, Thirty Three and A Third, which is being released this week.

Falsetto

In one number called The Song, the ex-Beatle is teamed with Eric Idle of the Monty Python comedy troupe, who offers an amusing falsetto commentary on the court proceedings at the end of one verse.

George also unburdens himself. He said : 'I get my digs in with lines like, "This song has nothing tricky about it / this song ain't black or white and as far as I know, don't infringe on anyone's copyright.". . .

George said he produced the record using session men, but he conceded that there are times when he has a hankering to work with John, Paul and Ringo.

'I definitely do miss it in some way,' he said. 'When you have a band, there's a certain amount of knowledge you have about one another and ...

you can fit right into a slot.

'There's a certain starting point that's already established that you don't have to spell out, as you do with new musicians.

Doubts

'I liked having the instant situation we got into with the Beatles, but at the same time, I don't think I could stand it again. It was too confining.

'The good thing about being on one's own, is all the time being able to use the other musicians ...

Warner Brothers, he would be able to join another label if the dreamed-for reunion with the other Beatles ever became reality.

He seriously doubts, however, that it will come about.

He doubts, too, that the proposed charity concert—aimed at scooping an incredible £150 million in one night—will work out.

'He's put us on the spot,' says George of US impresario Sid Bernstein, who ...

George Harrison: 'I'm not going to get hung up'

EXTRA 2   *Daily Mail, Wednesday, December 1, 1976*

Mrs LULU'S SECRET

LULU, the perky rock singer, was keeping a secret under her hat when she married John Frieda in London yesterday. For husband John is a hairdresser . . . and Lulu, wearing a head-hugging bonnet, was keeping him guessing on her choice of hair style for their big occasion.

Picture: KENT GAVIN

YOU MEET THE **NICEST** PEOPLE IN THE MIRROR

DAILY MIRROR, Saturday, October 9, 1976   PAGE 11

DAILY EXPRESS Tuesday February 8 1977

Wings are spreading

New baby to join the McCartney family band

By Judith Simons

ANOTHER baby is on the way for Linda McCartney, wife of ex-Beatle Paul, leader of the Wings group.

The addition, due in September, will bring the count of little Wings to four.

And nobody is more pleased than the eldest of them, 14-year-old Heather, 34-year-old Linda's daughter by her previous marriage to geologist Melvyn See.

"I am good with babies," said Heather yesterday. "I like the idea of having one in the house again."

So do the McCartneys, married eight years, and parents of two other daughters, Mary, 7, named after Paul's mother, and Stella, 5, named after Linda's mother.

Paul's world

The couple have always said they want a large family. Jokingly last night 34-year-old Paul explained why.

"The idea of a big family is to have a band," he said. "We're providing for our old age—when we're 64!"

As Linda cooked dinner at their home in St. John's Wood, London, Paul said: "This is lovely news for us.

"Do we want a son or ... Well, be happy

DAILY EXPRESS Monday September 27 1976

Sinking Venice rises to new height on Paul McCartney's Wings of song

PAUL McCARTNEY had just seduced the most romantic city in the world, and wore the smile of a satisfied lover.

He had at first charmed, then aroused, an unresponsive crowd of 30,000 which normally live more comfortably with the works of Mozart.

For a man who at 34 has become the most successful rock songwriter on earth and has lived with an almost embarrassing adoration since 1962, it was a moment to cherish.

"This concert," he declared, went beyond just entertaining an audience. It was like happening or very special festival."

McCartney had decided that he and Wings would give their services free, with profits of £25,000 from ticket sales going towards the UNESCO fund-raising for Venice, which is steadily dying through high tides and pollution.

CONVOY

barges

meant performing in a twelfth-century St. Mark's Square, into which a barge had been allowed for the first time to set up 40 tons of stage equipment worth £1million.

It had been brought

6 . . . with blinding flashes of light and a thin red laser beam the show took off 9

McCartney's own money to set up.

As to his own involvement, he is pointedly casual.

"It is for a good cause" he says simply, "and the chance to play in a setting like that was a wonderful experience.

"We were all very conscious that nothing like this had ever been done before," he adds. "The whole band was determined to respond to that."

And respond they did. The concert brought 350 journalists and six television crews to record the spectacle.

Aesthetically, to stage rock music in this beautiful square, with its

(coffee 50p a cup), and of shops selling Venetian glass, Capodimonte figures and the very best in Italian leather.

The 15,000 limit set by municipal authorities as the maximum weight the ancient flagstones (perched on foundations of logs) could take was doubled long before the show was due to start.

CLASSICAL

had been sold at up to £10 each, but as security was almost non-existent it was an open house.

For a city renowned for its palaces and classical culture, it was an unusual audience.

Expensively dressed northern Italian women, in silk scarves and Gucci shoes, jostled for places alongside youngsters from the

the square were replaced with red, yellow and blue spotlights being bounced off a huge global-shaped mirror above the stage.

ORIGINAL

setting

with fascination, rather than get involved. McCartney was going to have to work hard to win them.

But he remained relaxed and happy, as is his style. He's having a good time and wants the crowd to enjoy themselves too.

Ironically, it took the former Beatles hit "Lady Madonna" to get things going. And with "Live and Let Die," which included Bond-like effects with blue

McCulloch and drummer Joe English.

Their songs have instant impact, are quickly remembered and are delivered with a professionalism and panache, which McCartney particular has developed to a fine art.

Last week, when played in Communist Russia, the audience wild. They have as big appreciation of our music Britain and America.

At least, Russia agreed offi

WORLD

tour

They are basically just the West. It's only politics which make seem grey and drab.

SHOW BUSINESS EXTRA By Garth Pearce ———Venice, Sunday

Taking Venice in a more classic style . . . Paul McCartney and Wings relax in a quiet backwater before their breathtaking concert

EXPRESS PICTURE BY JOHN P

Kisses all the way

By KEN IRWIN

THEY'VE got Europe in a spin . . . and, Man, what a welcome home they got yesterday.

Britain saved her kisses for the Brotherhood of Man pop group as they flew back in triumph from the Eurovision Song Contest in Holland.

The champagne flowed. Offers of work came pouring in.

And the group's manager, Tony Hiller, announced that they had been booked for a special week-long show at the London Palladium.

The group wooed the Euro-judges with their song "Save Your Kisses For Me."

And manager Tony, 49—who also co-wrote the song—was cock-a-hoop yesterday that the group had found fame at last.

He said: "We had been in the shadows for too long—now I'm just knocked out at our win."

There were special private celebrations yesterday, too.

One of the group, 25 - year - old Nicky Stevens, announced her plans to wed in June.

And blonde Sandra Stevens just couldn't hold back her tears of

HOME: THE HEROES OF EUROPE

joy as she was given a real North Country welcome at her Wakefield home.

But the party will soon be over. Sandra will tonight join Nicky and the other members of the group—Martin Lee, 26, and Lee Sheridan, 29—for a cabaret spot in Manchester.

Bill Cotton, head of BBC Light Entertainment, said last night that the BBC will stage next year's contest.

TURKISH . . . blacked out the Greek entry on Saturday in a protest over Cyprus

Man in London yesterday. Picture: VICTOR CRAWSHAW.

EVENING STANDARD. MON

Marvin's golden oldies are back in demand

By James Johnson

BESPECTACLED Hank Marvin—the guitarist who inspired a thousand others—must be alone in being surprised that the Shadows golden hits are about to be relaunched.

From this week EMI Records plan to spend more than £100,000 on promoting an album entitled The Shadows 20 Golden Greats which includes nearly all the group's early instrumental hits.

It comes as the next logical move on the nostalgia bandwagon that has recently even put veteran Bert Weedon at the top of the charts.

"Apparently EMI carried out a survey and found there was a huge demand for the old records," says 35-year-old Hank. "I must say it's all very flattering."

The EMI survey also discovered a number of people who fondly remembered the days when they used to mime along with cricket in front of

That 60's guitar Marvin to Ma me

"At whether or not on records, "It was only by chance we were given Apache that

was our first big hit. That really went on to set the style for the others."

Marvin originally became involved in music when he bought a £2 banjo from his French teacher in Newcastle. there he graduated to and skiffle in a late 50's.

MY TEN YEARS WITHOUT SEX.... by Cliff Richard

'I DON'T BELIEVE IN SLEEPING AROUND AND I'M DAMNED IF I'LL MARRY JUST TO PROVE I'M NOT GAY'

Daily Mirror

54

BRITAIN'S BIGGEST DAILY SALE

6p
Thursday, December 2, 1976

No. 22,658

TV's Bill Grundy in rock outrage

?!★!

THE FILTH AND THE FURY!

THE GROUP IN THE BIG TV RUMPUS
Johnny Rotten, leader of the Sex Pistols, opens a can of beer. Last night their language made TV viewers froth.

When the air turned blue..

A POP group shocked millions of viewers last night with the filthiest language heard on British television.

The Sex Pistols, leaders of the new "punk rock" cult, hurled a string of four-letter obscenities at interviewer Bill Grundy on Thames TV's family teatime programme "Today"

The Thames switchboard was flooded with protests.

Nearly 200 angry viewers telephoned the Mirror. One man was so furious that he kicked in the screen of his £380 colour TV.

Grundy was immediately carpeted by his boss and will apologise in tonight's programme.

By STUART GREIG, MICHAEL McCARTHY and JOHN PEACOCK

Uproar as viewers jam phones

Shocker

A Thames spokesman said: "Because the programme was live, we could not foresee the language which would be used. We apologise to all viewers."

The show, screened at peak children's viewing time, turned into a shocker when Grundy asked about £40,000 that the Sex Pistols received

from their record company.

One member of the group said: "F---ing spent it, didn't we?"

Then when Grundy asked about people who preferred Beethoven, Mozart and Bach, another Sex Pistol remarked: "That's just their tough s---"

Later Grundy told the group: "Say something outrageous."

A punk rocker replied: "You dirty sod. You dirty bastard."

"Go on. Again," said Grundy.

"You dirty f---er."
"What?"

"What a f---ing rotter." As the Thames switchboard became jammed, viewers rang the Mirror to voice their complaints.

Lorry driver James Holmes, 47, was outraged that his eight-year-old son Lee heard the swearing . . . and kicked in the screen of his TV.

"It blew up and I was knocked backwards," he said "But I was so angry and disgusted with this filth that I took a swing with my boot.

"I can swear as well as anyone, but I don't want this sort of muck coming into my home at teatime."

Mr. Holmes, of Beechfield Walk, Waltham Abbey, Essex, added: "I am not a violent person, but I would like to have got hold of Grundy.

"He should be sacked for encouraging this sort of disgusting behaviour."

INTERVIEWER Bill Grundy introduced the Sex Pistols to viewers with the comment: "Words actually fail me about the next guests on tonight's show."

The group sang a number — and the amazing interview got under way.

GRUNDY: I am told you have received £40,000 from a record company. Doesn't that seem to be slightly opposed to an anti-materialistic way of life.

PISTOL: The more the merrier.

GRUNDY: Really.

PISTOL: Yea, yea.

GRUNDY: Tell me more then.

PISTOL: F---ing spent it. didn't we.

GRUNDY: You are serious?

PISTOL: Mmmm.

GRUNDY: Beethoven, Mozart, Bach?

PISTOL: They're wonderful people.

GRUNDY: Are they?

PISTOL: Yes they really turn us on. They do.

GRUNDY: Suppose they turn other people on?

PISTOL, (in a whisper): That's just their tough s---

GRUNDY: It's what?

PISTOL: Nothing—a rude word. Next question.

GRUNDY: No, no. What was the rude word?

PISTOL: S---

GRUNDY: Was it really? Good heavens. What about you girls behind? Are you married or just enjoying yourself?

GIRL: I've always wanted to meet you.

GRUNDY: Did you really? We'll meet afterwards, shall we?

PISTOL: You dirty old man.

GRUNDY: Go on, you've got a long time yet. You've got another five seconds. Say something outrageous.

PISTOL: You dirty bastard. You dirty sod.

GRUNDY: Go on. Again.

PISTOL: You dirty f----er.

GRUNDY: What?

PISTOL: What a f----ing rotter.

GRUNDY: Well, that's it for tonight . . . I'll be seeing you soon. I hope I'm not seeing YOU again. Goodnight.

WHO ARE THESE PUNKS? PAGE

DAILY MIRROR, Monday, December 19, 1977 PAGE 11

THE MOST BANNED BAND: Rotten, Jones, Vicious and Cook

THE TRUTH ABOUT BRITAIN'S MOST NOTORIOUS BAND

Never mind the filth, here's the SEX PISTOLS!

THEY outrage and offend, but they are not going to go away. The Sex Pistols, four once-unemployed youngsters, today head the money-spinning punk revolution. Before their current British tour, writer GLORIA STEWART joined them in Holland to discover how shocking they really are.

STEVE JONES, the only handsome member of the Pistols, resplendent in tight black pink patterned shirt and an immaculate jacket, stands up, thumbs his nose.

Sid Vicious orders the first of a series Across the hotel dining room a large group of people are celebrating a silver wedding.

The Sex Pistols, the most banned band in Britain, were back in action, in Holland.

They had last appeared in Britain fourteen months ago.

When we left for Holland no one expected them to be playing again soon in Britain.

Rank, Mecca and Trust House Forte had banned them. Other places were hard to find.

Vast

After Holland at one day's notice, several bookings appeared in England—all of them in out of the way places. Yet vast crowds turned up.

Britain's radio stations aren't always keen to play the Pistols' records. The band's

leather jacket, talks to their manager Malcolm McLaren.

"I want some sweets!" The chorus continued until Malcolm bought a large tin of fruit drops. Sid, one of the band's two guitarists crammed them into his mouth six at a time.

I boarded their bus in Maastricht, a small town on the border of Holland and Belgium.

Aboard with Malcolm and Sid were Johnny Rotten, the raucous singer, Steve Jones, guitarist and Paul Cook, the drummer.

We all left together for the next gig at the Poziet Club at Tilburg, a tiny town in the middle of Holland.

Beer

ROTTEN: "Where's the beer? He's set off without any beer. Terrible organisation.

T... tall... nurse... the check... toddle

Paul the kid bikes.

Then numbe... sere ches... voice soun... bag. 'Tho...

THE SEX PISTOLS ON TOUR

OUR SONGS ARE ANTI-GOD, ANTI-QUEEN

The punk era might not be described as the most tasteful but it certainly gave the British music industry a much-needed shake-up. Punk offered a welcome change from pre-fabricated pop and outraged the music industry, which was long practised in deciding what music young people wanted to hear.

The music Press turned their backs on the industry and happily denounced some of the record companies' more conventional offerings. Endless small record companies, clubs and fanzines sprang up to support the new music and image, which was practically ignored by the established companies until it dawned on them that they could be missing out financially. They made belated attempts to sign punk groups and predictably eventually succeeded in making money out of them.

I'M A REVOLUTIONARY!

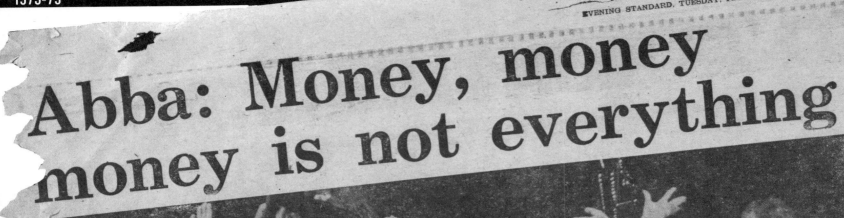

EVENING STANDARD, TUESDAY, FEBRUARY 15, 1977—3

Abba: Money, money money is not everything

ABBA take a bow—on stage at the Albert Hall last night. From left: Bjorn, Anna, Frida and Benny.

A RECORDING machine code-named ABBA bewitched the pop world last year.

One in 20 Britons bought an ABBA record in 1976, making the Swedish group the most popular since the Beatles.

They were out of the top 30 for only 12 weeks and had three number one singles.

The group also headed the LP charts, with "ABBA's Greatest Hits," the most popular album of the year.

And a new LP, "ABBA Arrival," which was released eight weeks ago, now stands at number one, selling 10,000 a day.

The result of their incredible dominance — revealed today in the 1976 chart return figures—is summed up in their latest single which made number two.

Blend

Its apt title: "Money, Money, Money."

Yet the ABBA magic is really a down-to-earth and unique blend of pop talent and astute business manipulation.

Guitarist Bjorn Ulvaeus, keyboard player Benny Andersson, and manager Stig Anderson write all the songs from a five-storey headquarters in Stockholm.

And with girl singers blonde Anna Faltskog, who is married to Bjorn, and Frida Lyngstad, who lives with Benny, they make their own films which are shown on television throughout the world.

A remarkable deal, negotiated by Stig Anderson, gives them a different record company in each of 34 countries.

This ensures intense competition to sell discs and keep the highly lucrative ABBA contract.

Yet the group has not performed live for two years and has shunned exhausting touring to spend only four weeks out of Sweden in 1976 —all for television shows.

Contract

A spokesman for CBS, which has the record contract for Britain, said: "It is like dealing with a highly efficient business machine.

"There can be no room for mistakes with ABBA. They direct weeks and sometimes months ahead on exactly what they want to do."

And 45-year-old Stig Anderson told me last night from Stockholm: "We are delighted with the British chart record.

"It has been so difficult to break the market because of the number of excellent British bands which normally rule the world."

ABBA'S introduction to Britain came in April 1974 when they won the Eurovision Song Contest with "Waterloo."

But with typical planning skill the group used the contest as a launching pad for world sales.

More than 100,000 copies of the record were exported to every European country before the contest.

The group were convinced that even if they did not win "Waterloo," would be the record most people would remember and want to buy.

The song was

in 11 nations — including Britain—within weeks.

Runner-up to ABBA in 1976 was singer Rod Stewart, with five hit singles which stayed in the charts for a total of 37 weeks.

His two LPs, "A Night on the Town" and "Atlantic Crossing" were also the third and 14th most popular.

Top single of the year was Pussycat's "Mississippi," which was in the charts for 15 weeks.

Eurovision Song Contest winners Brotherhood of Man, with "Save Your Kisses For Me" and ABBA's "Fernando" and "Dancing Queen" all tied for second place at 13 weeks.

The year saw the strong re-emergence of 33-year-old former Beatle Paul McCartney with his group Wings.

They came seventh in the most popular singles charts and their LP, "Wings at the Speed of Sound" was second to ABBA.

The returns reveal that the record and popular music industry is one of the most profitable in Britain.

More than 170 million records were pressed in 1976 with sales of over £130 million. Millions were exported.

Yet there is failure too. More than 4,000 singles were released during the year. Only 21 made it to the top.

TOP SINGLES

HERE are the Top Ten stars of 1976 singles. Details supplied by courtesy of New Musical Express:—

1 ABBA

2 Rod Stewart

The Teds jive again for Buddy

8—EVENING STANDARD, THURSDAY, SEPTEMBER 15, 1977

JOE MAULDIN—bass.

JERRY ALLISON—drums.

—guitar.

ALL ROCKERS together—left to right, Ron Wood and Mick Jagger of the Stones, Tony Barrett of the Eddie Cochran Fan Club, and Paul McCartney, who arranged the concert.
Pictures: Michael Fresco

HOLLY—died in 1959.

1957: Allison, Sonny Curtis (guitar) and Joe Mauldin (bass).

JUST LIKE 1958—girls jive to the Crickets sound.

Standard Reporter

BUDDY HOLLY may be dead —but his memory lives on.

Last night many of Britain's top rock stars joined rock 'n' rollers of all ages at a concert at the 'Kilburn State Theatre devoted to the music of the bespectacled singer who died in a 'plane crash in 1959.

Old Teddy Boys dug out their drapes and their boot-lace ties; girls tied their hair into pony-tails; rockers old and young donned their leather jackets and drainpipes and jived in the aisles to the music of the Crickets, Holly's backing group.

It was a night of nostalgia as famous songs from the formative days of rock rang round the theatre—songs like Oh Boy and Peggy Sue.

The line-up was the same as the one on Holly's first No. 1 record, That'll Be the Day, in

Last night's audience included Rolling Stones Mick Jagger and Ronnie Wood, guitarist Eric Clapton, Denny Laine of Wings, and former 10 cc members Kevin Godley and Lol Creme.

It wasn't just the Teds who responded with the 'fifties-style jiving in the aisles. Eric Clapton was seen happily rocking in his seat.

The concert was part of Buddy Holly Week, thought up by Paul McCartney when he took over the publishing rights for Holly's songs two years ago.

James Johnson—Page 21.

LONDONER'S DIARY

Paul McCartney buys up Holly song catalogue

I HEAR that Paul McCartney, one half of that once prolific Beatle song writing duo, has bought off a considerable coup in musical publishing by buying the rights of some of the biggest hits of the late and lamented Buddy Holly.

The works of the bespectacled Holly, both as composer and singer, have lived on long after his untimely death in an aeroplane crash in 1959.

Daily Mirror, Thursday, April 21, 1977 PAGE 15

A FAMILY TOUR of The Family

the show business story of the decade

by CHRIS HUTCHINS

THE MAN ON THE INSIDE

THE ROYAL PARDON

SHOW NIGHT: Tom shakes hands with the Queen at the London Palladium

TOM JONES and Prince Philip share one characteristic: they don't mince words. So when Tom heard that the Prince had made some insulting remarks about his Royal Variety Show performance, the scene was set for a right royal bust-up.

After the show, in 1969, Tom had been presented backstage to the Queen and Prince Philip. The Prince asked him: "What do you gargle with — pebbles?" Tom took it in the light-hearted spirit in which he thought it was intended.

But next day, at a lunch held by the Small Businesses Association, the Prince really put the boot in.

Not realising he was being reported, he said: "Last night we went to the Variety performance.

"The last man to come on was Tom Jones. Now there's a young man of about twenty-five or something, probably worth about £3 million.

"It's very difficult at all to see how it is possible to become immensely valuable by singing what I think are most hideous songs."

The Prince joined in the laughter which followed adding: "I would not say this about the Beatles."

Prince Philip tried to stop reporters quoting his off-the-record remarks, but a Sunday newspaper rang me

with them and asked for Tom's comments. Tom's "comments" were predictably explosive.

"I was giving my services to charity. What did he think it was—a bloody royal audition?"

If he'd told me his true opinion after the show at least we could have had it out man to man."

I cleaned up Tom's outburst and passed his comment on to the newspaper concerned, which—to the

great embarrassment of Buckingham Palace — ran the story of the verbal punch-up.

Four days later Tom received an apologetic if somewhat pompous letter from an aide at the Palace.

A year after that Tom met the Queen and Prince Philip again — when he was invited to a cocktail party at the Palace before another big charity performance.

Spotting the singer across

the reception room, Philip walked across.

"He said he was trying to encourage small businessmen and needed some comparison of earnings to make his point," Tom told me later.

"So you've kissed and made up then?" I remarked.

Tom smiled: "I could have forgiven the Prince anything when I noticed his shirt collar was starting to fray."

How Prince Philip said sorry about the row he had with Tom Jones

Philip . . . the jester

WHAT TOM JONES SAID

'I could have forgiven the Prince anything when I noticed his shirt collar was frayed'

A STAR LOST FOR WORDS

THE two years of schooling which Tom Jones missed when he was confined to bed with tuberculosis took their toll. He never mastered the simple art of handwriting.

The two words of his own name are about the only ones he can manage in other than block capitals.

And he can spell only the simplest words.

On rare occasions when it was essential that a written message went before Tom's block capitals, I usually wrote it, taking care to form the letters as he did to his signature.

When he was asked to write something in public we had a system.

With almost any word of more than four letters he would turn to me and say:

"How is that again?"

If we were in America it would be . . . "How do they spell that here, Chris . . ." and would then dictate the spelling.

Tom is a fighter, with great determination. The way he dealt with the writing problem is an example of his will to overcome personal setbacks.

I also admired his efforts to improve his learning by reading every history book he came across.

THEIR MASTER'S VOICE: SEE CENTRE PAGES

DAILY Mirror

BRITAIN'S BIGGEST DAILY SALE — 7p — Wednesday, August 17, 1977

ELVIS PRESLEY IS DEAD

THE IDOL: Pop king Elvis Presley as his millions of fans throughout the world knew him.

ELVIS PRESLEY, the king of Rock 'n' Roll, is dead.

The 42-year-old super-star who had millions of adoring fans throughout the world, was alone when the end came.

He collapsed yesterday afternoon in the sprawling mansion in Memphis, Tennessee, that he had turned into a fortress against the world.

Elvis was found by his road manager. He gave him the kiss of life, but could not revive him. Elvis was then rushed to hospi-

From ANTHONY DELANO in New York

tal, with his bodyguards following the ambulance

There, they broke down in tears as doctors pronounced him dead.

Later, a hospital spokesman said the rock king may have had a heart attack.

But it was an open secret that Elvis — a recluse hiding inside his palatial home for months — was using drugs, including heroin.

The star who never smoked or drank had been ill for months.

But for years before that, liver

trouble and increasing weight problems had led to fewer and fewer stage appearances.

In fact, the once slim and handsome singer who made untold millions with over 20 years of record hits like Hound Dog, Heartbreak Hotel and Blue Suede Shoes had become immensely fat.

He also had to live with the memories of a broken marriage.

While doing his army service in West Germany, he met and fell in love with the colonel's beautiful daughter, raven-haired Priscilla Beaulieu.

They married in 1967 and had a daughter, Lisa, whom he idolised. But then, in 1973, Priscilla left him.

After that, Elvis's problems started growing.

By 1975, it became clear that something was badly wrong.

He had to cancel a Las Vegas appearance for a stay in hospital, and for the first time fans noticed how flabby he had become.

Elvis insisted it just looked that way because he was wearing a bullet-proof vest. It emerged that he had a morbid fear of being shot while performing.

Health

After that, however, his deteriorating health made him stay in seclusion for longer and longer periods, broken by several stays in hospital.

Last night, after hearing the news of his death, Priscilla immediately left for Memphis. She said: "I am distraught."

Despite Elvis's failing health, his thousands of British fans continued to plead with him to give concerts here.

He never came . . . and now he never will.

THE ROCK WORLD MOURNS..

By JACK LEWIS

THE pop world was in mourning for the king of rock last night.

Disc jockeys on Radio Luxembourg and Capital Radio played Elvis records all night as a mark of respect.

Radio Luxembourg also cancelled all its advertisements for the night.

The Daily Mirror switchboard was swamped with calls from Elvis fans — many of them sobbing girls.

Todd Slaughter, secretary of the 12,000-strong Elvis fan club in Britain, said: "I am heartbroken. He was a part of our lives.

"Many of us dedicated our lives to following

him, and collecting Elvis records, books and posters.

"The roots of pop music have been taken away. He was the man who started it all."

Members of the British fan club are already planning to fly to America for the funeral.

Elvis's greatest fan in Britain — warehouseman Ron Elvis Presley—col-lapsed when he heard the news.

Ron, 33, of Winsford, Cheshire, changed his name last year. His home is a shrine to Elvis.

He said: "He was like a god to me."

Sales of Presley records are believed to have topped 500 million, making him the biggest-selling artist of all time.

Anniversary of death

ELVIS PRESLEY died two days after the anniversary of his mother's death on August 14, 1958. She died at the same age as he did—forty-two.

HUSBAND: Elvis with wife Priscilla, during their six-year marriage.

THE KING IS DEAD —See Centre Pages

THE ASTONISHING TRUTH ABOUT SEX MANIAC ELVIS

THE SUN, Monday, November 20, 1978   17

He wept down the telephone to me...he was very ill

DAILY STAR, Thursday, June 12, 1980

THE KING IS DEAD...

Panic hits Presley's pop empire

Presley was found dead in the bathroom of his home, Gracelands, on 16 August 1977. The world mourned the first real star of rock-'n'-roll. To many Presley's life had been under threat from possible assassination or kidnapping from the time he had left the US Army in 1960. Although he made some great singles and albums, his personal life wasn't so successful. He became progressively reclusive and by the end of the 1960s he was heavily dependent on drugs. During his last years he had returned to performing live, obviously very overweight and at times given to incoherence.

Not unexpectedly, in view of his influence and wealth, there were squabbles over his estate. The singer's manager, Colonel Tom Parker, and members of his family became involved in protracted law-suits. Presley's physician was taken to court on a charge of indiscriminately prescribing huge doses of pills but eventually he was acquitted. These and other stories of Presley's strange behaviour rather tarnished the artist's early wholesome image but most still remember him as the king of rock-'n'-roll and thousands go to visit his Gracelands home, which Priscilla Presley opened to the public in 1982.

DAILY STAR, Tuesday, June 10, 1980   12

DRUGS, GUNS AND THE MEMPHIS 'MAFIA'

Adapted by Jean Ritchie from the book Elvis: The Final Years to be published in Britain in August by W. H. Allen.

THE LAST ten years of Elvis Presley's life were increasingly dominated by drugs. He lived on a deadly diet of pills and junk food which put him in hospital time and again.

His other great addiction was guns — he never moved anywhere without them. There were happy times, too. Times when he was surrounded by his friends and hangers-on who made up the famous Memphis "mafia."

But towards the end a lot of them had drifted away, leaving him increasingly on his own. He was alone when he died.

Pills and junk food ... the deadly diet

OVER a period of eight years, Elvis Presley dosed his body with an incredible amount of drugs and junk food. And he ended up in hospital several times during those nightmare years.

He popped his first pill in Weisbaden, West Germany, as a corporal in the tank corps.

Like so many other American soldiers he took a stimulant to keep him awake at night while on guard.

The only surprising thing then was that

DAILY STAR, Monday, June 9, 1980   15

ELVIS... THE UNTOLD STORY

The last terrible years ... an orgy of drugs and food

THEY were the final terrible years. The year

Rod Stewart just used me, says bitter Britt

From RODERICK GILCHRIST in New York

ACTRESS Britt Ekland sobbed as she spoke bitterly last night about the break-up of her three-year romance with singer Rod Stewart. ' I feel I have been used,' she said.

'I don't think there is any chance of us getting back together again. It is over. We are finished. I have reconciled myself to that fact now.'

As she spoke at the Hollywood mansion she shared with Stewart for two years, the rock s... staying at a hacienda just a few minutes' walk ... in his life, beautiful Californian heiress Liz

... nsidering giving 34-year-old Britt the £500,000 ...reasures.

But Britt laughed the suggestion aside : 'Does that sound like Rod ?' she asked. 'Ask yourself what he did when he split with his previous girl friend, Dee Harrington.

'Did he give her the house and everything in it ? No he didn't. What he did do was go around changing the locks so she couldn't get in.

'He is not a generous man. My God, it even hurts him when he has to go to the bathroom.'

But urder Californian law Britt could sue Stewart for half his estate.

Stewart, thought to be worth at least £3 million, lived with Britt for three years. Their romance ended

Britt—ever a loser in love
See Femail Page 10

the day she left America to visit her parents in Europe.

While she was in Stockholm, Stewart was taking Miss Treadwell to fashionable discotheques and restaurants.

Britt did not know about their affair until a friend telephoned her when she returned to America a month ago.

Last night Britt, who has a 12-year-old daughter, Victoria, from her marriage to Peter Sellers and a son Nicholai, three, by record producer Lou Adler, said :

6 Before I began living with Rod he was worth about one mention in the gossip columns. He is now headline news around the world.

He has used my name and position to get publicity and I am very bitter about this.

Before me, most of his girl-friends were dumb blondes. But I am Britt Ekland. I was Britt Ekland before I

Turn to Page 2, Col. 1

DAILY MIRROR, Friday, August 26, 1977   PAGE 3

Footloose! It's Rod and Liz

THIS is the picture that heralded the break-up of rock star Rod Stewart's romance with Britt Ekland.

The blonde beauty he is dancing with in a New York disco is the new love in his life, 26-year-old Californian heiress Liz

Treadwell. Clubgoers thought she WAS Britt, but the jilted actress—then unaware of her rival—was away in Scandinavia.

Liz and Rod—whose new album may be titled "Footloose and Fancyfree"—danced the night away.

The rest is pop history.

JILTED! IT'S BRITT THE £6m LOVER

THE final break between Britt Ekland and Rod Stewart took place today in a Los Angeles courtroom.

Lawyers for the Swedish beauty and British pop star agreed on a temporary cash arrangement.

It will last until 34-year-old Britt's suit for £6 million worth of Rod's money and assets is heard, on September 12.

The singer will have to pay for the upkeep of the $2500,000 Beverly Hills mansion the couple shared for two-and-a-half years.

Rod, 33, must also hand over £2,500 to his ex-love before 5 p.m. on Monday.

An order was made restraining the pop star from transferring any of his money out of the country, or interfering with Britt's life.

During the time the couple lived together, Britt claims she helped Rod to earn almost £6 million, not counting a multi-million recording contract in the offing.

It is also claimed that it was agreed to play down her film career in order to help the rock star.

SUING: Actress Britt Ekland.

Meanwhile in Memphis

WEDNESDAY, MAY 25, 1977

Jam today .. the mods are booming again

FORGET teds and punks ... the mods are back.

The mod revival is being led by a London band called The Jam and followed by hundreds of fans who admire their clothes, haircuts and style.

"I know that the punk scene is really just a kind of follow-on from the mods and the skinheads — but I just don't like their clothes at all," says Paul Weller, The Jam's 19-year-old lead guitarist.

"I can't stand all those bondage things they wear. So now we get our clothes made

up in Carnaby Street and we wear all the mod things like dog-tooth check jackets and straight trousers.

"I even built myself a proper mod scooter with all the chrome and spot-lights.

"I'm doing it not because I want to start a huge mod revival or anything. It's just a cult that I've read and heard a lot about and it really interests me."

Nevertheless, if the band's superb new album, In The City, achieves the success it deserves I don't think I want to be a rocker this Summer.

WEEKEND STANDARD

Evening Standard

47,471

London: Friday September 16 1977   7RR   8p

CLOSING PRICES

GLORIA JONES

Mini driven by girlfriend hits tree

CRASH KILLS MARC BOLAN

MARC BOLAN—he took the full force of the crash sitting in the passenger seat.

Standard Reporter

ROCK star Marc Bolan was killed today when a purple Mini driven by his girlfriend left the road and hurtled into a tree on Barnes Common.

Twenty-nine-year-old Bolan, of T Rex fame, was sitting in the front passenger seat.

The car was reported to have been travelling between 40 and 50 mph, and the impact flattened the engine compartment snapping off the gear lever and forcing the steering wheel up to the roof. Bolan took the full force.

His girl friend, American singer Gloria Jones, 30, and mother of his two-year-old son Rolan, was taken to Queen Mary's Hospital, Roehampton, with a broken jaw and face injuries.

A Barnes police spokesman said: "As far as we know neither of the occupants of the car was wearing a seat belt."

Miss Jones was said by a hospital spokesman to be fairly comfortable. "She has her jaw wired up and she is on the mend."

Her manager Tony Howard said: "She does not know yet about Marc's death. She is in deep, deep shock. The doctors advise against telling her.

"Gloria had just got back from Los Angeles, where she had been for six weeks. She brought her brother Richard on his first visit to England. He was in a car behind the Mini. He came round the bend and saw the crash. He pulled them out of the car. He was first on the scene."

The party had been dining at Morton's in Barkeley Square. Tony Howard — also Bolan's manager—joined them with his wife for coffee. He left at 3.15 a.m. and Bolan left shortly after.

Marc and Gloria were driving back to their home in East Sheen.

Distraught Mr Howard said: "The party had not been drinking. Marc had given up drink as part of a slimming exercise. He had recently lost two stone.

Mr Howard went on: "Marc was doing very well with his television shows. We were going to do another series and were discussing a play with Granada Television. Then we had plans for a German tour, more recording and then a trip to the United States."

The remaining programmes in Bolan's series Marc will still go ahead next Wednesday and the week after. "That is what Marc would have said Mr Howard."

Mr Franco Ingrad, night manager of Morton's, said Bolan and two friends drank two bottles of wine and four drinks between them. Mr Ingrad added: "They had one bottle of white wine and one of red with their dinner and just four drinks—a scotch, a martini and two brandies between them.

"Marc was well known in the restaurant and always looked very smart. He usually wore tight silver trousers, a bright blue shirt and high boots."

Mr Harry Robinson, who lives near the crash scene, said: "This is a terrible road and it is the third accident involving the same tree within a year."

Police examining the crashed Mini found it littered with personal effects—a pair of girl's red leather shoes, a red and white striped shirt and a copy of the New Musical Express, opened at a full-page record review head-line: "Hope I grow old gracefully before I die."

Police said they had taken blood samples from Bolan and Miss Jones and were also Cont. Back Page, Col. 2

News on camera: Page 3

THE WRECK of the purple Mini in which Marc Bolan died.

Evening Standard: Ed Buziak

Maria Callas found dead in flat

From Sam White

MARIA CALLAS died at her Paris flat this afternoon. Police were called to the flat in the fashionable avenue Georges Mandel after her maid found her apparently unconscious.

The first theory regarding cause of death was that she died of a heart attack. Meanwhile no official statement as to the cause of death has been issued.

Daily Mail, Monday, January 9, 1978

From RODERICK GILCHRIST in Memphis

The faithful followers of King Elvis make sure the show goes on

Fan puts a rose on Elvis's grave.

THEY came from all over America bearing wreaths of red roses shaped like guitars, hound dogs and huge musical notes.

There were cars jammed bumper-to-bumper on Presley Boulevard with signs in the back windows saying: 'Mile high on Elvis.'

One woman from Kalamazoo brought a giant bedspread that had 134 squares with the title of one of her idol's songs in each square.

Elvis Presley, the king of rock and roll is dead but yesterday, on what would have been his 43rd birthday, he was far from forgotten.

Twenty-five thousand fans made the pilgrimage to Memphis to lay flowers at Presley's grave in the 13-acre grounds of Gracelands, his mansion.

As they filed silently past the grave — with the big white statue of Jesus, his outstretched arms pointing in the direction of the swimming pool, over-

shadowing everything — some were crying just like they were here on the day Elvis died five months ago.

All over Memphis there were shops selling mementoes of the city's most famous son. For £3.50 you could buy a ceramic decanter which chimed 'Love Me Tender' one of Elvis's biggest hits, and could be filled with cologne when the head was screwed off.

At cinemas throughout this rock and roll city, there were

showings of all his movies, sales of crocheted sweaters with 'Elvis Elvis Elvis' on the back, stuffed hound dogs and dollar bills with his picture in the centre.

Over at the Pinkins Fairground one of the biggest crowds of pilgrims gathered to look at Elvis's 1956 custom-built Cadillac, the first car he ever bought.

Presley's white-haired father, Vernon, occasionally appeared at the front door of his cottage on the

estate to accept gifts from fans.

The parade of adoring women with cameras and damp white handkerchiefs in their hands were allowed to stand by the grave and take pictures and tell one another about the last time they had seen Presley in Las Vegas or Des Moines or wherever it was. Naturally, the mood was sombre.

Vernon Presley said he wanted everyone to know how happy he was that they

had come and he hoped no one thought the sale of mementoes on Elvis Presley Boulevard was an exploitation of his son's name.

He said: 'I have always maintained that I would keep Gracelands as it was when Elvis passed away and as long my health holds up that is still my intention.'

The flower shop opposite Gracelands, which reputedly has turned over nearly £500,000 in business since Presley died, was glad to hear that.

DAILY MIRROR, Wednesday, August 16, 1978   PAGE 9

DAY THREE of the series they're all talking about

GREASE VERDICT ON TRAVOLTA
by Hollywood's star finder

ALAN CARR
Enjoying success

HE BUMPS, HE GRINDS, HE'S ABSOLUTELY FREE!

by JILL EVANS

ROBERT STIGWOOD, impresario, buys another yacht and adds to his properties in tax-free Bermuda and California. His Hollywood buddy Alan Carr, personal manager to a galaxy of stars holds court at his Beverly Hills mansion.

They are enjoying the runaway success of "Grease" their joint production which has become one of the top-ten box-office blockbusters in cinema history.

The two razzle-dazzle showmen who are putting new life into the Hollywood film sets, really picked a winner with a show which started as a glorified musical evening in a tiny Chicago theatre.

And they pulled a master stroke by putting John Travolta in the starring role, even before his rise to super-stardom in "Saturday Night Fever."

Deal

The story of "Grease" goes back to 1971 when two writers, Jim Jacobs tried

stars including Tony Curtis, Peter Sellers and Ann-Margret, took the idea for a film to Stigwood.

Between them, they devised something which is making millions — and starting a cult in Fifties' fashions.

Stigwood, 44, is best known in Britain for launching the Bee Gees and staging the long-running West End shows "Hair" and "Jesus

television series "Welcome Back, Kotter," America's answer to "The Fenn Street Gang."

"This guy," said Carr, "is beyond any male stereotype. He bumps, he grinds. He's absolutely free on the screen."

Carr selected Olivia Newton-John to co-star as Sandy after meeting her at a party.

He said: "At first she was her usual self, almost a waxen

telling a joke, screwing up that perfect face into cute and hilarious contortions."

She agreed to do a screen test and that was it.

And Carr altered the story line to make Sandy from Australia to fit in with Newton-John's accent.

Stigwood and Carr have become a couple of Hollywood's characters.

They are competing with each other for the title of "larger than life producer," calling Hollywood back to its traditional character, a superficial, tinsel town.

2—EVENING STANDARD, THURSDAY, MARCH 23, 1978

FILMS: ALEXANDER WALKER hails an exciting new yo[...]

Yes John, yes John, YES!

DON'T measure the size of a star by the dimensions of his Hollywood showcase. SATURDAY NIGHT FEVER (Cert. X: 120 mins.: Empire) amply confirms the truth of this.

It's a small movie, really. But the one talent it contains fills it to bursting point. It makes it seem in every way bigger, brighter and more zestful than it is. That talent is the electric John Travolta.

Just watch him in the early scenes, garbing himself from the skin out in fancy gear for a boogie session at the Brooklyn discotheque. Body cologne, jet-black briefs, glittering neck-chains and amulets, platform shoes, a suit like stretch elastic—finally a dry-blower to tease his hair into a pampered version of [...]

AUSTRALIAN FOOTBALL Pools check

TAIN'S GGEST HING LE

Evening News

LONDON: SATURDAY, JULY 15, 1978 10p

Road chaos as the fans flock to see Dylan

The fans yesterday—new generation, same hopes

250,000 GO ROCK CRAZY

MORE than 250,000 people flocked in today to pay homage to rock star Bob Dylan.

Six-mile traffic jams built up as thousands more headed for Dylan's concert at Blackbushe airfield, Hants.

Daily Mail, Friday, June 16, 1978

PAGE 3

Dylan last night—the greatest concert I have ever seen

By RAY CONNOLLY

author of the rock movies 'Stardust' and 'That'll Be The Day'

THEY gave Bob Dylan an ovation simply for existing last night.

At first the sound of the ecstatic thousands at Earl's Court was an affirmation of loyalty, a thank-you to him just for surviving.

But by the end of a two-hour show the enthusiasm had generated into wild appreciation beyond anyone's expectations.

Because last night Bob Dylan gave, I think, quite the most exciting, vibrant concert I have ever seen. It was a celebration of a form of music—rock music — which Dylan took 12 years ago and made literate.

Daily Mail, Tuesday, September 19, 1978

Wedding plans, then a huge overdose

Moon the Loon's last party—by Anette

Anette, the girl Moon was to marry, with Richard Dorse, right, his personal assistant.

By THOMSON PRENTICE

THE last bizarre performance of rock star Keith Moon was to swallow more than 30 sleeping tablets after cooking himself a steak breakfast.

But why he did it will always be a mystery.

The 33-year-old 'wild man' of rock was found dead in bed a few hours later by his Swedish fiancee, Anette Walter-Lax.

Anette, Moon's doctor, Geoffrey Dymond, and his personal assistant - cum - bodyguard all told the inquest at Westminster yesterday that he had no worries, and no death wish.

He had proposed to Anette

KEITH MOON
'No worries'

only the day before he died. That night they had danced together at a lavish show-business party and Moon was planning enthusiastically for his role in a new Monty Python film.

Dr Dymond did add, however, that Moon thought the tablets were 'fairly harmless.'

In a voice little more than a whisper 23-year-old Anette told of their last night out together—at a party given by Paul McCartney.

'Keith was not drunk party. As far as had only a few been on

The to a the p died height through decided was tire

Back Place, M light supp bed. 'I k some sleep said.

'He woke morning, got steak. It wa

for him. He usually wok hungry.'

After eat to h

Daily Express, Friday, September 8, 1978

hell-raiser Keith Moon the night before tragedy

PARTY'S OVER

Girlfriend finds pop idol dead

his Mayfair flat

Moon's last night out... with party hosts Paul and Linda McCartn

got to know so well... with girlfriend Annette and bearded David Frost at McCartn

---

SUNDAY MIRROR, September 10, 1978 — PAGE 3

Behind the mask.. Moon the sad clown

IT'S Moon the Loon on the loose. The Who's tragic drummer is pictured in Hollywood indulging his twisted sense of fun. His favourite prank was to don a monster mask and cruise along

Keith Moon

Sunset Strip in his vintage Rolls scaring people. Keith could always raise a laugh. Now friends say that behind his mask the clown had tears in his eyes.

Picture:
MICHAEL BRENNAN

I STILL LOVED HIM—KIM

By TONY FROST

KEITH Moon's ex-wife Kim revealed yesterday that she had never stopped loving the bizarre star.

Her voice

death at the age of 32. she said: 'I really thought he was indestructible but in the end all those

hours after whooping it up at a party in a London restaurant.

Among the guests at the party were Paul McCartney, David Frost and girlfri

DAILY Mirror

Saturday, February 3, 1979   8p

Britain's best guide starts on Page 9 **tv**

SID VICIOUS DIES IN DRUGS DRAMA

Mum finds him in his girl's arms

FREEDOM: Vicious with his mother after his release on bail — just one day before he died.

SID VICIOUS, the tormented star of punk rock, died of an overdose of heroin yesterday.

He was found naked in the arms of his latest girl friend in her New York flat less than twenty-four hours after he was released from jail on bail.

His mother, Mrs. Ann Beverly, took the couple a cup of tea in bed and frantically tried to wake Vicious.

The girlfriend, Michele Robison, was completely unaware that he had died while they slept.

Police said last night that he had taken the heroin overdose by accident.

Vicious, 21, guitarist with the now defunct Sex Pistols, had been allowed £30,000 bail on a charge of murdering his former girlfriend, "Nauseating" Nancy Spungen, last October. His earlier bail had been revoked when he was accused of assault

By CHRIS BUCKLAND and STUART GREIG

during a night club brawl.

After walking from the courtroom on Thursday, Vicious and Michele went off to celebrate his freedom at a party in her seedy flat in fashionable Greenwich Village.

Later he injected himself with heroin and then had a 45-minute seizure.

But friends managed

● **Continued on Page Three**

Bass player of sorts, Vicious replaced Glen Matlock in the Sex Pistols when the latter was sacked on 5 March 1977. Vicious, formerly with Siouxsie and the Banshees, joined three months after the Pistols had been abusive on the live Bill Grundy *Today* programme on British television. It was Vicious who wrote the song *Belsen was a Gas* that eventually found its way into the Pistols' repertoire.

Vicious attempted a solo career after Rotten disbanded the Pistols on 14 January 1978. However, his life style was to lead to an early death. On one occasion he tried to commit suicide by jumping from an hotel window but was prevented by his fiancée, Nancy Spungen. He was arrested soon after on charges of murdering her but before he could be tried he took his life through a heroin overdose.

POLICE FILE

For a band largely ignored by the music press for being "punk bandwagon jumpers" with two singles about a whore and suicide banned by the Beeb, THE POLICE are doing very nicely, thank you. It's been a long, hard slog but Summers, Sting and Copeland have finally joined that small elite capable of producing singles which chart in the Top Five one week after release. JAMES PARADE plots POLICE progress in our special feature

ANDY SUMMERS

STEWART COPELAND

STING

N O BAND in history has ever been unluckier mom... Police then...

Pic by Fin Costello

DAILY MIRROR, Saturday, May 26, 1979   PAGE 9

How Elton John rocked his way through the Iron Curtain

RUSSIA is in the throes of a new revolution . . . thanks to rock superstar Elton John. Of course the fans have heard the music before.

Expensive cassettes recorded from black market albums or from crackling, distorted broadcasts by the BBC World Service circulate among young people.

But until now they haven't had the chance of seeing the phenomenon of a live rock concert. Elton John came and conquered.

The pop group Boney M came and performed. The Russian Press and TV did not mention his arrival. There were no posters about the eight concerts in Moscow and Leningrad. When Radio Leningrad announced the concerts, hundreds of fans went to the ticket office only to find that all the best seats had already gone to the Communist party elite.

Symbolically, one of the highlights of Elton's performance is the old Motown hit: "I Heard It On The Grapevine."

In this country that's just how the youth of Russia will get the word that Rock has broken through the Iron Curtain.

The Soviet youngsters, with no experience of behaving like rock fans, tried to live up to the history of the moment—with some touching results. When drummer

Music Mania in Moscow
Special report by ALASDAIR BUCHAN

Ray Cooper invites them to clap along, they try . . . woefully. When Elton announces his song, there is silence followed by loud cheers when they recognise the first few bars.

It's not because they don't understand English. It's because they know his hits as well as his "Cosmonaute" ("Rocket Man") "Temporary Love" ("Part Time Love"), "Pigeon on the Horizon Road Out of Yellow Brick" ("Skyline Pigeon") and "Goodbye ("Goodbye Yellow Brick Road").

If they get past the cordon of attendants and plainclothes police in front of the stage, they expect him to kneel down and sign autographs.

And because it's all new to him, too, he does.

In return, the fans press bunches of flowers into his hands and he places the blooms on top of the Steinway piano.

The novelty and relaxation of it all has affected Elton. Each night he stays up late, joking and joining in a jam session with the restaurant band, playing backgammon in the bar or doing brilliant Edna Everage monologues.

Best

"I'm over the moon now but I was terrified before the first night," he says. "I felt nobody really knew me here and that it could all go terribly wrong.

"I'm always making sweeping statements, but I can say it has been one of the best experiences of my life.

"Doing the tour with Ray and without a band was an attempt to get back to doing what I want to do.

"And at last I'm happy. Russia has proved I was right."

That confident cheerfulness is best demonstrated by the fact ... can even joke ... time

ROCKING IT TO 'EM: Elton delivers his musical message.

be on sale in Russia at normal prices. But that won't help the ones who have paid over the odds for them already.

Embassy magazines in Russian with articles about him, they wish him luck.

And one superfan explained how much of a sacrifice he made to hear

Trucks

Although the Russians have tolerated ... sented excesses ...

surround the back door as Elton left.

By the third cordon of police ... by two ... positioned ... trucks kept the ... place.

Elton ... problem ... window ... drove ... flowers ... to ...

Gun girl's family fight to ban this Boomtown Rats disc in America

Keep this killing off the record

FAR LEFT: Brenda Spencer is led away from the court after being remanded in custody. **LEFT:** how the Mirror broke the story of the San Diego attack. **ABOVE:** the cover of the Boomtown Rats' controversial single "I Don't Like Mondays"

MONDAYS these days are just like every other day for Brenda Spencer, the mousy-haired, bespectacled teenager who brought terror to a Californian school in January.

She sits morosely in her cramped cell-like room inside a juvenile jail, sometimes sobbing sadly to herself, rarely saying a word.

Even the child psychiatrists assigned to her case struggle to get through to her. One of them said she seems determined to pull up an emotional drawbridge and cut herself off from other people.

Sixteen-year-old Brenda isn't allowed newspapers or radio, so she knows nothing about a pop song which has set the British charts alight and looks likely to do the same in the States.

The song, "I Don't Like Mondays," by the Boomtown Rats, is all about the dull Monday morning she shot dead her headmaster and school janitor, and wounded eight school children aged between seven and ten, and a policeman.

BURTON WRAGG, 53-year-old dedicated headmaster of San Diego's Cleveland school and likeable janitor Michael Suchar, 56, lay dead as shocked police asked Brenda Spencer the reason for her orgy of violence with a .22 automatic rifle.

The cold reply was: "I don't like Mondays. They give me the blues. This was to liven up a dull day."

Stupefied Americans heard the news and did their best to forget the meaningless carnage.

Until the British Band, Boomtown Rats turned it into the most controversial hit record in years—one that has been inter-

From PAUL CONNEW in SAN DIEGO

TWO PEOPLE were killed yesterday when a schoolgirl sprayed a playground with bullets.

Later the girl, 16-year-old Brenda Spencer, said: "I don't like Mondays. They give me the blues.

"This was to liven up a dull day."

VICTIM: An injured girl after shooting.

preted as an anthem to teenage disillusion, with school and boredom prime targets.

Brenda's family, with the help of prison authorities, are fighting frantically to keep the news of the record from her. This fight will almost certainly be lost if Columbia Records go ahead with plans to release "I Don't Like Mondays" in the States.

"We've made a rule never to mention it during family visits. It wouldn't thrill Brenda. It would only sicken her still more," said the girl's devoted maternal grandmother, Mrs. Trudy Hobel, at her San Diego home.

"That's why we kept the record barred here.

"It's the sickest, most gruesome example of cashing in on people's personal misery that I've heard in a long time. For heaven's sake, the child hasn't even gone for trial yet.

"In America we have a saying 'Anything for a buck.' But I always figured you British—and I've visited England four times—had a lot more good taste and sensitivity than to go in for something like this.

"Even without parents or radio, there is a grapevine in these correction units, especially among new prisoners are brought in.

"Think of the effect on our family if the horror record is released here.

"We were subjected to crank telephone calls after the shootings.

"We would get people saying things like: 'What are you gonna use the suicide plugging.'"

Daddy doesn't understand it. He always said she was good as gold.

Brenda's elder sister, who is working her way through college, has also suffered. She has had to endure a lot of painful remarks. This is why we still revive the shootings. Meanwhile, Columbia still insists that "I Don't Like Mondays" will be released in America in time for the family's protest.

But no final decision has been reached whether the shock record will also become a US single release.

The Spencers—and the family of Headmaster Wragg—have independently taken legal advice to see if the record's release can be blocked. They have been warned that it will probably be a costly and ill-fated attempt.

Mrs. Hobel said: "What Brenda did was a terrible, tragic deed. But she is a sick, emotionally disturbed kid rather than a homicidal monster.

"The real story behind the shooting isn't that of a girl who hated Mondays or school. Brenda, you see, hated every day, not just Mondays. She hated so much of her sad and unhappy life.

"The truth is that she was a young girl caught up in the middle of a bitter family crisis. Her parents were living apart. Her mother was fighting through the courts to get custody of Brenda. She felt the girl badly needed a mother's love and guidance.

"Her father was opposed to the move and prevented Brenda seeing her mother. He lavished her with presents, including the gun she used on that terrible Monday, which was a Christmas gift.

"In the end my granddaughter simply snapped under the strain. She was a desperately unhappy, lonely girl who took that gun while possessed by the uncertainties of her life. I'm convinced it was really a terrible panic cry for help.

"Even now she resists talking about what happened. Her eyes just glaze over and she trembles and says she can't really remember exactly why or how she shot those poor people.

"We just pray that one day she'll recover enough to be rehabilitated into society. But we accept that day is probably a long way ahead.

"Sick, sick, sick," was

DEAD: Michael Suchar.   **DEAD:** Burton Wragg.

AFTER TERROR: A girl is comforted by her mother at the San Diego school.

also the bitter reaction of the families of headmaster WRAGG and the wounded schoolchildren.

Speaking for the first time about her ordeal, widow Mrs Kathe Wragg said bitterly "I was just beginning to come to terms with my husband's senseless death . . . and now this."

"I just feel sick to the pit of my stomach. It is horrible and hurtful to everybody concerned. It's a sick voyeurism and bad taste in society.

"I can never forgive Brenda Spencer for killing my husband. But she

Tell me why. I don't like Mondays. Tell me why, I don't like Mondays. Tell me why, I don't like Mondays. I want to shoot. The whole day down.

is a sick child whose senseless crime doesn't qualify her for exploitation in this way.

"If the record industry has a Soul taste award it should give to these people right now."

"I would just like to appeal to millions of youngsters and their parents to respect my grief in just one special way. By refusing to buy this sick, sick record."

*Extracts from "I Don't Like Mondays"
© Copyright Sewerfire-Zomba*

"I would like to sock these Boomtown Rats on the jaw. The last thing Brenda—or anyone else associated with those awful events—needs is this glib, nauseating, commercialisation of a tortured young girl's tragedy. It's obscene.

"If they claim their record is some worthy work of art or social comment I say they're liars. It's just a cheap, nasty gimmick aimed at making a fast buck out of other people's suffering.

Both of Brenda's parents, mother Dorothy and father Wally Spencer, California State highway supervisor, have sworn, on lawyers' advice, not to talk about the shooting before Brenda's trial. But both broke their vow and said they were shocked and sickened after being told of the 'I Don't Like Mondays,' disc.

The silicon chip inside her head. Gets switched to overload And nobody's going to school today. She's going to make them stay at home

And he sees no reason 'Cos there are no reasons What reasons do you need to be told?

'She hated so much of her sad life . . . she simply snapped, it was a terrible panic-cry for help'

Keith Moon's death suggested the Who's touring days were over but at least one member of the group, John Entwhistle, was determined they would hit the road again. The former Small Faces' drummer, Kenney Jones, was admitted to the group's previously unaltered line-up.

However, the group received a set-back when 11 concert-goers were killed at Cincinnati's Riverfront Coliseum on 3 December 1979. The doors had been opened late and, in the ensuing rush for seats, many were crushed and trampled on.

KILLER STAMPEDE!

Drinks, drugs and hysteria.. then eleven Who fans die

From EDWARD VALE in Cincinnati

AN ORGY of drink and drugs was partly blamed yesterday for a horrific stampede which killed eleven youngsters at a pop concert.

After a wait of six hours, thousands of hysterical fans tried to burst through the doors as the top British pop group, The Who, were about to take the stage.

The screaming and shouting youngsters went down like ninepins at one of the entrances to the 18,000-seat riverside Coliseum in Cincinnati, Ohio.

Horrified fans who tried to hold back were forced on.

The eleven victims—four of them girls—were trampled, crushed or suffocated.

Police and officials decided the concert should go ahead to prevent a riot.

Blamed

The group—leader Pete Townshend, Roger Daltrey, John Entwistle and drummer Kenny Jones—did not know of the tragedy until the concert was over.

Last night the blame for the disaster was being handed around.

POLICE blamed drink, drugs and the fact that the fans were kept waiting for the doors to open.

PARENTS blamed the handling of the crowd by the Coliseum staff.

Only twenty-five security men were reported to be in control of 18,000 fans. Because of the staff shortage, only three of the fifty turnstiles were opened.

Whoever was to blame, the cause was undoubtedly the rush by the fans to get the best of the unreserved places—more than half the seats in the hall.

One fan caught up in the stampede, 22-year-old Jeff, of Manchester, said:

"I felt myself going over and I just grabbed at anything to stay on my feet. I was grabbing at hair, at bodies . . . grabbing at anything to save my life.

"I knew some of the people under me were dying but there was absolutely nothing I could do about it.

THE WHO—Top: Daltry, Jones.   **Bottom:** Entwistle, Townshend.

CARNAGE: Bodies litter the entrance to the concert hall as firemen and helpers try to revive the victims.

'I was grabbing at hair, at bodies.. anything to save my life'

rida — 12.30 pm Monday

LLETS
ULDN'T
L HIM

— Cancer did

**BOB MARLEY'S
FINAL
RETURN HOME**
King of Reggae laid to rest in Jamaica

p (18p L.I.)

AND
OF

Another
pictu
exclus

'BOY GEO
IS EVI

could raise
for Ethiopia

SKY and GEOFF BAKER

agers are set to raise a
starving people of Ethiopia
of one record.
y It's Christmas, by superstars
played by Daily Star columnist
Radio One programme earlier
this week.
Withi

**JOHN LENNON
shot dead
in New York
Dec 8 1980**

There have been a number of major pop events during this period that, due to the widening use of satellites, have often been screened world wide. Live Aid was unquestionably the largest gathering and brought together many of the biggest names in the music industry. Despite a few egotistical tantrums, it was an outstanding success story. It was the rock musician Bob Geldof who brought the problem of famine relief before the world and whose brainchild it was. South America played host to Queen and other western rock groups at a spectacular concert in Rio de Janeiro. Another landmark in pop's history was Wham!'s visit to China in 1985.

This anti-Establishment stance of the late 1970s quickly faded once the 1980s dawned. Billy Bragg, the Redskins and Paul Weller were among those who tried to mix music and politics but a group's image became the most important ingredient for success. Many groups dressed very stylishly, even Weller come to that. The music of the new pop heroes, which included George Michael, Dire Straits, Tears for Fears, Paul Young, Sade, Sting and King, appealed to the 25 to 45 age group as well as to the teenage market.

The only controversial affair was the removal from the daytime radio playlist of Frankie Goes to Hollywood's *Relax*. The ensuing publicity helped only to vastly increase its sales. Frankie Goes to Hollywood's other single *Two Tribes* had enormous sales and, like Paul Hardcastle's *19* was accompanied by a disturbing video.

The video became an expensive but compulsory way of selling artists. It helped to establish Adam Ant, gain Talking Heads a wider audience, aid a come-back for Kate Bush and promote teen pop's latest group A-Ha. Certainly, it was the video that saved groups endless time in recording for television shows but, at the same time, it removed the 'live' element.

The Band Aid charity single *Do they know it's Christmas?* sold over three million copies at the end of 1984 and beginning of 1985 and overtook the previous best-selling British single *Mull of Kintyre* by Wings.

Sadly, there were several deaths during this period. John Lennon's assassination by a former fan outside his New York home was the most shocking. The rock-'n'-roll veteran Bill Haley died as did a newer luminary, Sid Vicious of the Sex Pistols. Manchester's Joy Division seemed to be heading for world fame until its talented lead singer, Ian Curtis, killed himself. Bob Marley's death from cancer was a great loss as was Marvin Gaye's murder.

British artists in the mid-1980s increasingly saw Britain as the springboard to success elsewhere, particularly the United States, and many spent less and less time in this country. In 1985, 12 of the 27 US number-one records were by British acts. One in every three overseas hits had a British connection, if not by artist then by songwriter, producer or recording facilities. Sales of British material were worth some £1.5 billion in exports. Even politicians praised the contribution made to the country's coffers by the music industry. The prestigious US Grammy Awards – the 'rock oscars' – in 1986 saw seven British acts sweep the board with one artist, Phil Collins, collecting three Grammy awards.

However, many of the singles in the British pop charts were bland and unoriginal, which was a direct result of record companies' reluctance to take risks or to fund innovative talents. As in many other fields, 'cost effectiveness' threatened to bar the different and the individual. Too many high album sales were of endless compilations of hit singles gathered together under a particular theme. Many singles relied on good producer-engineer-studio innovations with the artists useful only for the product's marketing and promotion. None of this made newspaper headlines but it did help some like Madonna and Prince who succeeded in gaining enormous Press coverage. Many have found the lack of musical originality of some of the artists rather dispiriting and it seems as if the British music industry is moving towards the contrived. On the other hand, who knows what new bands and ideas are waiting to burst onto the scene?

DAILY Mirror

Thursday, January 17, 1980   9p

Today's paper is wo... TO YOU... 50p SEE PAGE 2...

HANDCUFFED

DRINKS SPREE KILLED ROCK STAR

DAILY EXPRESS Wednesday October 8 1980

JOHN BONHAM
Carried to bed

JIMMY PAGE
'John was tipsy'

By ALEX HENDRY

ROCK superstar John Bonham died from a massive overdose of vodka and orange in a 12-hour drinking spree, an inquest heard yesterday.

The millionaire Led Zeppelin drummer had drunk so much—about 40 measures—that his blood alcohol level was at least three-and-a-half times over the legal limit for drivers.

Pathologist Dr Edmund Hemsted told the inquest at Windsor, Berkshire, that drink made Bonham sick, waterlogged his lungs, and killed him.

...am, 32, was found dead last ...e £900,000 Windsor home of ...a guitarist, Jimmy Page.

...ession

...al assistant, ...ng session ... near ... or-

Paul ... held i... jail on... drug charge...

By TOM MERRIN

POP star Paul McCartney wa... taken to a Japanese jail i... handcuffs yesterday.

The ex-Beatle was arrested b... drugs-squad police minutes after h... stepped off a plane in Tokyo.

The drama came when custom... men allegedly found half-a-pound... of marijuana in a plastic bag inside... one of his suitcases.

McCartney was said to hav... admitted: "I brought some hash... for my smoking."

His wife Linda and their four... children watched the arrest with... members of McCartney's band... Wings. They all flew into Tokyo... together for a two-week concert... tour of Japan.

Millions of TV viewers also saw... the 37-year-old star being led away... in handcuffs with a policeman on... either side of him.

Last night, as McCartney was... ...nally charged with drug-... Japanese tour promoter

...urn to Page 3

ZEP SPLIT! (OR DO THEY?)

THE STATEMENT was brief, zeroxed and to the point.

"We wish it to be known that the loss of our dear friend and the deep respect we have for his family together with the sense of undivided harmony felt by ourselves and our manager, have led us to decide that we could not continue as we were."

It was signed Led Zeppelin, dated December 5, 1980, and written on a WEA Records news sheet which still had John Fruin listed as a director.

Thus ended a week of speculation during which Cozy Powell, Paul Thompson, Carmine Appice, former Kiss skin-basher Peter Criss, Aynsley Dunbar, Ian Paice and even Ringo Starr had been mooted as possible replacements for the late John Bonham.

Contacted earlier that week by NME, former Roxy drummer Paul Thompson insisted that he wasn't in a position to either confirm or deny speculation that he was the odds-on favourite. He was extremely optimistic, but at the same time didn't want to queer his pitch with his prospective employers.

Within 24 hours the above somewhat ambiguous official statement was circulated.

Efforts to contact manager Peter Grant and individual members of the group to confirm whether or not Led Zeppelin had actually broken up were intercepted with polite replies of "We'll pass your message on". WEA Records, who distribute the SwanSong label, were unable to expand on the subject.

It could well be that the press release was circulated to alleviate mounting pressures and to give the band time to resolve the rift that allegedly now exists between Plant and Page before actually getting round to the selection of a new drummer.

On the other hand, it could be that Led Zeppelin has been permanently grounded. If so, what are the immediate options? It's no big secret that Robert Plant has often toyed with the prospect of fronting a Rockpile-styled band and, on occasion, has guested with Edmunds, Lowe and Co.

Similarly, Page could take a leaf out of Ritchie Blackmore's back pages and form a new touring band.

There's also the possibility that Plant, Page and Jones are attempting to gauge public reaction to a possible split in the anticipation that groundswell opinion will reach such a level that they will have no alternative but to return to the stage.

AND THE REST OF THIS WEEK'S NEWS

'I've learnt my lesson' — LYDON

WILD MAN OF PUNK GOES FREE

By BILL GRAHAM

IN STARK contrast to the courtroom melodrama of John Lydon's October conviction for assault in Dublin, his appeal last week against the resulting prison sentence could hardly have been more anticlimactic.

No one in the city, Lydon included, had anticipated such a quick, or indeed as favourable, an outcome to the appeal.

After only a five-minute hearing in the Circuit Court, Judge Frank Martin granted the appeal against the three-month sentence dished out by the lower District Court and then, with a benevolence totally unexpected by Lydon and his legal advisors, the judge also acquitted him of the charge.

So short and sweet was the hearing, that the two publicans who claimed that Lydon had assaulted them — Eamonn Brady and Eamonn Leddy — were completely wrong-footed: they arrived minutes after the decision was announced and were left fuming outside.

The case was conducted in low tones, hardly audible in the body of the court. Judge Martin, who had previously enhanced his street credibility by banning the last Boomtown Rats concert in Dublin, heard only the evidence of the prosecuting Irish garda.

Satisfied of the petty nature of the incident and of the fact that neither of the publicans had been injured in the alleged fracas, he cut short the hearing and acquitted Lydon.

The judge did, however, invite Lydon to

contribute £100 to the court's "poor box" as a token of his goodwill. Such informal face-saving mechanisms may not exist in British law, but they are far from unusual in the lower Irish courts.

On top of that, it is estimated that Lydon is down £2,000 due to his legal and travel costs.

Afterwards Lydon, wearing a sober grey suit and shirt and tie, admitted he was "dumbfounded" by both the decision and its speed. "I didn't know what the hell happened," he said in smiling confusion at Dublin airport as he prepared to take an early flight back to London.

His nightmare, he said, had been that the court "might double the sentence or give me the same and fine me as well."

Lydon and his advisers

Don't Walk Away In Silence

IAN CURTIS, lead singer of Joy Division and one of the most talented performers and writers in contemporary rock music, committed suicide on May 18th. PAUL MORLEY & ADRIAN THRILLS pay tribute to the man and the group.

Manchester's Joy Division seemed to be heading for world fame but their future was curtailed by the death of their 23-year-old lead singer, Ian Curtis. He committed suicide on 18 May 1980. Their music reflected the social and economic hardship of the times and was a mixture of the brutal and the tender. For many people Joy Division offered the best in British music at a time when the industry had again become over-commercialised and lacking in integrity.

SO WHY do we get so animated and enthralled by Joy Division?

Rock's such an infuriating thing it's a marvel we get so consumed. Mostly rock is an unstable, stale slab of crudity and stupidity; an endless roll of superficiality and lies. Some people, though, achieve something more than the usual

pushed its possibilities to the limits.

The very best rock music is art, and that is nothing to be ashamed of. Good rock music is entertaining and amusing, legitimate and intelligent, and from week to week, single to single, upset to upset, it keeps us going. The very best rock music — that is because of the roots, the hedonism, the delinquency and the screaming of rock tradition — is dramatic, neurotic, private, intimate and draws out of us more than just admiration and enthusiasm.

Whether it's Jimi Hendrix or Joy Division it suggests infinity and confronts squalor. In direct opposition to the impersonal exploitation of the rock structure it miraculously comes from, it cares for the inner

Dickensian warehouse converted into a rehearsal studio — seemed the ideal place for a Joy Division video. But the band's attitude to proceedings was withdrawn and disinterested. Even on camera, they seemed to have little time for such promotional niceties.

Such lethargy could hardly have been further removed from the mood in the university dressing room later that week as the band prepared for the Birmingham gig; Joy Division, despite the myth of romanticised individuals, despite their reputation as sober gloom that seemed to extend way beyond their vivid musical imagery, despite the cryptic humour of manager Rob Gretton, were earthy and easy-going people.

As Tony Wilson says, "To people they seemed a very gloomy band, but as human beings they were the absolute opposite."

The absolute opposite. Indulging in the

to warm to the dark dance music as the swirling, shifting guitar and drum patterns of the hypnotic '24 Hours' give way to the pulsebeat of the throbbing bass introduction to 'Transmission'. The band's third single suddenly seems to take on the aura of the hit it should have been as the audience finally begin to respond with any real vigour for the first time during the entire gig, their reticence melting in the face of the frightening intensity of Joy Division's performance.

The euphoria rises through 'Disorder', Curtis's flailing robotic juggle dance taking on almost violent proportions as Morris and Hook hold down the backbeat with precision and power and Albrecht studiously picks out the purest improvised guitar solos.

The guitarist takes over on synthesiser for the two closers, both again from the new LP, the translucent 'Isolation' and the serene 'Decades', a track, like the awesome 'Atmosphere' or 'Love Will Tear Us Apart' that accentuates the delicate side of the group and provides a sharp counterpoint to the more physical hard rock that comprises most of their set.

Curtis, however, stumbles from the stage at the end of the song, totally exhausted

---

The short goodbye....

The last JOY DIVISION feature by DAVE McCULLOUGH

LAST TUESDAY I was filling in an expenses form when somebody told me a joke. They said they'd had a phone call from Scotland saying The Teardrop Explodes had dedicated a song on stage the previous evening to Joy Division's Ian Curtis who was dead. I laughed, and half self-

this isn't yet verified, that his wife had left him on Saturday afternoon and he'd committed the deed later that evening. The band were preparing to fly to America the following morning.

These are the shadows of

it too will be released in the coming months. On Sunday the band were going to America for three weeks of touring, so there is every reason to conclude that it was a hectic time for the

DAILY Mirror

SPECIAL ISSUE

Wednesday, December 10, 1980   12p

JOHN LENNON shot dead in New York Dec 8 1980

DEATH OF A HERO

MURDERED SUPERSTAR: One of the last pictures of ex-Beatle John Lennon, taken in New York three weeks ago

Please turn to Pages Two and Three

NME

NEW MUSICAL EXPRESS

A BAD TIME IN NEW YORK

NEWS DEREK JOHNSON

THRILLS CYNTHIA ROSE

Doorman: "Do you know what you've done?"

Chapman: "I've shot John Lennon."

JOHN LENNON MURDERED

leaves Roosevelt Hospital comforted by record company boss David Geffen

JOHN LENNON gave his last autograph in New York on Monday night.

In exchange, Mark David Chapman, 25, white and Hawaiian, thanked him with five .38 calibre bullets to the upper torso, inflicting seven wounds and severing a major artery.

The suspect, who had been in New York for two weeks, had been stalking Lennon for days outside the Dakota apartments on 72nd Street, Central Park West.

Lennon had spent the evening with Yoko and producer Jack Douglas at the Record Plant studio, and departed at 10.30 pm with the intention of getting something to eat before going back to the Dakotas.

When John returned

New York report by JOE STEVENS

time. Chapman made no attempt to escape. He threw his gun down, and was grabbed by the doorman and a passer-by while Yoko, understandably distraught, clutched Lennon's body, screaming: "He's been shot! Someone help! Someone help!"

One of the Lennons' neighbours called the police, and a passing patrol car arrived and Lennon in the office. As

His final wish: 'I want to die before my Yoko'

THE SUN, Wednesday, December 10, 1980

105

Page 12 – MELODY MAKER, February 14, 1981

BILL HALEY in London for the first and last times — 1957 and 1979.

The rock 'n' roll innocent who shook the whole world

by Colin Irwin

THE news of Bill Haley's death was headlined with characteristic relish by the daily tabloids on Tuesday morning. They seemed to have acquired quite an affection for rock 'n' roll departures, and phrases like "father of rock 'n' roll", "king of the teds", "first king of rock", "The man who changed the face of music" were bandied around with lavish extravagance.

Such claims aren't so inaccurate when the facts are examined. A genuine rock 'n' roll legend, Haley initiated and came to symbolise the rock 'n' roll revolution of the late Fifties, yet he was a curious symbol of the rebellious stance increasingly associated with the growing youth culture.

He was chubby, he was married, and he greased a lock of hair over his bald-

BILL HALEY, one of the first of the rock 'n' roll pioneers, died on Monday night after apparently suffering a heart attack in bed at his home in Harlingen, Texas. Haley, 55, made his living as a singer for 40 years, starting at the age of 15 singing country songs, but didn't come to prominence until he recorded "Rock Around The Clock" in 1954, aged 28.

The single has since sold an estimated 23 million copies around the world, charting six times since 1955.

by John Orme and Carol Clerk

He opened up the world of live rock 'n' roll with U.S., British and European tours in the late Fifties, and his concerts were often marked by the first real violence and hysteria to be attached to the new youth music of rock 'n' roll, much to the astonishment of the quiet, unassuming singer on the stage with the Comets.

His concerts tailed off in the Sixties but in the late Seventies he started a rock 'n' roll comeback

and last visited Britain in 1979, when he played a sell-out house at London's Southgate Royalty, the centre of the rock 'n' roll revival in the capital. That show, on March 8, was filmed for a movie called "Blue Suede Shoes", which covers the life and work of the founding fathers of the music. Although current details of the film are not clear it is understood that the film has been finished, and that a release is likely in the next few months.

Haley was due to play at London's Hammersmith Odeon last November, but he was taken ill with a suspected brain tumour ten days before the concert and his health declined since then.

Haley played country and western and was even briefly a disc jockey before he realised post-war teenagers wanted something more exciting, perhaps a white version of R&B. He was 28 when *Crazy Man Crazy* became the first 'rock-'n'-roll' record to make the US *Billboard* pop charts in 1953. *Rock Around the Clock* became his biggest hit of the 1950s but *See You Later Alligator*, *Rock-a-Beaten Boogie* and *Rockin through the Rye* also did well. Haley was hugely popular in Britain and fans went wild when he toured the country in 1957.

The 1960s and 1970s saw little chart life but when he was able Haley toured extensively. Even in his forties the famous kiss curl survived but then, as before, it was hard to associate this pleasant, balding, family man with the teenage rebels who went to his concerts, tore up seats and damaged cars and anything else in their way outside.

DAILY Mirror

Tuesday, February 10, 1981   12p

BILL HALEY IS DEAD

From NIGEL NELSON in New York

PIONEER 'rock 'n' roll star Bill Haley died last night. He was 55.

Bill Haley and his band, The Comets, shot to fame in the fifties with their recording of Rock Around The Clock, theme of the film Blackboard Jungle.

It has sold 22,500,000 copies since it was released 25 years ago. The band was in the

HALEY: Top rocker

forefront of rock 'n' roll in the fifties. As the new wave of pop arrived, the Comets' popularity waned.

In recent years Haley

lived quietly at Harlingen, Texas. He was found dead in bed of natural causes. The rock king —See Page 7

BOB MARLEY 1945-1981: FOUR-PAGE MM TRIBUTE

'Sometimes when I think about it, I think maybe I can help bring mankind together'

rom Jamaica's slums to reggae Master Blaster

Miami, Florida — 12.30 pm Monday

16th May, 1981 New Musical Express — Page 3

BULLETS COULDN'T KILL HIM

— Cancer did

SEVEN MONTHS AFTER he had been diagnosed as suffering from the disease, Bob Marley fought his last fight with cancer when he died at the Cedars Of Lebanon hospital in Miami early last Monday afternoon.

The death of the 36 year-old Jamaican folk hero occurred only four days after he had flown to Florida, following what several sources close to him believed to be the successful conclusion of a five-month course of intensive treatment at the Bavarian clinic of unorthodox cancer specialist Dr Josef Issels.

It was not to be, however: a spokesperson at the Cedars Of Lebanon hospital said on Monday that Bob had arrived in Miami last Thursday specifically to be admitted to the hospital.

"He was in extremely poor condition when he arrived here," commented Karen Buschbaum. "When he got here it was determined there was not much we could do for him except keep him as comfortable as possible."

Reggae has always had to fight for airtime and apart from a few specialist programmes, it has largely been ignored by British radio and television. Relatively few reggae artists have managed to break down airtime barriers but when they have it has been mainly because they have had a more popular appeal. Undoubtedly, Bob Marley and the Wailers were the best-known group of this musical and social genre.

Marley's death from cancer in 1981 was greatly mourned in both Britain and the West Indies. His body lay in state in the National Arena, Jamaica before being buried in the north coast parish of St Anne's, close to where he had lived during the early years of his marriage. Shortly before his death he had joined the Ethiopian Orthodox Church and had taken the name Berhanie Selassie, meaning Light of the Trinity.

Pic Adrian Boot.

BOB MARLEY'S FINAL RETURN HOME

King of Reggae laid to rest in Jamaica

'Head banging' probe as pop boy dies

DAILY MIRROR, Saturday, January 2,

CHRISTOPHER: Hoped to become a draughtsman.

A NIGHT out at a rock concert ended in tragedy for schoolboy Christopher Tyrer.

He died after joining in a "head banging" session.

Now doctors are hoping to find out whether the dance, in which youngsters shake their heads violently from side to side in time to the music, led to 15-year-old Christopher's death.

They believe he died from a brain haemorrhage.

Christopher, of Wednesfield, West Midlands, seen "head banging" as 1,000 fans watched the rock group Saxon at Wolverhampton Civic Hall.

Next morning his parents found him paralysed down one side.

He died in hospital eight days later.

Christopher's mother, Mrs. Pauline Tyrer, said: "It's so easy for youngsters to get carried away at a concert. When the excitement reaches fever pitch they don't know what they are doing.

"If head banging did cause his death we hope

By ROD CHAYTOR

it will serve as a warning to other young people."

Her husband John said he had often seen his son shaking his head and dancing to music at their home and had warned him that it was dangerous. Christopher's friend Adrian Bibb, 15, said there had been a scramble after one of the rock group threw a towel into the audience.

It was possible that Christopher had taken a knock on the head as he grabbed a piece of the material as a trophy.

Doctors hope to establish exactly what caused his death after a postmortem next week.

Stevens struggled through the second half of the 1970s as a lively rockabilly artist in rock and roll clubs. However, in the 1980s he has proved one of the pop chart's most consistent hit makers. His rockabilly style has been refined to become more acceptable in the discotheques. He has largely modelled his act on Presley's and not surprisingly he played the role of Elvis in the musical of the same name that enjoyed a successful London West End run in the early 1980s.

WILLIAM MARSHALL meets the new King of Rock
SHAKIN' ALL OVER

"I won't lose touch like Elvis. I will always be part of the real world"

JEREMY CAMPBELL reports from Washington on the eclipse of Elvis Presley's manager

How Colonel Tom was rocked to his roots

THE CURTAIN is finally coming down on the razzle-dazzle career of Colonel Tom Parker, the publicity-shy publicist and opaque master of ballyhoo who built Elvis Presley into a legend and placed him among the immortals.

A recorded voice answers the telephone at the Colonel's Palm Springs, California home, saying tinnily that the line has been disconnected. But I am told on excellent authority that the U.S. immigration and naturalisation service is seeking a court hearing to deport him to his native Holland.

In a sparse Press release Parker had been identified as good American stock, son of a West Virginia couple who had been on tour with a carnival when he was born. Court records reveal that he is actually Andreas Cornelius van Kuijk, a native of Breda, Holland, who came to America in 1929, at the age of 20.

THE STANDARD, WEDNESDAY, JULY 7, 1982—7

PARKER: lawsuits and accusations.

Elvis's manager, Colonel Tom Parker, suffered a severe battering to his reputation during the early 1980s. He was accused of exploiting the singer's 'name and image', of taking an unduly high percentage of royalties (50 per cent) and of defrauding the Presley estate of some $5 million. Court battles ended in June 1983 after 21 months of litigation. Parker had filed a counter suit and offered a detailed rebuttal of the charges made. The eventual agreement contained numerous clauses but one of them demanded that Parker should turn over a substantial part of his interest in Elvis's recordings to RCA and the Presley family. For this he received a large money settlement.

A FRIEND DROPPING IN

Manchester Evening News

FINAL

35,050

TWENTY-FOUR HOUR RADIO & TV GUIDE PAGE 3

WEDNESDAY, JANUARY 20, 1982

STILL 12p

BRITAIN'S BIGGEST REGIONAL EVENING NEWSPAPER

Court threat as Manilow fans get warning

STAR IN 'LIGHTED CANDLES' STORM

Youth escapes shotgun blast

RAIDERS blasted the pay-desk window at a petrol station with sawn-off shotguns last night and then held the lone teenage attendant on the floor with a gun to his head.

Bill Bailey, aged 17, told today of his narrow escape when the two masked men opened fire.

A Rover saloon had pulled on to the forecourt of Boadon filling station on the A6 Chester road, near Altrincham. The gunmen leapt out and fired at the security window.

"I was very lucky," said Bill, back on duty today. They just blasted the flap of the security window as they leapt from the car. They could easily have hit me.

"They told me to let them in. When someone tells you they are going to blast your head off with a shotgun, there's not much you can do.

They forced him to the floor and put the gun to my head."

After the blast at window, Bill, who as of Timperley with his parents pressed a panic but under the kiosk till to

MANY of Barry Manilow's faithful fans are female. But faithfulness or femininity cut no ice with the American pop-star's muscle-men, as they sweep their grim faced and silent charge through the foyer of Manchester's Hotel Piccadilly. BELOW, the frowning crooner reaches the safety of the lift, leaving behind angry Pressmen, some of whom had waited for six hours.

Pictures : CLIVE COOKSEY

Gee! £1,200 for a night

By ANDREW NOTT and GEOFF GREEN

BARRY MANILOW promised today to warn his fans not to light candles during his first Manchester concert tonight.

If they ignore him, the US superstar's concerts at the Apollo Theatre tomorrow and Friday may be stopped by a court injunction.

The threat to the sell-out concerts materialised at today's meeting of the city's Environmental Services committee.

Councillors were "horrified" when they heard that local radio stations had been telling fans that candles had been lit at other Manilow shows.

Committee chairman Roger Delahunty was instructed to ask the Apollo management to persuade Manilow to withdraw the "candles" number from his act.

Earlier he told the meeting: "The thought of three or four thousand candles being lit and waved in the air horrifies me. The possible hazards are horrifying to contemplate.

The committee was told that legally the council was the licensing authority and if the candle number

---

Stones fan shot dead outside U.S. concert

ONE man was shot dead and another wounded outside a Rolling Stones concert in America in what police believe was a row about tickets.

Richard Wright and his companion, Andy Ulsaker, were attacked by two men in woods outside the Capital Centre as the band was playing to a sell-out audience in Largo, Maryland, last night.

Mr Wright died in hospital of multiple gunshot wounds shortly after the attack. Mr Ulsaker is "stable" in hospital.

THE STANDARD, MONDAY, NOVEMBER 8, 1982—7

The Beatles are back in the charts and is 21 years old. But how many of us recall what our lives were like

Private Eye can really 21 years ago?

THE BEATLES: "Still twisting madly at midnight."

Twenty years after the Beatles' first single release, EMI began reissuing their records in picture disc form with the result that *Love Me Do* went into the charts once more in October 1982. Subsequent releases have done well but have not repeated the number-four position attained by *Love Me Do*. Beatle songs have continued to sell heavily and especially in the United States where new compilations have added to the sales of records issued during the Beatle years. There is still a considerable amount of Beatle material that has not been released but, to fans' sorrow, agreement has not been reached about how it should be marketed.

Happy days... when we didn't have to look behind us

by VALERIE GROVE

DAILY Mirror

Saturday, February 5, 1983   16p

Heart attack at 32 kills pop superstar

SINGER Karen Carpenter of the chart-topping Carpenters pop duo died of a heart attack last night.

Karen, 32, who had suffered from the slimmers' disease anorexia nervosa, collapsed at her parents' home in Downie, California.

She was found in a bedroom by her mother who tried frantically to revive her as she gasped for breath. Her father and brother Richard, 35, were sitting downstairs.

By the time ambulancemen arrived Karen had sunk into a coma. She died in hospital 30 minutes later with her family at her side.

Last night, hospital officials refused to give details. Karen's Press agent, Paul Bloch, would only say: "It's a great shock to all of us."

Karen and her brother had sold 60 million records worldwide with hits like Yesterday Once More, On Top Of The World and Close To You. She had suffered from anorexia—which can cause heart problems—for two years, and at one time her weight fell to six stone.

Coroner's officials said last night that she weighed 7 stone - 10 lb when she died.

Press spokesman Paul Bloch said: "She lost a lot of weight over the last year. But she was under treatment and had gained most of it back."

Divorced

Karen's illness became worse after the break-up of her two-year marriage to property developer Thomas Burris, 42. The couple divorced last year and Karen lived alone in a high rise flat.

Karen and Richard soared to fame after they were spotted by Herb Alpert who offered them a contract with A and M Records.

They had a fresh-faced wholesome look which won the hearts of fans and their songs reflected it.

The image worked so well that the then President Nixon said: "The Carpenters represent

From PAUL CONNEW in New York

all that is true and best in America."

But soon the duo got fed up with their "whiter than white" image.

They announced that neither of them was a virgin, that they had affairs and believed in pre-marital sex.

Albums

Their popularity remained undiminished and they went on to become the world's No. 1 vocal duo.

They won three Grammy awards and made eight gold albums and ten gold singles. Their hits included Rainy Days

● Turn to Page 3

STARS: Karen and Richard at the height of their fame in the seventies. Yesterday she died of a massive heart attack at her parents' home in California.

Karen of the Carpenters dies

DON'T BE SHY . . . IT'S ONLY DI—See Page

Yes sir, this IS my baby!

By ALASDAIR BUCHAN

OUTRAGEOUS OZZY'S THE DADDY OF SHOCK ROCK

WE'VE all heard of the Beauty and the Beast. But this ridiculous!

The creature cradling Aimee Osbourne in hairy hands is actually her doting dad, Ozzy.

Not the sort of snap you expect to find in most family albums, of course . . .

But when your dad is a bloke who's been known to bite off a bat's head on stage, and throw lumps of raw liver at his audience, you learn to cope with his little eccentricities.

Three - week - old Aimee obviously has, because she managed to sleep through the entire proceedings.

And by the end of the extraordinary picture session, 33-year-old Ozzy must have felt like doing the same.

For all that monster make-up had taken a full FIVE HOURS to put on, and a further hour and a half to scrape off.

But the wildman of head - banging, heavy metal rock still managed to keep his zany sense of humour.

Hairy

As those hairy hands were finally fitted into place, Ozzy declared: "Gosh, this is handy! Now I can scratch my knees without bending over.

"Mind you, I'm going to have problems changing Aimee's nappy."

Predictably, the Beast had some shocking ideas on how to bring up his beautiful daughter.

"My missus, Sharon, doesn't agree," he growled. "But I hope she is going to grow up to look just like her daddy—fangs and all.

"Though it would help if we could change her diet to rusks and bat's blood—instead of all this filthy milk."

But not even Outrageous Ozzy could hide his true feelings for long.

"Actually, Aimee's a lovely baby," he said. "She's really beautiful.

"Though she doesn't say much yet — apart from the occasional 'Kajagoogoo.'"

Ozzy's werewolf look will also be seen on his new album, Bark at the Moon, which goes on sale next month.

And despite his hairy reputation, the former Black Sabbath lead singer does NOT look like this naturally.

So he had to call in top Hollywood make-up expert Greg Cannom to (literally) lend a hand.

"The first step was to make a cast of Ozzy's real face," explains the 32-year-old Californian. "I then took that back to America and began building the make - up around that.

"I also had a mould of Ozzy's teeth to work from."

Back at his Los Angeles laboratory, Greg created false noses, false foreheads, false fangs and several sets of contact lenses. Real human hair was sewn together into wigs for Ozzy's head and body.

Greg also made a full, foam latex mask to fit over the whole of Ozzy's face.

And last week, in London, Greg and his two assistants — Mark Mayling and Janice Barnes — completed the £50,000 transformation.

Ozzy's only protest came when they sprayed glue on to his body to fix the patches of blond hair in place.

"Here, why's it so bloody cold?" he shrieked.

Mammoth

"Because it's full of alcohol," explained Greg.

"Funny," muttered Ozzy. "It usually causes me pain on the way out."

The mammoth make-up session had started at mid-day and finally ended at 5 p.m., when Ozzy was ready to be photographed.

Like a true professional, Aimee, the first child of Ozzy's marriage to his manager, Sharon, was ready right on cue.

And as you can see, the pictures were a howling success.

Pictures by KEN LENNOX

STAGE THREE . . . but the full horror of Ozzy is lost on sleeping beauty Aimee

... as himself

Greg puts the first layer of make-up on Ozzy   STAGE TWO . . . the patches of hair are glued in place

Only in your . . .

PLUS buzz from Simon Bates PLUS Rick Sky's Pop the Question

BAT-BITE OZZY GETS IT IN THE NECK!

By SUN REPORTER

ROCK star Ozzy Osbourne is in hospital after a studio accident almost as bizarre as his wild stage act.

Ozzy, who once bit the head off a live bat, was making a video in which a mirror was exploding in front of his face.

The mirror should have been harmless plastic—but real glass was used and needle-sharp fragments were blasted into his throat.

After the accident in London, 34-year-old Ozzy was cleaned up and caught a Concorde flight to America, apparently feeling fine.

But pressure in the cabin forced more hidden shards of glass deeper into his throat.

A spokesman for the star, who is on a nine-month concert tour of America, said: "He was in agony on Concorde and the pilot radioed for an ambulance to meet him in New York."

Ozzy had emergency treatment followed by a long and delicate operation at the Mount Sinai Hospital on Thursday.

Weird

"At the moment we don't believe any permanent damage has been done. It has not affected his vocal chords," the spokesman added. But at least a dozen gigs will be cancelled as a result of the accident.

Ozzy was lead singer with Black Sabbath for ten years before going solo in 1979.

He is notorious for his weird and unpredictable performances — and was banned from several American states after biting the head off the bat during one concert.

Corporate pop and Image styling have gone hand in hand during the 1980s and Dressing Up rather than Dressing Down has been the norm for pre-packaged pop. Stars have either adopted designer clothes or worn the fashions of the new-style chain shops and, when Duran Duran had their first hit in 1981 with *Planet Earth*, cynics said they looked as if they had just stepped out of a high street fashion boutique.

In the *Virgin Yearbook* Vici MacDonald reckoned that they and others like them were simply apeing the values of the 1970s' rock scene and that in their vulgar displays of conspicuous consumption they would have disgraced Led Zeppelin and the Stones in their heyday.

Duran Duran, at least, have redeemed themselves more recently by demonstrating their considerable musical ability.

Some might doubt the age of Tina Turner as 45 in 1985 but no one would quibble that the enduring lady has enjoyed an incredible career revival that began with the hit single *Let's Stay Together* at the end of 1983. Much of her come-back is due to her recording in Britain. She toured the country in 1985, playing to overflowing houses and earning ecstatic reviews.

Monday December 5 1983
TV and RADIO GUIDE
Leisuretime
AND CLASSIFIED ADVERTISEMENT SECTION

TONY JASPER begins a special two-part series on the supergroup about to visit Manchester

DURAN DURAN: THE IMAGE IS THE MESSAGE !

These were the scenes when Duran Duran were in Manchester last — the fan-worship is looking almost like that of the Beatles.

Duran Duran — the 'dishy guys' are Nick Rhodes, John Taylor, Roger Taylor, Andy Taylor and Simon Le Bon.

NINE singles, three albums, 12 shorts in their video library, a video album, and a biography *(Duran Duran, Their Story* by Kasper de Graaf and Malcolm Garrett) give you five-guy Duran Duran on plastic, paper and film.

But to true fans even the accumulation of those things could not compensate for missing the band "live" in Manchester tomorrow and Wednesday.

Duran Duran is today's supergroup — the band for whom manager Michael Berrow sold his house to finance the support slot in the nationwide tour by Hazel O'Connor in the autumn of 1980.

His risk proved well-founded for today he is rich. So likewise the band — their fame has become worldwide with records and concerts everywhere and the band drawing huge crowds.

To detractors like me, Duran Duran is an average musical band who have been spent into popularity, but I know a few million people have no truck with this viewpoint. Fans worship the looks and music of keyboards man Nick Rhodes, John Taylor the bass guitarist, drums and percussion player Roger Taylor, lead guitarist Andy Taylor and lead vocalist Simon Le Bon at 25 years of age.

Duran Duran formed in 1978 and by the summer of 1980 had stabilised into a formation that continues. Musical taste and stylish ambience drew the interested who were looking for a smart good-looking outfit, others drew the best of the new crop which emerged as the last decade drew to a close.

"We are dead serious about what we do. Today we've much more confidence and feel our new album Seven And The Ragged Tiger is the best thing we've ever done.

Suzi Rome have worked themselves hard in telling the Duran Duran message, for the group have been "placed" time and again on media

...group's videography, alongside Lonely In Your Nightmare and In disc Boat. The latter, in disc form, is on the group's first album and the former on Rio. The video album Duran Duran is a summation of their first 11 stretches to March of this year it does not include the new one for Union Of The Snake.

The videos are excellent and reveal how the pictorial is now a major backcloth to current record success. More than most Duran Duran

...have caused a revolution in record buying habits — for fans now expect more than mere black vinyl, and high in the priority listing is to hear a record with a visual accompanying it or at least being there in the mind.

The good looks of the five members have been...

DAILY RECORD, Wednesday, February 15, 1984   17

TINA TURN-ON

Those rock 'n' roll thunder thighs are heading your way

ROCKING THE NIGHT AWAY ... Tina's special style of entertainment, aided by backing singer Lejeune Richardson.

By BILLY SLOAN
Scotland's No. 1 Pop Writer

FOR reasons I can only describe as purely professional, I was standing just 18 inches away from Tina Turner's trembling thunder-thighs.

And if you believe that excuse — you'll believe anything.

The super sexy 44-year-old American singer is the kind of woman we boys dream about.

REACTION

But if Tina wickedly winked an eye and invited us into her lair we'd probably run a record-breaking mile — in the interests of self-preservation, of course.

She's at Glasgow Apollo on Saturday, Aberdeen Capitol on Sunday, and Edinburgh Playhouse on Monday — and she's NOT to be missed.

For in nearly 15 years of concert-going, Tina Turner puts on the sexiest, raunchiest and most highly-charged rock 'n' roll show I've ever witnessed.

Last week I caught up with the Queen Of Bump And Grind's appropriately-titled Captured Live tour at Leicester's De Montfort Hall — and I've never seen an audience reaction like it.

Grown men abandoned their girlfriends and stormed the stage throwing bunches of red roses.

Others clambered on to each others shoulders trying to reach Tina.

Some drowned our her between song announcements with sexual suggestions the Kama Sutra would be proud of.

And who can blame them, when she seductively struts up to the microphone, scantily clad in torn animal skins, and purrs:

"Now, now boys—you know I like it ROUGH."

The temperature and excitement level goes through the roof.

Squatting invitingly near the edge of the stage, Tina storms into her version of David Bowie's Cat People and when she spits out the line "I've been putting out the fire with gasoline," it becomes one of pop's most memorable understatements.

The way she clutches the mike could be classed as a criminal offence, and her dynamic, high velocity vocals singe the eardrums.

CRIMINAL

Musically she's brilliant—powering her way through Rod Stewart's Hot Legs, the Beatles' Get Back, John Fogerty's Proud Mary and The Who's Acid Queen.

Tina has the unique ability to take pop classics, turn them inside out and inject them with an overdose of sensuality to make them her own.

Surrounded by a dynamic five-piece band, and flanked by two shapely female backing...

There, after cooling down, she soothes her throat with a bowl of hot mushroom soup and talks about her Scottish visit.

"All I've heard about the country is that the weather is cold and the men wear kilts," she says in a sexy, rasping voice.

EXERCISE

"The tour has been fantastic so far — I've enjoyed every show and just want to keep on playing."

That's exactly what she's been doing for the past six months.

With just three days off at Christmas, spent in the quietness of her Los Angeles apartment, Tina's been permanently on the road in Europe, the Far East and America.

She's a Buddhist, doesn't smoke, drinks only the occasional glass of white wine, and doesn't need to exercise to keep her amazing body in shape.

Entertainment
Boy George wins the hearts in Redneck City

day, April 8, 1984

'BOY GEORGE IS EVIL!'"

Boy George and Culture Club enjoyed a series of seven top-three British singles between October 1982 and December 1984. The group also featured prominently in the British invasion of the American music charts in 1983. Once a minor figure on the rather posy London club scene under his real name of George O'Dowd, Boy George's make-up and clothes were the subject of considerable Press interest. While his looks and dress were admired by teenage girls, he was often viewed with distaste by adults. He asked politely, 'What's being heterosexual got to do with dressing up?'. In 1985 he continued to gain gossip column inches but he didn't have another hit until 1986.

DAILY STAR

16p (17p C.I.s)   Printed in London

MONDAY, APRIL 2, 1984

Tuesday September 11 1984

POP
Half the people who laugh at me look awful

Page 20—New Musical Express 24th March. 1984

THE

CLONE

RANGER

1. DREAMY DESIRE AND LEGS

Now

SUPER STAR COLOUR INSIDE TODAY

IT'S BOY GEORGE THE SOLE SINGER!

By RICK SKY

BOY George took Canada by storm last night—in his bare feet.

Wearing a baseball hat and a dazzling new smock covered in dollar signs, he bounced about the Montreal Forum's stage as the fans screamed in delight.

It was the first concert of Culture Club's sell-out three-week tour of North America.

Earlier the flamboyant singer told Canadians: "Princess Diana is the most fashionable person in the world today. She's very good at making the best of herself."

He added: "Everybody has this illusion that all rock stars are sexy. That's rubbish. Most rock stars are vulgar and decadent.

"For instance, I don't particularly find Mick Jagger sexy."

Boy George the Bitch—Centre Pages

I WANNA KISS THE BRIDE

Elton and Renata ... sealed with a kiss.

ROCK superstar Elton John married his secret sweetheart in Sydney last night.

It was a whizzbang flamboyant affair ... and the Australian city had never seen a wedding like it.

More than 1000 adoring fans waited outside St Mark's Church to see the happy couple.

But Elton only had eyes for Renata Blavel, the German-born girl to whom he proposed four days ago.

And as soon as they left the church, a happy Elton, 36, beamed: "I wanna kiss the bride."

Earlier, Elton was first to arrive at the church, rigged out in a white silk coat, black pants, a purple silk shirt, a purple band.

He was every inch the pop world king.

But it was Renata, 30, who brought a gasp of admiration from the fans.

She wore a magnificent, full-length, white lace gown. A delicately woven white lace veil covered her face and her dark shoulder-length hair.

Inside the church — decorated with lilies of the valley, carnations and ferns — the Rev James Whild conducted the 50-minute service.

Strangely, for the world of pop stars at least, the only music was provided by the organist.

ROSES

It was decorated with thousands of red and white roses, huge clusters of carnations and white orchids — all flown from New Zealand.

The bridal table, sur-

I DID IT! Waves after the ceremony.

IT'S LOVE—IN WEEK

There was a big burst of cheering as the newly-weds emerged from the Church and got into a white Rolls-Royce for the ride back to their luxury hotel.

There Elton had taken over the entire ballroom for the £100,000 reception.

Rock star Elton does it in style

rounded by 11 others, had a six-foot high floral centrepiece bearing the letters E and R. And the wedding cake—described as "truly monumental"—stood five tiers high.

The wedding breakfast included venison, pork, truffles, lobster, quail, Queensland mud crabs, Tasmanian scallops, mountain trout and tropical fruit.

All the champagne and wine had been flown in from France.

ALBUM

A seven-piece band played old-time music from the 1890s to 1930s.

Among the distinguished guests were singer Olivia Newton-John, Barry (Dame Edna Everage) Humphries and Michael Parkinson.

They were joined by four tennis stars — John McEnroe, Ivan Lendl, Guillermo Vilas and Mats Wilander.

But Elton's best friend, Rod Stewart, was not there. Rod's record company had insisted he stay in California to finish his latest album.

CLUB

Yoko Ono phoned to give the couple her best wishes. She said that John Lennon would have loved to have been at the wedding.

And officials of Elton's football club, Watford, also phoned their boss.

It's understood that Elton and Renata are planning a second wedding in London, possibly in April.

And there will be no honeymoon at the moment. The whole Elton John team fly to New Zealand later today at the start of a new tour.

■ Smiles all the way from the superstar of pop and his attractive new wife Renata.

Despite this headline, Dennis Wilson's death caught many by surprise. Drug usage had mainly been associated with his brother Brian and the ever unfolding story of how he was faring 'on' or 'off' drugs. However, in 1983, Dennis's condition became so bad that other group members and the management banned him from concerts. He was told that he must follow Brian's path and go through a 'detox program'. He checked in and later out of hospital. His last hours were spent sailing and diving and reports said that he had been drinking heavily. He did not resurface from one of his dives and his body was eventually pulled from the water; he was pronounced dead three minutes later.

The Beach Boy Who Went Overboard

Dennis Wilson was the wild one. He could never get enough of anything—drugs, women or booze. But in the end, he had nothing. He was homeless, penniless, and his own family had booted him from the group he originally inspired. By Michael Goldberg

Many have compared the invasion of the US charts by British artists since 1983 with the influx of acts that came after the initial Beatle foray into the United States in 1964. Among the high-selling British acts in the States during this latest period have been: Culture Club, Tears for Fears, the Pretenders, the Eurythmics, Wham!, Duran Duran, Spandau Ballet, the Thompson Twins and Dire Straits.

SPECIAL ISSUE!
ENGLAND SWINGS
Great Britain invades America's music and style. Again.

MONDAY, APRIL 2, 1984   16p   (17p C.Is)   Printed in

POP STAR SHOT DEAD

Marvin Gaye: Row with father

POP STAR Marvin Gaye was shot dead by his father early today. Police in Los Angeles said an argument broke out Sunday lunch and C... pulled out ... would have been 45 today, was best known for his hit "I Heard ...through The Grapevine." His ...r will be charged later today.

FULL STORY PAGE 11

...orror as

...our die

...married just over a year ...oney was from St Felix ...old, Suffolk, which has ...s Grund.

...ue team leader Gnos ...Daily Star last night of ...nents when the top of ...ted — and the silent ...wards the skiers.

...'ve never experienced ...It was almost com- ...ones that died were ...low and rock. ...ny of 60 volunteers

...ge Two

DAILY STAR, Monday, April 2, 1984   11
S/BS

POP STAR MARVIN SHOT DEAD BY FATHER

By LIZ HODGSON in Los Angeles and JIM MURRAY

2 a.m.

POP singer Marvin Gaye was shot dead by his father last night.

The star was killed after an argument at his home in Los Angeles.

He was rushed to the California Hospital and Medical Centre with a single wound in the chest.

But he was declared dead within 10 minutes.

Last night his father, Marvin Gaye Snr, a retired Pentecostal preacher was under arrest.

A row broke out over Sunday lunch and the singer's father grabbed a pistol and fired several shots.

A police spokesman said: "He is to be charged later."

Gaye, who would have been 45 today, was best known for the 1968 hit I Heard It Through the Grapevine.

He sold millions of records and two years ago climbed up the British charts with Sexual Healing.

Gaye had fallen out with his father in recent years.

"My father was a very strict disciplinarian against whom I rebelled," the singer said in a recent interview.

"The star found difficulty coping with his wealth and fame.

At one time he left California to live in a motor van in Hawaii. While there he tried to kill himself by taking an overdose of cocaine.

On another occasion a nervous breakdown forced him out of show-biz for several months after his wife Jan left him for singer Teddy Prendergrass.

Gaye leaves his third wife Janis, 27, and their ...old son Frankie.

Marvin Gaye ... row over Sunday lunch

Sad end for a giant

A SMALL army was called in when Peter Yarnall died. Firemen, police and workmen with a crane ended up helping the undertakers.

For Peter, 35, weighed 59 stone — and lived in a third-floor flat.

A plan to remove bannisters and lower his body ...failed when the rope broke.

...d a full-length window ...Ham, London.

JACKO'S STAR WARS SHOW TAKES OFF

On tour with the world's top pop act

POP superstar Michael Jackson has driven his fans wild with the launch of his fabulous Star Wars spectacular rock show.

It was the first concert of the Jackson family's much-heralded three-month tour of America, but predictably Michael stole the show. And WHAT a show!

The dazzling two-hour open-air performance blasted into action with lasers, huge banks of moving lights and fireworks.

And Michael displayed the full range of extraordinary talents that have made him the biggest earner in rock music, worth some £190 million.

The locals here in Kansas City claim to be a sceptical lot—even their car licence plates say Missouri is the "Show Me State."

But seeing was believing. All around me grown-ups were gawping like kids, with their mouths wide open, as the show got under way. First, armour-clad

Fans are thrilled by space special

From GERALDINE HOSIER in Kansas City

Michael slays five eerie space monsters with a laser sword.

Then a mass of coloured lasers starts to zig-zag everywhere and the audience find themselves part of an illusion — being inside a space invaders machine filled with deafening sound.

As that subsides, three huge banks of lights begin to rise around the 100-foot stage to reveal the five Jackson brothers — Michael 25, Jermaine 29, Tito 30, Marlon 27 and Randy 22.

The sixth brother, Jackie, missed the gig because of a knee injury.

Michael, at this point wearing a black and white striped outfit and of course The Glove—white and layered with 1,200 rhinestones — has the audience in a frenzy before he opens his mouth.

Face to face, superstar Michael looks frail.

But on stage he changes beyond recognition. Snake-hipped and twinkle-toed, he strutted and boogied, dominating the entire event.

At one point he appears in a pink space suit.

It is the signal for an astonishing space fantasy to begin, with two enormous electronic spiders swinging menacingly up and down.

And the whole extravaganza ends with a bang in a glorious firework display.

WHY CLOSE FRIENDS ARE WORRIED ABOUT SUPERSTAR JACKSON

Michael the Hermit's sad farewell

AT THE end of The Jackson's spectacular rock tour, Michael Jackson announced to the crowd: "This is our final show together at the end of 20 wonderful years."

The 6,000 fans packed into the Dodgers Stadium, Los Angeles, applauded loudly. Yet they were seeing not only The Jacksons' last live show, but Michael Jackson's last live performance.

Jackson tour a "hell on wheels"

The Jacksons' 1984 summer tour of the United States was one of the pop industry's largest and most extravagant affairs. It was news long before the first chord was struck as commercial interests fought bitterly for the right to make millions of dollars. The tour took in 20 cities, was attended by an estimated 2,700,000 people and grossed $41 million. When the tour finished the group's charismatic vocalist Michael announced it would be their last. However, some still doubt that this is the case.

When the copyright for the majority of the Beatle song catalogue came on sale Paul McCartney was outbid in his attempt to buy it by Michael Jackson, who later caused much consternation in the British music industry by closing down the respected ATV music publishing company.

Both events were heavily criticised in the British trade magazines and were seen as the bad face of American capitalism. For a short time Michael Jackson's image suffered but it was not long before the affair was forgotten.

Beatles' songs go up for sale

MICK AND JERRY: The baby was two weeks late.

My girl—hat-trick for Mick

MICK JAGGER'S girlfriend Jerry Hall gave birth to a baby girl today — the Rolling Stone's third daughter. The baby, Jerry Hall's first, weighed 8lb 2ozs. She was born just before 7 am at New York's Lennox Hill Hospital.

● TURNED ON . . . like his audience, Prince gets excited by his sexy songs

The Prince of sex

To him, it's the most important thing of all

BY RICK SKY

". . . but he's not gay. He's very masculine."

". . . when I con . . ." about his . . . man . . .

Prince's women come in again.

He lets them tell the world just a little about his superstar life . . . and . . . the . . .

VANITY . . . . "He's very powerful"

SUNDAY MIRROR, February 17, 1985   PAGE 13

Britain's No 1 pop columnist

CLOWN PRINCE OR NEW KING?

JUST how big is Prince? Is he really the new monarch of rock — or merely a clown, huddled under a blanket that hides his face if not his ego?

His zany antics in London last week, when he hid from the cameras at Heathrow on his arrival to attend the BBC record awards cere-

Zany antics that hide a giant talent

mony, set a lot of people giggling.

There was something incongruous about a strutting purple peacock acting the shrinking violet.

But superstars Mick Jagger, Simon le Bon and Boy George aren't sneering.

They recognise that 5ft 4in-tall Prince has scorched past all of them and has taken over the crown once worn by

Michael Jackson to become a giant of the rock world.

Prince has already topped the U.S. album, singles and film charts simultaneously—something no one has managed since The Beatles.

His Purple Rain album topped the U.S. charts for nearly six months and it has already sold more than 15 million copies around the world.

The LP has yielded three smash hit singles in the States—Purple Rain, When Doves Cry and Let's Go Crazy. And it looks as though there are more to come.

"Not only is he very successful," says Mick Jagger, who knows a thing or two

PRINCE—he's the new king, say rivals

about stardom. "He's also very, very good."

Prince has already proved himself to be a more prolific and inspired song-writer than Michael Jackson.

Yet both share many qualities beyond their stardom.

They share the same half-white, half-black, half-male, half-female beauty which has made it possible for them to hold sway over just about every section of the rock record buying public. Both are deeply religious.

But there the similarities end. Prince is as filthy as Michael is wholesome. His songs are about passion and kinky sex.

PERSONALLY I'm more than prepared to forgive Prince all his childish shenanigans.

He is, quite simply, the most important new rock star of the eighties.

His manic intensity gives his records an edge that makes most of his so-called rivals look like the ephemeral pap they are.

As a close friend told me: "Music is so important to him. It is a cloak and a shield—a womb, that makes him hard to get to."

BEST QUITS HIS JOB

FALLEN soccer idol George Best has quit his job as front-man for the snazzy West End club Blondes.

"There are no hard feelings," says Joe McManus who co-owns Blondes.

"Just before George went to prison he decided it would be better if he didn't have any more to do with the place.

"Obviously the temptation to drink is always there."

Best—tempted

Phil Collins tie

But last time out he and his band were rather more formal and had special ties designed to be worn on the tour.

Today we've got TWO of these exclusive ties up for grabs as well as FIFTY

copies of their great new album.

To enter, just answer these questions about Phil:—

1. How high did he get with You Can't Hurry Love: (a) No. 1, (b) No. 5, (c) No. 10?

2. What is his current hit?

Send your answers on a postcard to Phil Collins Contest, The Club, PO Box 642, London EC88 1SX, by February 28.

The senders of the first two correct answers drawn then will both win a tie and album and 48 runners-up will each win an album.

● Don't miss The Club in the Daily Mirror every weekday!

Phil—with that tie

D DOWN

f George pop star nning to mmer off. to relax, e "fairy writing." about Diana n the

George

During 1984 the American artist, Prince's, decadent act attracted lengthy coverage in the Press. Clever hype made him an overnight sensation. He became a household name in Britain after appearing on the televised award ceremony of the British Phonographic Industry. A giant 'minder', accentuating Prince's 5-foot 4-inch stature, accompanied him on his long trek up to collect his two awards. This unnecessary performance did not go down well with the Press but it certainly made him the most talked-about star for years.

PRINCE OF DARKNESS

Rock star flies out in a blanket of security

By JOHN BLAKE

MAKE way for the Prince of Darkness! Startled air-line passengers had to do it that yesterday when American pop star Prince left Britain with a blanket over his head and a minder by his side.

The rocky horror show at Heathrow airport was as bizarre as Prince's TV appearance on Monday night.

The seven-stone singer was guarded by two murderous-looking heavies as he stepped up to collect two trophies from Britain's record industry.

And his acceptance speech sounded as though his tongue had been superglued to his teeth.

But Prince's popularity speaks for itself. The 26-year-old singer recently topped the US film, album and singles charts, a feat previously achieved only by the Beatles—and he's No. 6 in today's British charts.

● Top 40—Page 17

VICTOR CRAWSHAW

HEAVY BACKING: Guard as Prince goes on TV

DAILY STAR

FRIDAY, NOVEMBER 30, 1984   17p (18p C.I.s)   Printed in London

BAND OF HOPE

Another Star picture exclusive

Singing for Ethiopia . . . Boy George making his contribution to the record

Hit could raise £1m for Ethiopia

By RICK SKY and GEOFF BAKER

BRITAIN'S teenagers are set to raise a fortune for the starving people of Ethiopia . . . all because of one record.

Do They Know It's Christmas, by superstars Band Aid, was first played by Daily Star columnist Simon Bates on his Radio One programme earlier this week.

Within hours, his listeners had pledged £35,000 for the famine appeal.

Simon said last night: "I'm totally overwhelmed.

"I didn't make an appeal for money. I just played the single and talked to Bob Geldof about it.

"To have £35,000 pledged like this, without asking for it, is marvellous.

"But it's typical of my listeners to open their hearts and their wallets."

Simon . . . "overwhelmed"

It was Geldof who brought together the galaxy of stars who form Band Aid, including Boy George, Simon Le Bon of Duran Duran, George Michael, Wham's Status Quo, and Sting.

They hope the record will reach number one in the charts and raise at least £1 million for the nation-wide appeal.

Geldof said last night: "Every pound raised will go to the Ethiopians.

"I wanted to alert the world to the tragedy. Unlike other people I'm in a position to do something about it.

All together now . . . Sting, Bono of U2, and Simon Le Bon in the studios

"It was wonderful the way the bands involved gave up their commitments to record the song."

A half-hour video of the band recording the song will be shown tonight on Channel 4's pop programme The Tube, when Boy George says :

"I am sure the record will go right to number one. Bringing everyone together was wonderful and we got on like a house on fire. It was quite amusing.

"Because people like Duran Duran, Culture Club and Wham are so famous we

Turn to Page Two

Frankie Gets Shirty

ANGRY POP IDOLS IN STREET FRACAS

FRANKIE Goes to Hollywood stars Paul Rutherford and Mark O'Toole have been involved in an amazing street brawl.

They lost their rags when a freelance photographer snapped them trying on shirts in an exclusive West End shop.

Maurice Conroy, 20, was grabbed and ordered to hand over his film.

Then, in front of about 50 young girl fans, the two Frankies let fly with a string of four-letter words.

Finally police arrived and broke up the fracas in South Molton Street, Mayfair.

"Paul and Mark seemed to go berserk," said Maurice, from Muswell Hill, North London.

"The language was appalling and they kept waving their fists in my face.

Jumping

"They tried to g___ my £400 camera ___ said they'd beat ___ unless I handed ___ the film.

Student Andy ___ of Eltham ___ London, wh___ incident, se___ a very nas___

"Paul ___ jumping ___

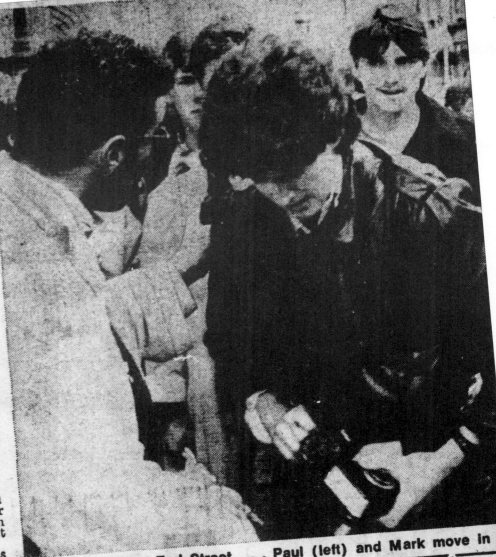

Fury in a West End Street . . . Paul (left) and Mark move in o___

Mr Smooth rips off 20 hotels

A CONMAN with a taste for good food and fast cars was ___ing sought last ___ after fooling ___ 20 hotels.

___est caper, ___anished ___ bill. ___ts ___

If t___

ROYAL ROW AS FRANKIE GO TOO FAR

MPs rap group for Prince Charles disc

By FRANK CURRAN

POP superstars Frankie Goes To Hollywood were at the centre of a royal sex storm last night.

The band's controversial debut LP features a Prince Charles impersonator talking about orgasms and ejaculation.

Scores of angry mums complained to the Daily Star after buying Frankie's album Welcome To The Pleasure Dome, which has

recently sold more than 700,000 copies in Britain.

EXCLUSIVE

DAILY STAR, Friday, December 28, 1984

___y Rights were brought out into the open in the music world by Tom Robinson and the Village People in the late 1970s. Their ___uccessor in the 1980s was Frankie Goes To Hollywood who highlighted the considerable homosexual undercurrents of the disco and club scene.

Their first hit, *Relax*, came towards the end of 1983. Its suggestive lyrics were not much noticed at first until BBC DJ Mike Reid refused to play the single on his show. This merely stimulated interest in the record and almost toppled their other hit *Two Tribes* to regain its number one position.

Michael Jackson to co-write America's Band Aid single for famine victims

THE STANDARD, FRIDAY, JANUARY 18, 1985—11

U.S. pop stars follow Geldof charity lead

COMPOSING: Michael Jackson, who will help write the song.

PERFORMING: Tina Turner, one of the many star singers.

AMERICAN pop stars, including Michael Jackson, Tina Turner and Bruce Springsteen, are to take up Bob Geldof's challenge and release a record to raise cash for Africa's famine victims, it was reported today.

Jackson is to team up with Lionel Ritchie and Stevie Wonder to write the song and a number of top pop, rock, country and R and B artists have agreed to sing on the single, to be recorded later this month.

Plans are also underway in America for a charity album, according to reports in the Los Angeles Times.

The American project follows the success of the Band Aid single Do They Know It's Christmas which has sold more than 6,000,000 copies after topping the British charts, and is currently in the U.S. top ten.

Proceeds from the record go to help famine-stricken already reached £8...

The Times... to be...

Rogers, Linda Ronstadt, Willie Nelson, Turner and Quincy Jones were among the artists expected to sing on the record, to be produced in Los Angeles.

Geldof, the Boomtown Rats leader who headed the British team, which included Sting, Boy George, Paul Young, Duran Duran's Simon le Bon, and U2's Bono Hewson, recently challenged U.S. pop stars to make a record of their own to aid famine victims.

Although plans for the African famine drive apparently were already under construction by some American musicians, the success of the Band Aid project has given impetus to their effort.

Geldof has said he intend to sue pirates in Singapore, where thousands of illegal copies of an album including the song Do They Know It's Christmas flooded the market in December.

Singapore is notorious as a base for record pirates and it's estimated that 20,000 copies of the Band Aid tapes were sold before the authorities managed to clear the rest from the shelves.

INSPIRATION: Bob Geldof in Ethiopia.

BLAME IT ON RIO

Elton John, Paul McCartney and Cliff Richard have played in the Soviet Union, the Police in India and Wham! in China and Japan. However, perhaps Rock in Rio can lay claim to being the most spectacular concert outside of Live Aid. In January 1985, 300,000 nightly attended a series of concerts that starred some of the biggest bands in the West. The stage, at 21,000 square feet, was large enough for a jumbo jet to land on and there were 20 tons of lighting equipment and 160,000 pounds of sound equipment emitting 500,000 watts of power.

In total, 3 million people attended and the figures easily overtook the previous highest attendance of 600,000 at the Watkins Glen Festival in the United States in 1973. Whitesnake and Iron Maiden were among the British stars but in the South Americans' eyes Queen towered above them all, the group having already undertaken a huge tour of South America.

PopLine AWARDS OF THE YEAR

It's Wham by a whisker!

The young guns scoop the titles

Wham's George Michael and Andrew Ridgeley . . . four titles

★ WHAM! and Duran Duran have emerged as the most popular groups of 1984.

That is the choice of thousands of Daily Express Popline readers, who have voted for their favourite stars and records in our second annual poll.

While Duran Duran's single Wild Boys topped the Best Singles section, Wham! scored with having produced the Best Albums of the year, Make It Big.

The two groups were also battling it out for Best Live Act—Wham! George Michael and Andrew Ridgeley, finally pipping Duran Duran to the post by just four votes. Yes, it was that close.

Twenty - one - year - old George Michael for the first time won the Best Male Singer title from Duran Duran's heart-throb, Simon Le Bon.

Twenty - three - year - old Alison Moyet, who sang with Yazoo until 1983, ran

By DAVID WIGG

remained loyal to their home - spun British stars. Not even America's Michael Jackson, who sold more than 25 million copies of

Later, bored with being on the dole, George wrote a number, Wham Rap, about the problem. They raised £20 to make a

A word from the winners

Rock stars happen to the nicest families

IT must be pretty disconcerting, come to think of it, when a favourite son, the boy you nurtured through sickness, health and 11-plus, suddenly confronts you as a long-haired, guitar-wielding pop-star, cavorting around on The Box mouthing incomprehensible lyrics for an audience to whom he has become a cult figure.

David Crosby, 30-year-old rhythm guitarist, singer and composer of Crosby, Stills, Nash and Young, agrees: 'In some ways,' he says, 'I must be such a mystery to my father (former film-maker Floyd Crosby, pictured left with his super-star son). But what I like best about him is that he seems to feel no need for me to be like him — so we're not offended by each other's differences.'

How do others conquer, or come to terms with, those differences? And how does a family relationship withstand the test? Talking here are some of today's brightest, and most idolised, stars . . . and their parents.

Prison for rock singer

ROCK STAR David Crosby has lost his battle to stay out of jail.

A judge in Dallas, Texas, refused the singer's request to be sent to a special drug rehabilitation centre instead of prison.

Crosby, aged 42, was jailed for eight years in 1983 after being found guilty of drugs and arms offences. The sentence was later quashed pending appeal.

But Crosby, a founder member of the '70s rock supergroup, Crosby, Stills and Nash, was arrested on drugs and arms charges last year in California and Dallas authorities demanded his bail be withdrawn.

Deputy District Attorney Jim Nelson yesterday told the Texas court: "We have proved he is a criminal and he should be treated as one."

Judge Pat McDowell agreed and ordered Crosby, who has been fighting cocaine addiction for 20 years, back to prison.

Later Crosby said: "I just want to get off drugs and back to playing music."

POP STAR'S PLEA IN HIS DRUGS CAMPAIGN

We must face this heroin tragedy together

TOWNSHEND: Urging more help for victims

I BELIEVE that no misfortune is so bad that it cannot be joked about. So for someone who was once a heroin addict I felt I had the right to make a crack about heroin.

I was little prepared, therefore, to the reaction to my jokey, ironic statement on radio last week: "Teenagers should never experiment with heroin — they should stick to the tried and tested pastimes like sex and housebreaking."

Politicians, however, lack a sense of humour, and I woke up the following day to discover that I had muffed my lines. The political roof had fallen in.

I remain, however unapologetic. The trouble is that the politicians who, like Luton North Tory MP John Carlisle, say that I am exaggerating the problem of heroin addiction, themselves have no answers or, where they do, attach these to their own political banner.

The Hard Left want to tell us that the increase in drug abuse amongst the 18 to 25-year-olds is due to unemployment. Maybe there is something in that, but speaking for myself, I resent those who see this desperate battle as merely another political problem, as a weapon with which to beat this present Government.

They offer miracles, but there will be no miracles from either side of the political spectrum for hundreds of thousands of heroin addicts.

Utterly universal

Lots of my Socialist friends told me that I had lost all credibility by talking about the drug problem under a Conservative banner. Who gives a damn about banners?

We are talking about our own young people. About kids who may never ever write a cheque, never mind walk into a polling booth.

Heroin is aloof from politics and politicians. It is utterly

By PETE TOWNSHEND

The Who guitarist and a reformed addict now trying to save others

that it would matter how your advisors voted. To whom do you turn? To an MP, or an errant pop star?

Let's go back to my joke. If your daughter becomes prematurely pregnant, Society can help you. If your boy breaks into a house and gets caught, Society will mete out harsh treatment. But at least he'll get treatment.

The young person who becomes addicted to heroin will find hardly any clearly signposted routes for long-term help.

This Government has at least shown that they are aware of the almost unbelievable scope of the heroin problem, particularly in our depressed areas.

They plan several information films for teachers, parents, social workers and the probation service. They are spending money on a campaign to discourage experimentation with heroin by the young. They clearly care about the addicted.

helped to consolidate Britain's trade with the East in the 1890s, used opium as currency in their trade with China.

Now we pay such a terrible price — and receive an ironic bargain. For the street price of heroin has never been lower.

Easy access

A Customs officer at Heathrow told me that he was quite sure that if every Jumbo jet from Pakistan could be thoroughly searched, heroin would be found every day. There are still too few Customs officers, but in any case, no airport in the world is capable of handling such delays.

Anyway, the tragedy has already happened and we might as well face it. It doesn't matter who we point a finger at.

The people who have succumbed to heroin in the last few years of easy access and

crutch quickly evaporates. We must be ready, as fathers and mothers, as friends and lovers, and doctors and social workers, police and priests. We must remember who these people once were that are now lost: they are victims of a tragedy and they need our help.

That fact must never be buried under the polemic speeches of politicians on the Left or Right.

The Government must do even more: specialised drug-withdrawal centres must be made available. I believe that at least a thousand beds will be needed. That could mean 500 reoriented and specially-trained doctors and nurses.

The Government must also provide enormous rehabilitation programmes. My peritsonal theory is that work in the open air is the best rehabilitation for city-scarred drug abusers.

Perhaps part of the Youth Training Scheme could be revamped to accommodate young people in forestry, farm labouring, sea fishing, National Trust path maintenance — yes, even training for the Home Guard!

Once detoxified, addicts must be given back their lives. They need dignity, purpose, a role and a belief in their own power to change the world. Let's face it, they need jobs.

I once believed that I could laugh at any difficulty, that politicians were boring because they were too serious. But heroin addiction can

---

DON'T BE A DOPE JOIN THE STAR AND RADIO ONE CAMPAIGN

THE FACTS NOT THE FICTION

SHOP A PUSHER

YOU can help save lives today

We're wild about Wham!

WHAM! sent 12,000 Chinese wild last night in the first major rock concert ever staged in Peking.

By the end of the two-hour show most of the packed audience were on their feet and dancing ... to the delight of WHAM! and the dismay of Peking police.

Dozens of youngsters were thrown out of the People's Gymnasium when they ignored police orders to sit down and insisted on boogeying.

One determined bopper was beaten to the ground by six policemen when he refused to return to his seat.

Right from the opening chord of Wake Me Up Before You Go-Go, when George Michael and Andrew Ridgeley bounced out on stage with huge grins, the audience were spellbound.

At first it was through sheer bewilderment.

TRIUMPH: Wham last night.

Picture: KENT G...

JOHN BLAKE reports from Peking

When George told them: "We hope you are all going to dance and clap your hands," no one appeared to have the slightest idea what he was talking about. His request was simply met with polite applause.

But soon they were clapping along with the songs. And when Western tourists started to dance the Chinese began to copy them—cautiously at first, then more and more wildly.

Even with the volume turned way down low to minimise the culture shock, the thirty tons of lights and sound system knocked the breath from people whose idea of a wacky night out used to be watching an opera.

Just a year ago dancing was illegal in Peking. And there were screams of amazement as Shirley and Pepsi, Wham's two dancing girls, slipped into ever-more revealing outfits.

The ten-song show climaxed with a sizzling version of Young Guns ... and then, suddenly, it was all over.

The Chinese did not realise that all big bands expect to be called back for at least two encores.

But everyone was happy. A leading politician, Xiao Hua, said: "It was very successful, you could see it on the people's faces."

Andrew said: "I thought the Chinese audience were absolutely marvellous."

NO GO-GO: Police evict a Wham fan who insisted on dancing.

Wham at the wall

WHAM'S George Michael and Andrew Ridgeley scrambled up the 2,000-year-old Great Wall of China yesterday ... and loved it.

Andrew said: "It's unbelievable that someone should build a wall that's longer than the distance from London to New York."

The pair dined on 1,000-year-old

SNAP HAPPY: George poses with two Chinese fans

From JOHN BLAKE in PEKING

eggs and Peking duck as they finished plans for their concert in front of 15,000 people at Peking's People's Gymnasium tomorrow.

More than 1,000 Chinese people queued through the night for tickets for the first concert ever played behind the bamboo curtain by a major western rock band.

Though tickets cost nearly £2 each—three days' wages for a manual worker—the fans were promised a free Wham cassette with every ticket.

Later a lavish banquet was staged for the duo by the Chinese government.

After listening to speeches of welcome Andrew told the hundreds of guests: "This concert may be a small step for the youth of China, it is a giant step for the youth of the world in bringing our cultures closer together."

The Communist Party is worried about the moral risk of allowing a western pop group to play to the city's young people.

Just 12 months ago dancing was illegal in Peking and discos were banned even in tourist hotels because they were "decadent."

Wham will strike all sexual innuendos from their stage show and they are expected to turn their sound system down to half volume.

● The Club—Page 15

I'll never

SPECIAL REPORT ON ROCK STAR'S FIRST CONCERT

● A SUNNY day and 65,000 people pack the grounds of Slane Castle, County Meath, Ireland, for rock idol Bruce Springsteen's first concert of his European tour. They came from all over the world and the Boss had them dancing with delight. Among the hordes was Starman John Beattie and here is his account of that memorable event ...

Dear Editor

I reckon I've done my bit for the Daily Star over the years.

You've sent me to the hotspots of Belfast, the North Pole and the Falklands (twice).

Never once have I moaned.

But to send your opera cruise, as self-appointed, to a rock concert — well, I went with great interest to Sky's report on last year's Glastonbury Festival. Or, perhaps, Joe Ashton's coverage of a meeting of the Tory Monday Club.

Anyway, as correct I went to see the Bruce Springsteen fellow at his appearance at Slane Castle.

Reaction

It is in a very pretty part of Ireland, overlooking the River Boyne, where King William fought the battle of the Boyne in 1690 and more. My reaction on seeing 65,000 people jammed into the castle grounds was that it was like a medieval jamboree compared with the new ...

N/AS   DAILY STAR, Monday, June 3, 1985   5

forget Bruce Whatsisname

Sea of fans

WHERE POLITICS HAVE FAILED THE POP STARS AND YOU WILL SUCCEED

THE STAR

THE FACTS NOT THE FICTION · SATURDAY, JULY 13, 1985 · 18p (19p C.I.S)

LIVE AID

16 HOURS TO ROCK THE WORLD

By RICK SKY

● THE GREATEST show on earth gets off the ground today. The world's top rock stars are coming together for the biggest concert ever staged. They will appear simultaneously at Wembley Stadium and in Philadelphia in the Live Aid televised spectacular. And they will all give their services free to raise an expected £10 million for the starving.

● A cavalcade of stars are performing in the Wembley concert, and to see them when they arrive at 11 a.m. will be the Prince and Princess of Wales.

● Up to 80,000 fans are expected at the stadium. Status Quo start the extravaganza rolling, followed by the best in rock and pop and ending with Paul McCartney.

● Last night Live Aid organiser Bob Geldof warned fans to beware of touts, and said: "Only buy souvenirs from officials." He added: "Let every penny go to those who need it most."

AND THE STAR GETS IT ROLLING WITH A GUIDE TO THE GIGS

Jerry . . . she's expecting Jagger's baby any time

Jerry gets a baby minder

By TONY BROOKS

MUM - TO - BE Jerry Hall will defy doctors to watch boyfriend Mick Jagger perform in the Live Aid concert.

The blonde Texan model is expecting the couple's second baby "any day now," say friends.

But she has insisted on being at the side of the stage when rock star Mick sings for 92,000 people at the John F. Kennedy stadium in Philadelphia.

Doctors begged 28-year-old Jerry to stay away, but she told them: "This is the event of a lifetime and I must be there."

She has agreed to compromise by having a nurse at her side throughout.

And a Jagger aide will be posted high in the stands, ready to telephone doctors if he's told the baby is on the way.

Mick and Jerry, joined by their 16-month-old daughter Elizabeth Scarlett, arrive in Philadelphia from New York today, four hours before he goes on stage.

Now Reds raise the curtain

THE big show will be beamed live to Russia and China, it was revealed last night.

Russian fans will see the full 16 hours while the Chinese have agreed to take four.

The Soviet deal was clinched after a frantic round of phone calls between London and Moscow.

It was a triumph for Live Aid's super-salesman, Bernard Docherty, who declared: "It's fantastic news.

"We will now be reaching 80 per cent of television sets around the world."

He said Russia's eleventh-hour decision

Turn to Page 2

Pages 13, 14, 15 and 16

FRANK
FEARLESS
FREE

Sunday People

FORWARD WITH BRITAIN   28p ★ L

JULY 14, 1985.   No. 5395

'Now I think I'll have to buy some denims' says Charles

ROCK'N ROYAL!

From the inside
MYRA'S STORY

Brady would have murdered me

AMAZING CONFESSION
PAGES 18 AND 19

★ PLUS ★ PLUS ★

Torvill without Dean

ME, MEN AND MARRIAGE

CENTRE PAGES

★ PLUS ★ PLUS ★

Dallas picture exclusive
INSIDE SOUTHFORK
Pages 8 and 9

ROYAL RAVERS: Charles and Di join Bob Geldof to acknowledge the cheers of 85,000 rapturous rock fans.

POP PRIDE: Wembley stars Phil Collins and Sting

THE GREATEST Rock Show on Earth ended last night with two billion people listening to a billion pounds of talent.

The stars at the amazing Live Aid concert at Wembley joined forces for a rousing chorus of the fund-raising hit Do They Know It's Christmas?

And what a right royal rave-up the whole 10-hour show was!

GREATEST SHOW ON EARTH
Pages 4 and 5

As Prince Charles watched the jean-clad rock fans enjoying the show, he said:

"I'll have to buy myself a pair of denims".

The royal couple clapped and tapped their feet along to the music. They left to cheers after an hour.

Nearly two billion people worldwide tuned into the extravaganza, which raised an amazing £15 MILLION.

And the profits from the twin Live Aid concerts at Wembley and across the Atlantic in Philadelphia could eventually be trebled when the cash is totted up from donations, TV rights and souvenir sales.

Boomtown Rats star Bob Geldof, who organised the event in aid of Africa's starving millions, summed up: "To me it is not a pop concert. To me it is not a TV show. To me it is simply a means of keeping people alive."

● WILTING UNDER 90° of dehydrating heat, 90,000 screaming Americans couldn't quite comprehend what they were seeing. It could've been a heat-haze induced mirage: just about every artist that ever figured in US pop culture was onstage at JFK stadium in Philadelphia. Every man (and woman) jack from Joan Baez to Madonna, from Neil Young to Hall And Oates. Woodstock was never like this.

Black Sabbath reformed for a day, so did Led Zeppelin. Robert Plant couldn't reach his high notes, but what the hell. Crosby, Stills and Nash were tedious beyond words, but for this day they were heroes like everyone else.

Even the fact that a selection of unscheduled acts (Thorogood, Rick Springfield, REO Speedwagon) were appearing didn't dim the collective sense of purpose.

Photography courtesy of RETNA Pictures Ltd

Photo: Sam Nix

● LAST ONE in close the door... JFK Stadium, the view from the rear... "can't even see the screen, man, but sure can feel the vibes..."

Photo: John Bellissimo

● MICK JAGGER: the eternal youth, saucy as ever

Photo: John Bellissimo

● MADONNA: NO longer blonde, fully clothed and dazzling billions with her self-assurance

Six satellites beamed Live Aid from Wembley Stadium, London and later from the JFK Stadium in Philadelphia to more than 100 countries around the world with an estimated television audience of between 1.5 and 2 billion people. During the whole ten hours, transmission was lost only twice: during five minutes of the Who's set and for part of McCartney's solo *Let It Be*. Live Aid was the greatest charity event ever and its audience one of the largest in history.

DAILY RECORD, Saturday, March 30, 1985 13

LADY MADONNA!

She's hot property —but not all that sweet..

SHE'S the hottest sex symbol to hit America, a curvy combination of singing and dancing, christened Madonna by devoutly religious parents.

With a siren-like voice and sexual, hip-thrusting gyrations which send video fans dizzy, she is the name on DJs' lips on both sides of the Atlantic ever since her single, Like A Virgin.

The critics, however, charge that 26-year-old Madonna has been hardly girlish in her dealings with those in the tough music business.

On her way to the top she has ruthlessly followed ambition wherever it takes her — leaving behind the original musical associates who helped launch her career.

"Have I exploited people?" she asks. "People say that, but that's just resentment of someone who's got the drive."

TEASING

"It seems like I'm leaving people behind or stepping on them. The fact is that I'm moving and they're not. I don't care if I ruffle someone's feathers."

Born in Bay City, Michigan, the eldest girl in a family of six children, she grew up in Detroit — then known musically as the pop world as Motown.

It was on the floors of discos in the city's nightclubs that people in the music business first noticed Madonna.

Her dance style comes through on her videos — harsh, raw sex-appeal, breasts and bottom thrust at the camera, with an index finger teasing her mouth.

She has single-handedly brought back the harem look, with two-piece outfits designed "; expose her naked stomach.

"When I stick a finger in my belly button, I feel a nerve in the centre of my body shoot up my spine," she reveals.

Her video act is not just a three-minute put-on for the cameras. She has experienced the more seamy side of life.

She once appeared nude in a porn movie, but brushes that part of her career aside.

"It was something I did—I don't lie awake worrying about it. It was part of growing up."

After minor success in New York she was asked to go to Paris to

By STEWART DICKSON

do back-up singing and dancing for Frenchman Patrick Hernandez, who had one disco hit, Born To Be Alive.

Video made her a star — record bosses realised they had one of the hottest properties in the industry.

Madonna has had a long line of boyfriends, the most permanent being New York disc jockey "Jellybean" Benitez.

She's recently been seen with actor Sean Penn, star of the

current American film hit The Falcon And The Snowman.

"I am a flirt," Madonna admits "Any men around me must remember my one guiding emotion — ambition."

Marketing Madonna is just one aspect she has ideas on—including the ever-popular doll.

"It will be a doll whose hair you won't have to comb," she says coyly.

"The things it will say will include 'Stop pulling my hair, leave me alone, how much money do you make?' "And 'Come here.' "

TEASING ... that's Madonna—but she's an ambitious ga[...]

.. AND IT'S Mr [...]

YOU could be maki[...] a grave mistake [...] you've written Marily[...] off as a Boy George copy[...] cat whose pop care[...] started and finished with [...] his only hit — Callin[...] Your Name—18 months[...] ago.

Diana Ross hasn't. In fact, when she heard he was in New York and looking for somebody "strong, wise and experienced" to manage his career, she had him flown down to Pennsylvania in her private helicopter to discuss the [...]

Marilyn — under new management.

Plea to mums

DOCTORS investigating why some children do not develop properly have found evidence that many babies are affected while in the womb.

A medical team in Dundee studied 4852 children born in 1974-5 and followed them up to their seventh birthdays, says a report in The Lancet.

They found the mothers of the 322 children who did not develop normally often had complications in pregnancy.

Dr David Taylor, of Ninewells Hospital, who led the team, said: "I appeal to all pregnant women to contact their doctors immediately if they feel unwell."

The bleep of hope

A GIFT of radio pagers to Scottish hospitals means that some transplant patients will only be a "bleep" away from vital surgery.

British Telecom gave 250 pagers to the NHS and in Edinbu[...]

Madonna was undoubtedly the big pop success of 1985 if hits and general media coverage are anything to go by. Five British hits came off her album Like A Virgin which sold over three million. In the United States she became the first singer to have had top hits in Billboard's five major charts of pop, black, country, dance and adult contemporary. She hardly pleased American feminists with her portrayal of the female singer as a sex object. She provided a female version of the male master of 'flirt rock', Prince.

SUNDAY MAIL, August 18, 1985 3

CLIFFHANGER!

Wedding high spot as Queen of Rock Madonna takes her vows over the ocean

ROCK star Mandonna has married film star Sean Penn in a clifftop ceremony overlooking the Pacific.

Security was so tight that famous guests such as Cher and actress Diane Keaton had to produce their driving licences to gain admission.

The 250 guests were told by phone only an hour before Friday night's ceremony that it would take place in the mansion of film producer Kurt Unger in the film star colony of Malibu.

SERVICE

Madonna, whose hits include "Like A Virgin", "Material Girl", and whose three records have reached top of the US and British [...] wore what was described [...] ugust to the closely-g[...]

The heavy fantastic

SEE when you climb on a chair to change a light-bulb and come down with a heavier thud than you care to admit?

My only regret at seeing Rudolph Nureyev dance at the Edinburgh Festival is that he now comes down to earth just like you and me—bang!

The difference is that at 47 he can still get himself into the air with ease.

And that's more than can be said for any football or rugby player of his age—so who says ballet is cissy?

DOROTHY YOUNG

The woman writer men can't ignore

MADONNA IS NO LADY..

COUNT me out when it comes to bending the knee to this madam they call Madonna.

Even if she DID sing like an angel, she would STILL come across in every other respect as a loud-mouthed self-publicist.

All right, she has three singles in the charts — no mean achievement.

But do we have to listen to her off-stage warblings about being a bit of a guru? Her singing is one thing; her PREACHING is quite another.

Samples: "I was always very conscious of God watching me. Oh really?

SECULAR

Or ... "Even when I put on a hat and pull it down low, the minute I step out of a cab, everyone says: "There's Madonna".

Well, it doesn't wash with [...]

[...]y go-getter like her a [...] a good agent and the [...] backing of the pop [...] and she becomes a cult [...] instead of just another

[...]nna's no idol, to my [...]. She claims her name is [...]. She insists there's nothing

Madonna — and crucifix —in action on stage

wrong with wearing a rosary or crucifix as a piece of ornamentation.

I might fall for either, but for the fact that a girl who maintains her religion's important could never—SURELY—have settled for that weekend marriage ceremony.

It was conducted beside the most secular imaginable status symbol — a swimming pool in Malibu.

Dressed to thrill

AS always, what the doctor orders takes no account of what patients might need.

Here's TV's Dr Vernon Coleman saying nurses in male wards should wear short skirts, black stockings and suspender belts.

Just to give the poor chaps a shot in the arm.

It's an idea that has sent the Royal College of Nursing reaching for their smelling salts.

But what pains me is that nobody has said women's wards could use a bit of uplift, too.

They can't all be Dr Kildares.

The Mail on Sunday, February 2, 1986

PHOTOS SOLD TO HIGHEST BIDDER AS SINGER WEDS MILLIONAIRE

THE new bride, Diana Ross

Diana the bartered bride

From PETER DOBBIE in Lausanne

DIANA ROSS married her multi-millionaire yesterday, and the best man was her bank account.

Forget To Have And To Hold and Until Death Us Do Part. This marriage may have been made in heaven, but it was sold to the highest bidder.

It put Joan Collins's antics in selling her own wedding snaps well in the shade.

Inside the ancient church at Romainmotier, about 20 miles from the ritzy lakeside resort of Lausanne, the moment of union between the 41-year-old soul singer and Norwegian industrialist Arne Naess, six years her senior, was recorded by a photo agency paying a six-figure sum for the rights.

One wondered whether the filthy rich Naess — his fortune is estimated at around £600 million — and his bride — resplendent in

an over-the-top £8,500 lace dress — really needed the money.

Outside the church, 100 photographers and reporters baying for blood after being excluded by private security guards clearly didn't think so.

Punches were exchanged between hired thugs and paparazzi as well as expletives foul in any of a dozen languages.

The couple's six children — they have three each by previous marriages — were held in a vice-like grip by the heavies as they sprinted the few yards from hotel to Cadillac.

A young man spouting Sloane talk delivered £5,000 worth of flowers to the church, all the way from London. They had been

brought in a refrigerated lorry three days earlier and looked it.

Back in the church, video cameras rolled for a company hired by the couple. Undoubtedly it will be part of a film package to be sold off — watch for it on Top of the Pops — although for a so-called star-studded occasion there were remarkably few celebrities. Only Gregory Peck and Stevie Wonder turned up.

The slick and sentimental Miss Ross reportedly turned down part in Dallas after finding true love with Arne Naess. To judge by yesterday's performance, she may simply have swapped one soap opera for another.

● In Oslo, Naess's first wife, who plays a Joan Collins character in a popular Norwegian soap, explained why she wasn't at the wedding.

Mari Maurstad said: "They won't miss me. There are enough bitches down there in Switzerland already."

FIANCEE AND BAND AMONG VICTIMS IN SINGER'S PLANE AS EMERGENCY LANDING GOES

Rock star Nelson dies in jinx crash

Scene of death: Tangled wreckage of the plane yesterday

SINGER Ricky Nelson died in a plane crash yesterday ... a victim of the death jinx that seems to plague American rock stars.

The private airliner of the '60s idol crashed in flames after an emergency landing went wrong.

Nelson died with his 27-year-old fiancee Helen Blair and five members of his band as his DC3 plane tried to come down on a rural highway in Texas.

And his death was tragically similar to those of fellow pop star air crash victims Buddy Holly, The Big Bopper, Jim Reeves and Jim Croce.

The Nelson tragedy brought the number of air travellers killed in 1985 to nearly 2,000, making it the rock...

Only the...
the un...
pilots...
and B...
cat...
with...

From PHILIP FINN in New York

Be Anyone Else But You, Hello Mary Lou and Garden Party... branched out into... co-starring with the Bravo...

£6

Dead: Singer Ricky Nelson

---

the Thin Lizzy singer who battled to help teenagers kick the habit

STAR PHIL'S ROCK AND RUIN ON DRUGS

Lynott dies in heroin battle

KING PHIL!

Britons grab the Grammys

By GEOFF BAKER

THE best of British pop stars swept the board early yesterday at the annual Grammy awards—the rock Oscars.

A magnificent seven British acts dominated the Los Angeles ceremony—beating the Americans in their own backyard. And the Mr. Polite of pop, Phil

Eric Clapton (left) and Ron Wood

Collins, led the way as he scooped three top awards.

The former Genesis drummer, who won the pop world's praise by playing at both Wembley and Philadelphia for Live Aid, took the Grammy as best male pop vocalist.

He was also named producer of the year and took the award for best album of the year with his smash-hit No Jacket Required.

Phil donned a plush tuxedo jacket for the ceremony, but it was a case of No Smart Shoes Required as he wore white tennis shoes with his glad rags.

He told the star-studded audience at the Shrine Auditorium: "I think my mum will be proud of me."

When Phil went up to receive his first grammy he said: "I really never expected anything."

On winning his second he said: "Am I glad I bought this Tux—"

And on receiving his third: "I've run out of things to say, to h—"

Dire...

The Grammy awards in Los Angeles

VISIT THE BOAT SHOW AT LONDON'S EARLS COURT—OPEN EVERY DAY UNTIL JANUARY 12

Why Geldof does not deserve medal, by MP

'He's had enough glory'

By LEON SYMONS and PETER HITCHENS

BAND AID campaigner Bob Geldof does not deserve an honour, a Tory MP claimed yesterday.

Former Minister Nicholas Fairbairn hit out as the row grew over rock star Geldof's omission from the New Year Honours List.

He said: "There are millions of people who work for charity and do not seek benefit for themselves. Very few of them are rewarded for their greatness.

"Those who attain glory in this way should in no circumstances be rewarded. Let us instead reward the great little people who go about this work in a quiet...

"I would award Bob Geldof a huge medal the day he never appeared again on television or visibly anywhere," said the former Solicitor General of Scotland.

Geldof: Left out

Ovation

He said: "I am... sixty one and experi... referring to the group... original jacket... dressed in his swimming pool.

The Stones celebrate with a sparkling array of special guests including... Dave Stewart of the Eurythmics... Daryl Hall... Kenny Jones, Francesca...

OUR RO...

Stars' night out at the Rock and Pop awards

GELDOF GIVES HIS GONG AWAY

Tribute of the Live Aid hero

Words: GILL PRINGLE
Pictures: ALAN GRISBROOK

ELTON JOHN: Special award

LIVE AID mastermind Bob Geldof finally got his gong last night — and promptly gave it away again.

The singer who organised the mammoth Pop concert which raised £100 million for starving villagers in Ethiopia was presented with a special prize at the prestigious BPI awards in London.

Then Geldof, who was robbed by the Nobel prize and New Year Honours List selectors, handed it over to concert promoter Harvey Goldsmith.

"Harvey worked so hard for the whole event. He deserved it more than me," he said.

Great

"I don't care about awards. It was great to see Harvey looking so happy.

"He's been in the business nearly 20 years and he's helped lots of groups in his time."

Geldof scoffed at reports that he will repeat the concert.

"Live Aid was like a shooting star," he said. "It was beautiful once—but it spoils it if you see it twice."

Geldof arrived at the ceremony, presented by the British Phonographic Industry, in a smart dinner jacket—with girlfriend Paula Yates on his arm.

Dozens of stars turned up for the £100-a-ticket bash at the plush Grosvenor Hotel in London.

Many of them, like superstar singer/songwriter Elton John were definitely dressed to thrill for the occasion.

"The Boss"—rock superstar Bruce Springsteen—was voted top international artist.

Annie Lennox and Dave Stewart of The Eurythmics picked up two awards.

Phil Collins did the double with Best Male Artist and Best Album.

Dire Straits, led by guitarist Mark Knopfler, won the Best Group award.

And new band Go West picked up the Best Newcomer prize.

BOB GELDOF: with girlfriend Paula Yates

EURYTHMICS: Annie Lennox and Dave Stewart

WINNER: Bruce Springsteen

WINNER: Phil Collins

GO WEST: Peter Cox (left) and Richard Drummie

☆ ★ ☆ **WHO WON WHAT** ☆ ★ ☆

BEST BRITISH MALE ARTIST: Phil Collins.
BEST BRITISH FEMALE ARTIST: Annie Lennox.
BEST BRITISH GROUP: Dire Straits.
BEST INTERNATIONAL SOLO ARTIST: Bruce Springsteen.
BEST INTERNATIONAL GROUP: Huey Lewis and The News.
BEST BRITISH SINGLE: Tears For

Fears' Everybody Wants To Rule The World.
BEST BRITISH ALBUM: Phil Collins' No Jacket Required.
BEST BRITISH NEWCOMER: Go West.
BEST BRITISH

Strawberry Fields forever

From Jane Rosen in New York

A NEWLY planted garden of trees and gently sloping meadows on the west side of Central Park was dedicated to John Lennon yesterday on what would have been his 45th birthday.

The New York City Council chose the 2½-acre tear-shaped plot as a memorial after Lennon was shot on December 8, 1980. It had been a favourite walking place of the former Beatle and his widow, Yoko Ono.

Miss Ono named the area Strawberry Fields and advertised in the New York Times asking countries to contribute plants and trees to an "international garden of

peace." The response was overwhelming—governments offered enough greenery, statues, and benches to fill Central Park.

Miss Ono's designers selected 161 species of plants for the 161 countries of the world—river birches from the Soviet Union, dogwoods, maples, and daffodils from the West, cedar from Israel, and fothergilla from Jordan.

The focal point of Strawberry Fields is a black and white mosaic sent by Italy with the word "Imagine" in the centre of a starburst pattern. Miss Ono contributed $1 million and New York City is spending $650,000 on the garden.